PRAISE FOR JESSICA SIMPSON'S OPEN BOOK

"Mesmerizing. . . . In 2017, something awoke in Simpson. She can speak honestly now. Is there anything else she wants to say?" —*THE NEW YORKER*

"*Open Book* explains what happened. . . . It just feels nice that one of the pop stars from our teendom has delivered on the twenty-year-old promise they're just like us." —*NEW YORK TIMES*

"In her honest new memoir, Jessica Simpson strips away the glamour associated with the blond hair, the clothing empire, and the early-2000s radio hits. . . . You'll see Jessica Simpson at her most authentic, relatable, and, yes, intelligent." —*GLAMOUR*

"Achingly honest. . . . A thoughtful and intimate portrait." —*TIME*

"A memoir that spares no one, not even herself. . . . Simpson breaks open the dam that is her personal history and the gossip surrounding her life, from the sexual abuse she experienced as a child to her alcohol addiction." —*LOS ANGELES TIMES*

"Powerful." —*PEOPLE*

"You may think you know Jessica Simpson . . . but it turns out there was a whole lot more going on than any of us ever knew. [*Open Book*] is a raw look into the lesser-known troubled side of her life, and how she still manages to see the positive side of everything." —*COSMOPOLITAN*

"I kind of feel like we all owe her an apology." —*RONAN FARROW*

"Captivating. . . . In *Open Book*, Simpson's interior life is accessible and far more complex than her public performance as a relatable pop star." —*JEZEBEL*

"Her excellent memoir is everything you could want. . . . By the end, you marvel at her hard-won wisdom."
—*ROLLING STONE*

"The singer, actress, and entrepreneur reveals struggles her fans never knew about. Simpson shares her truth like never before." —*TODAY*

"Written with considerable hindsight . . . so revealing." —*BUZZFEED*

"Jessica Simpson gets very real." —*REFINERY29*

"A no-holds-barred memoir. . . . A journey through the thirty-nine-year-old's most challenging moments." —*O, THE OPRAH MAGAZINE*

"[Simpson] makes a point of reflecting on her mistakes but is cognizant of the pressures and expectations that others put on her." —*WASHINGTON POST*

"She's honest, genuine, unabashedly vulnerable, and she exhibits the same qualities in her writing."
—*HODA KOTB*, EXCERPT FROM *NYT* BESTSELLER *THIS JUST SPEAKS TO ME*

"Simpson's memoir contains plenty of personal and professional moments for fans to savor. An eye-opening glimpse into the attempted self-unmaking of one of Hollywood's most recognizable talents." —*KIRKUS REVIEWS*

OPEN BOOK

JESSICA SIMPSON

with KEVIN CARR O'LEARY

DEY ST.

An Imprint of WILLIAM MORROW

DEY ST.

OPEN BOOK. Copyright © 2020 by Sweet Kisses, Inc. All rights reserved. Printed in the United States of America. No part of this book may be used or reproduced in any manner whatsoever without written permission except in the case of brief quotations embodied in critical articles and reviews. For information, address HarperCollins Publishers, 195 Broadway, New York, NY 10007.

HarperCollins books may be purchased for educational, business, or sales promotional use. For information, please email the Special Markets Department at SPsales@harpercollins.com.

A hardcover edition of this book was published in 2020 by Dey Street, an imprint of William Morrow.

FIRST DEY STREET PAPERBACK EDITION PUBLISHED 2021.

Designed by Renata De Oliveira
Bird illustrations © Cat_arch_angel/Shutterstock

Library of Congress Cataloging-in-Publication Data has been applied for.

ISBN 978-0-06-289997-2

21 22 23 24 25   LSC   10 9 8 7 6 5 4 3 2 1

To sweet Sarah, my angel.
And to those who are lost and hope to be found.
I pray my truth will help.

CONTENTS

introduction

If you feel like I wrote this book for you, it's because I did.

I spent more than a year on *Open Book*, and I thought about you the whole time. During that time, you became like a sixth member of my family, and I was always thinking of things I had to tell you. Sometimes it was a funny story I knew would make you laugh, and other times I needed to say the scary stuff out loud, so I'd be accountable for creating change in my life. And then there were nights I would pick up my pen and be surprised by something I didn't know that I knew. I would write a sentence, then two, and gradually find an answer for myself that I could share with you. Because that was my intention with this book: To pack all I'd learned the hard way into something I could give you as you start—or restart—your own journey. Not a map or another to-do list, but something to help as you make your own way.

That was a lot of time to spend with somebody, so I got used to having you around. Part of me didn't want to finish the book because I knew how much I'd miss you.

I didn't know it was the start of the conversation.

I first saw this at the book signings. At the very first one, there was the woman who told me she knew she had a problem with alcohol. She'd never said it out loud before.

We hugged, and I started crying, of course. "You have the power within yourself to make this change and to make this change for *yourself*," I said, looking her right in the eye. "I don't know where your struggle lies under the alcohol, but if it's something that you feel compelled to give up, you should embrace that."

"I can't believe I'm saying this," she said.

I smiled and leaned in. "Kind of makes you wonder what else you're going to do to surprise yourself, right?"

In that moment, it all made sense. The timing of everything. Every pain and trial I've gone through made sense so I could be there for that one conversation.

That was just the beginning. There was the man in Nashville who waited in line forever to tell me that he served at Camp Anaconda army base in Iraq, and he remembered my visit in 2005. "When I read what you said about your trips, I called the guys I served with and told them to get your book. They were like '*Jessica Simpson*?'"

I laughed, and he added, "I'm sorry, that didn't come out right—"

"No, I get that a lot," I joked.

"It's just nice that someone remembers we were there," he said.

In Chicago, I had a woman come up to say she was the girl in the stands at the football game, the one that wore the blonde wig and the number-9 jersey. Throughout the game she'd yell at Tony Romo, the Dallas Cowboy I was dating at the time, to distract him. Video of her had gone viral, because at that time people were calling me a jinx for the team. "From the deepest part of my heart, I want to say that I'm so sorry," she said. "I jumped on the bandwagon and I dressed up as you, not knowing that you were . . . uh, human."

We hugged, two humans. Yes, I bawled. But I held it together at another signing, when my then seven-year-old daughter, Maxwell, joined me at the table. People who'd waited in line wanted her autograph in the book, too. "Mom, I don't think I really have an autograph," she whispered to me, "but I love to write in cursive."

"That's perfect," I told her.

A woman stood in front of us. "Thank you for talking about what you went through as a child," she told me. I knew she meant the sexual abuse I'd endured from age six until I was twelve. She cleared her throat. "I've been through the same thing and I'm a mother now," she said, barely getting the words out. "I was scared it might happen to my children because I just couldn't talk about it with them."

She began to cry. Maxwell nudged my leg. "*Mom*," she whispered. "You should hug her."

I jumped up, shaking my head like I'd lost my manners. "I'm so sorry," I said, moving around the table to give her a real hug. "We're okay now." She said she'd told her husband about what happened, and how they needed to have that talk with their kids. Plus, she was going to see a therapist. "It happened so long ago." she said. "I thought it was too late for me to talk about."

When she walked away, Maxwell asked, "What was she talking about?"

I motioned to the event manager to just give me a minute. "Well, in the book Mommy talks about when she was a little bit younger than you . . ." I paused. This was going to have to be the time for our talk. "I struggled with somebody touching me in an uncomfortable way."

"Oh, that's so sad, Mommy," she said. This is my sweet girl who starts praying on November 1 for Santa Claus, Mrs. Claus, the elves, and all the reindeer to sleep well so they can rest up for their busy time at Christmas. "That won't happen to me."

I wanted to smile and say, "You're right," and move on. But I couldn't. "We don't want it to, no," I said. "And if it ever did, I want you to be able to tell them to stop and tell me or Daddy right away. Okay?"

She nodded. Parents have to seize these moments when you have your kids' attention. Time goes by so fast. She is eight now, my son Ace is seven, and our Birdie is just a few months from turning two. Eric and I had her as I worked on this book you're holding, and she just now came toddling into the study where I write. Which means Ace, her best friend, will not be far behind. The sun is going down and it's almost bath time, so that's my cue to go.

I am so grateful to you and to everyone who's read *Open Book* or may still. I hope you'll let me know what you do to surprise yourself, or what you decide it's not too late to do. Or who it's not too late to *be*. I can't wait to find out. I was afraid to stop talking to you last time, but now I know this isn't goodbye.

We're just beginning.

Jessica Simpson
NOVEMBER 2020

PROLOGUE

The kids are asleep, and my husband is reading in the other room. So, it's just you and me.

Every night after we put our children to bed, I come down here to the study to write. It's cold here in Los Angeles, so bedtimes have been creeping later. My daughter Maxwell is six now and my son Ace is five, and they have the kind of energy that needs to be burned off outdoors or it will just add up like a bill that needs to be paid at the end of the night. The poor kiddos have to be at school at seven a.m., so getting them down by eight or eight-thirty is tough. Swimming has always helped—my kids are fish—but it's been too chilly for the pool. Sometimes, as they are racing around the house, I think back to when I was their age in Texas, and I can't remember having all this energy. But I guess I was busy, at dance class every day and then nights at church.

This afternoon my husband Eric set big drop cloths in the backyard as an activity for them. He's done this for years, laying out paints and brushes so they can have at it. He says it's like therapy. A way to get out all your emotions. I panicked the first time I saw them throwing paint.

"It's washable, babe," Eric said.

"Don't do this at anybody else's house, okay?" I yelled, pulling a face as Ace upended a cup of yellow paint on a canvas. "This is just for here." I am Southern, so manners matter. Say please and thank you, and don't throw paint at playdates.

Eric would let them paint the whole house if I'd be okay with it. He's this amazing blend of athlete and hippie, a pro football player who did yoga on the sidelines at Yale while everyone else ran sprints. I usually join in on painting, but I am so pregnant with our daughter Birdie that today I just sat and watched, hoping that if I just shifted one more time, I would somehow get comfortable. Spoiler: Nope.

Still, I was present. I kept a promise I made to myself a little over a year before to show up in my own life. To feel things, whether they were the result of bad memories, or good ones in the making. Like the gold of the setting sun hitting Maxwell's face as she knelt on the grass to draw freehand, the quick moves of a girl who is sure of herself. And Ace, stepping back to look at all the paints before committing to action. Just like me, he quietly observes and then has that moment where he tilts his head back and just *does*, every premeasured stroke of color seeming spontaneous.

We divide and conquer at bedtime. Eric takes Ace, who wants every minute he can get playing with Dad. I take Maxwell, who still lets me sing "Jesus Loves Me" with her every night. I know you might be thinking of the singsongy "Jesus Loves Me," but I do the version from *The Bodyguard*. The one where Whitney and her onscreen sister whisper-sing a slowed down, wistful version. Maxwell and I list off all the friends and family we are praying for, and then we sing, "Jesus loves them, oh, yes He does . . ."

Lullabies came hard for me. My first night home from the hospital with Maxwell, I was afraid to sing to her because I didn't know if I could sing quiet. I've never had to sing where I didn't have to *perform*. Aim my voice for the back of the arena. I remember thinking, *Should I just sing "The Star-Spangled Banner" quietly?* If I tried "Amazing Grace," I knew I would get the Spirit and bust her little eardrum. It was like I was in an *SNL* sketch about the over-singing pop-star mom. Whitney saved me.

Tonight, in Maxwell's room, when prayers were done, I got up from sitting on the bed—which takes some strategic planning when you are seven months pregnant—and I was about to slip out. Maxwell is not one of those kids who need you to stay until she's asleep. I love that she is her own girl *and* she will let you know it. But tonight, just as I went to turn off the light, I heard her little voice.

"Will you rub my nose?" she asked.

"Yes, baby."

This is something I did with both my kids when I breastfed them. I sat with them in my rocker, and stroked the bridges of their nose lightly, back and forth. Each stroke, an *I love you, I love you, I love you.* The times they ask for this are growing further apart, and I know that one of these times will be the last one. There are so many firsts to raising kids, and parents are told to catch them all. But they don't warn you about the lasts. The last baby onesie. The last time you tie their shoes. The last time they think you have every answer in the world.

As I rubbed her nose, Maxwell settled in to her pillow and sighed. I looked down at her closed eyes. *She is growing up so fast,* I thought. Just on the edge of the age I was when I began beating myself up when I fell short of perfect. A few months back, we were in the kitchen at lunchtime. I gave her tomato soup and I asked her if she wanted some bread.

"Bella told me bread makes you fat."

You are six, I thought.

"*Maxwell,* bread does not make you fat," I said. "And I don't understand why you would think about that."

"Well, Bella's mom does not eat bread."

"Well, you're gonna eat bread."

"Oh good," she said, and paused. "Because I really love bread."

"You listen to what *your* mommy says," I said. "Don't listen to someone else's mommy."

I even put extra butter on that bread. As I did so, I thought *How does she even know what "fat" is?* It was a wake-up call. She already has this world to grow up in, and I want her to feel safe enough to love herself and the body that God gave her. Not waste the time I did being cruel to myself. Standing in front of the mirror at seventeen, pinching a tiny vice grip of stomach fat until I bruised, because the first thing I heard from the record company after I signed was, "You've got to lose fifteen pounds."

Maxi is one of the reasons I am writing this book. It's also a commitment I've made to you, though it's hard sometimes to look back on some moments in my life that I spent years, okay, decades, trying to forget. For me, sitting down here with a piece of paper and a pen is like, "Hello, self! What are we gonna confront tonight?"

This was supposed to be a very different book. Five years ago, I was approached to write a motivational manual telling you how to live your best life. The Jessica Simpson Collection had become the top-selling celebrity fashion line, the first to earn one billion dollars in annual sales. I delivered the keynote at the *Forbes* Power Women Summit and *Women's Wear Daily* was talking up how smart I was to make clothes that flatter all silhouettes. (Hello, I've had every size in my closet, so I'd better be inclusive.) I was a boss, and I was supposed to tell you how to make *your* dream come true. You too could have a perfect life. Like me.

The deal was set, and it was a lot of money. And I walked away. Nobody understood why.

The truth is that I didn't want to lie to you. I couldn't be honest with you if I wasn't honest with myself first.

To get to this point, to talking to you right here in this moment, I had to really feel. And I hadn't been doing that. Up until a few years ago, I had been a feelings addict. Love, loss—whichever, whatever, as long as it was *epic*. I just needed enough noise to distract me from the pain I had been avoiding since childhood. The demons of traumatic abuse that refused to let me sleep at night—Tylenol PM at age twelve, red wine and Ambien as a grown, scared woman. Those same demons who perched on my shoulder, and when they saw a man as dark as them, leaned in to my ear to whisper, "Just give him all your light. See if it saves him. . . ."

For years, I occupied my time trying and failing to be the woman the men in my life wanted me to be. Never just me. I ran into situation after situation, telling myself that the reason I had so much anxiety and was scared to death to be alone at night was because I just needed to be a better person for whomever I was trying to please at the time.

When I found the love of my life in 2010 and started my family, I could just be me. I took myself out of the music industry to be normal and be the kind of mom I wanted to be. I had to change all my numbers and my email address so none of my exes had any hope of contact. It sounds dramatic, but I had dated a guy who had a habit of showing up out of nowhere to mess with my mind.

It was a good plan, but without the creative outlet of making music or the distraction of cryptic man texts to decipher like riddles, my anxiety took over. I didn't know what to do with all that energy. I was like a lot of women who get their wish: I loved being a mom, I just didn't love being me.

To avoid feeling, I numbed myself with alcohol. For about three years of my life, up until Halloween 2017, I had an unhealthy relationship with alcohol. I never hid it. "I know, I know," I told my friends, "I just need another one." I had given up drinking so easily when I was pregnant and never craved it, so I didn't think it was a problem. But our house was the gathering place for all my friends, the place where everyone always ended up. I had a prescription for a stimulant, which gave me the focus to never get messy. I'd look around at my friends getting sleepy and/or sloppy and think, *I'm just an ox, I guess*. Then at night, still flying from the second stimulant that I had maybe taken at six p.m. with tons of alcohol in my system, I'd take an Ambien.

Yes, I realize I am very lucky to be here with you. Even then, I knew it was getting out of hand, but I put that on the back burner. I told myself, *Eventually, you'll get it together.* There was always a later. *Soon the kids will notice,* I worried. I never grew up with alcohol in the house, and we had *so much.* If the kids started questioning us about why, I wouldn't have the answer. Because I didn't know why we had so much alcohol. Except that our house was always the party house for all our friends. When the kids notice, I promised myself, I'd stop.

There was no time, though. I was juggling relationships, my business, motherhood, and the needs of anybody but me. I didn't think I was enough, so I overcompensated by making my life a series of experiences for everyone else. There was always another friends-and-family getaway overseas, and then I'd come home to plan an over-the-top kid's birthday party.

Maybe you'll relate: It's like when everything is moving really fast, but you've created that speed. You're the one who set all these great things into motion, but now they're spinning all at once. You take a step back to try to make some sense of it, and before you know it, you've accidentally become a spectator to your own life, unsure how that woman who used to be you plans on doing it all. You stand there thinking, *Okay, when am I gonna jump back in?*

And when I did, I knew I had to face my fears and do it sober.

Or else I'd be a hypocrite.

I can't really stand in front of the world and say how much I love myself when I'm destroying myself. I had to strip away all the self-medicating to feel the pain and figure out what was wrong. I'm still doing the work in therapy two times a week resolving those issues. Honestly, I am not sure if I'll have another drink in the future. Will I have a glass of wine in the South of France in two years? The last thing I need is another reason to feel self-conscious about paparazzi catching me doing something and proclaiming, "Oh, she's off the wagon." But then I remind myself that life is really just about one moment at a time. To not think about two years from now, but to think about me right now. Two years from now will figure itself out.

Right now, with this book, I want the freedom to say, "Well, there are no more secrets." I have grown into myself and come to a place where I want to be honest about my flaws. If I can do that in front of the world, then I can remain honest with myself. I like to say stuff out loud so then I can be accountable, but that also leaves me open to criticism. I beat myself up enough with this fight club in my head that I know what can happen if I invite new members. My purpose, however, is bigger than my fear of judgment. Someone, maybe you, needs me to say the things that are scary to admit. If I go there, maybe I can show you that you can, too. I don't live in a fantasy world—it might seem that way to other people, but I don't. All of us are so much more alike than we want to accept.

I always knew I was going to be a writer. Even though I'm Southern and sometimes say things in an off-kilter way, I do like the romance of the hard stuff in life. I know there are people who think I can't string two thoughts together, let alone sentences. In the beginning of my career, somehow, I was always the joke. Everybody made fun of something I'd say, and I admit, I definitely played into it. People's laughter meant a lot to me, and being the joke validated me being smart to myself. It felt like I could pull one over on somebody. I thought, *How dumb are you to think I'm that stupid?*

The fact is that I have kept journals since I was fifteen. I started the year my cousin Sarah was killed in an accident. Two years and three days older than me, she was like a sister to me. Sarah left behind a ton of journals, listing off the people she was praying for. When I read her journals, I saw that she had prayed for me. Every day. I inherited her purpose, and I still feel a need to see through what she had started in so many ways. As I wrote about situations in my life and the people I was praying for, the journals became a safe place for me to talk through things without putting any pressure on anybody. And crushes. Oh, so many crushes.

I dragged out a huge box of journals to read through as I started writing to you. The first one has a cover of smiley faces, but in my early twenties I began to fill up Mead Five Star spiral notebooks. I had a few pretty ones I got as gifts, but they always had like one or two pages of notes in them before I gave up. I needed the drugstore kind with hard plastic covers in different colors, a code that only I understood. A black one for the end of my first marriage, red for the hope of a love affair, blue for when I wanted to focus on my career and song lyrics . . . I often wrote in pencil, so I could go back and erase it if I wrote something grammatically incorrect or spelled a word wrong. Partly because I am so self-conscious, but also because, if I died like Sarah, I wanted people to think I was smart.

It upsets me to read some things I said about myself. In the journals from 1999, I beat myself up about how fat I was before I even gave the world a chance to. Ten years later, I wrote about the world telling me exactly what they thought of me when I wore size 27 "mom jeans" to a Chili CookOff concert in Florida. The sad thing is that I talked about finally feeling confident in the pages before that. That ended. "What percentage of the day do I think about my body on a scale of 1–100?" I wrote. "80%. I hate this."

But there are good times to relive too. There are moments when I read what I wrote now and I say, "Wait, I like this person. We could make a good life together if we were friends."

I also hope to be your friend. I am going to need you to hold my hand through some memories, and there may be times that I'll end up holding yours as we confront similar things that scare us. I've come to recognize fear when I see it. It may show itself in different ways, but it's a familiar face, isn't it? I have a different relationship to fear now. I've learned that we grow from walking through it, and a lot of people don't even know they have that option. You either conquer it, or you let it destroy you. So, let's do this together. I promise we'll laugh, too, because I do get myself into situations. I mean, it *had* to be a Chili CookOff of all places. Most of all, I promise to be totally honest with you, so you can feel safe to be honest with yourself, too.

When I told my closest girlfriends I was writing a book, they all came up with possible titles. One wanted it to reference the breakout moment on *Newlyweds* when I wondered aloud—and on camera—if the Chicken of the Sea I was eating was tuna or chicken.

"Call it *I Know It's Chicken*," said one girlfriend, and everyone started saying it loudly to themselves. "*I Know It's Chicken*."

"Guys, it's tuna," I said. "I should know." We all about died laughing.

See? Life's taught me a few things. Here's my story. I'm not afraid of it anymore.

part one

1

A LESSON IN
SURVIVAL

Ace was in the backseat, recounting an episode of *Wild Kratts*. At four, my son lived for his cartoons, and could reel off facts about all the animals he saw on the nature show.

"Did you know there are fish that can fly?" he asked us.

"Fish that fly?" I said.

"Yeah, they're called flying fish."

"That's a good name for them," I said. Eric was at the wheel, driving us to a Tuesday morning Halloween assembly at our daughter Maxwell's school. I sat on the passenger side, absently practicing my "I have it together" face.

It was seven-thirty in the morning and I'd already had a drink. I always had a glittercup in reach at home. That's what I called the shiny tumblers filled with vodka and flavored Perrier.

At that time, the flavor was mostly strawberry, but by then I didn't care what it tasted like. I just needed a drink every morning because I had the shakes.

My anxiety always kicked into high gear before school functions, and there had been a few performances since Maxwell started kindergarten in September. I knew how important they were, even if they made me nervous. All these five-year-old kids in their navy-blue school uniforms, learning not to be scared to perform in front of so many people. Maxwell was going to sing at the Halloween assembly, and I'd tried to get her to practice the song in front of me at home the night before.

"I want to surprise you," she said.

"No, but, I really want to know what you're doing," I said. "I want to know if I can help out."

"I got it," she said.

That is my daughter. Maxwell is so like my younger sister Ashlee, and I love them both for their independence. I constantly find myself calling Maxwell "Ashlee" and vice versa. Maxi is in control, and I never want to be overbearing. It was hard for me not to try to protect her when she was too young to understand nerves yet. When she would say, "Why is my tummy upset?' before a performance, I'd feel a sympathetic flip of my own stomach remembering all the times I had nerves before going onstage or doing an interview. Eric knew what that was like, too, that feeling right before he went on the field playing football at Yale or for the 49ers. That pressure of everyone looking at you.

I felt it then in the car headed to school. By then, I had engineered my life so the world mostly came to my house, a comfortable hangout place for my family and friends, and I had the ability to do almost all the business side of my collection there, too. I even had my own recording studio. I could be safe at home. It was almost a shock that morning to realize, *God I have to put myself together.* Put the pieces of the puzzle together from a memory of who people expected me to be. I knew I was falling apart, but I had to look like a good mom who was present for her children. Which I was—I am—but I was just never going to be the cupcake mom or the arts-and-crafts helper at school. Even then, when I knew I was operating at about fifteen percent, I knew I was a good mom.

We pulled into the lot and I spotted my dad's new Mercedes. It was hard to miss, a bright-green, custom sports car I recognized from his Instagram. I had not seen much of my father since my parents split in 2012. They were married for thirty four years, and I had a hard time being around them together since they'd stopped loving each other. My father decided to tell me his plan to leave my mother when I was at Cedars-Sinai hospital, a week before I delivered Maxwell. No spotlight is safe around a Simpson—we'll steal it every time.

I was blindsided by this news, which triggered his natural salesmanship. He pitched it to me as a positive thing. "You gave me the confidence," my father added, quietly. "You gave me a way out."

Great, I thought to myself, *I broke my own heart.* When he left the room, I broke down. I gave my father a way out of his marriage to my mother.

I didn't want to be thanked. I wanted them to be grandparents. I wanted them to be there for me as I was about to have my first child. Eric had to hold me as I repeated over and over, "It's not my fault."

Five years later, my dad was inside waiting for us in the gymnasium at Maxwell's school. The performances are usually in the school auditorium, but for some reason they switched it that morning. I had the feeling I did when I was just starting out. There would be a sudden venue change for a showcase, or you thought the stage would be higher—it just threw me. The seating was in the bleachers and I walked in to see everyone looking down on me. Sounds were ricocheting off every surface and the place was lit up so bright I wanted to put my sunglasses back on.

I hugged my father quickly, and we all made our way up to find spots in the bleachers. Dad sat directly behind me, and I was relieved my mother wasn't there. Even choosing who to sit next to seemed to send a message about whose side I was on. Honestly, since the divorce, I'd chosen my mother, period. She was someone I dealt with day-to-day running the Jessica Simpson Collection. When I saw them together with Maxwell and Ace, instead of appreciating it I found myself mourning my old normal. The new normal sucked. The new normal was the role reversal of my parents coming to my house separately for the holidays like they were teenagers. *This is what life is,* I would say to myself. *Forget what life* was.

Even if I tried to be impartial, I could see how my mom was blindsided and hurt. Tina Ann Drew was seventeen when Joe Truett Simpson started working as the youth minister at her church in McGregor, Texas. He'd only taken the job out of desperation. The youngest son of a Baptist preacher, my dad had done everything he could to avoid following in his dad's footsteps. But his scholarship to Baylor didn't cover room and board, so he finally asked my grandfather to get him a job. His first night on the job, he went back to Baylor, told his roommate he met the girl he was gonna marry, and broke up with the Tri Delta sorority girl he'd been seeing. He waited six months to ask my mom out, and first checked with the pastor to see if it was possible. He told my dad he had to ask the permission of the youth committee chairman. Which happened to be my mom's mother.

Nana said yes, which surprised everyone. My mom's parents were strict—my Papaw was a principal and Nana was a librarian who required order in her life. Mom was the youngest of three girls and had the most drive to start a life away from home. And there was Joe, who believed that since all things were possible in Christ, why not dream big? They married right away, and along came me.

"Well, she was a busted condom," Dad would say in my earshot when I set out to do something big. "So, she came with purpose." My mom always told me I was the fastest swimmer. I was an accident, but it really did just reinforce the idea that God sent me here for a reason. During Sex Ed in school, they told us all to use condoms. "They're ninety-nine percent effective."

I stood up. "I'm the one percent," I yelled, "so it can happen to you! Let's be abstinent." I was a witness.

I always felt that need as a preacher's daughter. If I thought that was a lot of responsibility, try being a preacher's wife. Mom was the first to tell me her life was all about business. The business of the church, and then the business of their children. And then it all ended, and she hadn't seen it coming. She spent decades putting her brilliant business mind to work for our family behind the scenes. Dad had the ideas, she would fine-tune them and pull them down a bit from the stratosphere. Then Dad would sell it. He was the pitchman who could sell anything. *If my dad can make people believe in God,* I always thought at the start of my career, *he can surely make people believe in me.*

He did for a long time, but I had to fire him as my manager in 2012. He thought I was following my mother's wishes, but he had made some bad deals for me. Just stupid stuff that people promised to him and he believed. Bridges were burned, and I didn't know how many until I tried to cross them. It took about five times to really fire him before the message stuck. The first time I chickened out and did it in an email. I finally just said it to his face.

Now, in the gym before the concert, I realized my dad was talking to me. I turned to face him and answered, something about the performance. His face changed, and I realized he smelled the vodka on my breath. His eyes widened in surprise, and then narrowed in a look of concern or pity, I wasn't sure. I turned quickly, glancing at two cupcake moms eyeing me. They sat next to each other and chatted through smiles as they went up from my shoes to my dress to my hair. I smiled back at them and they looked away. I wished I had a girlfriend here with me. I blamed myself for not making more of an effort to get to know other moms at school, but I also knew I was barely hanging on. I just wasn't capable of small talk with strangers.

I leaned over Ace to whisper to Eric. "I feel like everyone's staring at me," I said through a closed smile that matched the cupcake moms'. He gave me a look that told me that was because they were. My husband can always tell what's on my mind.

Finally, the kids started the performance and everyone cheered. Maxwell spotted us in the crowd, and I let out a "Whoop" when we made eye contact. I was so proud of her.

It's enough that this piece of my heart walked around outside of me, but to see her be so confident and happy was a blessing. I felt real joy. I was pulled into being present, forgetting everyone else around me. Just there. I wished it could be like that all the time.

When I performed, I was always present, but it had been years since I was onstage. My kids had never even seen me perform. The only time Eric had seen me sing in front of an audience was when I was promoting my second Christmas album in 2010, but that had been on a Macy's Thanksgiving Day Parade float surrounded by dancing muffins and gingerbread men. Eric couldn't really get a sense of me as an artist in that setting. For about a year, I'd been writing and recording music in my home studio—raw and from the heart. It was music I was really proud of. But I still worried that to my family I was like a pop star in theory only.

The assembly ended, and my anxiety returned. Stronger now. Parents descended from the bleachers to greet their kids. The gymnasium seemed brighter, and even louder. I needed to get out of there.

Maxwell came over and we gave her huge hugs before the students needed to go back to class. Ace looked up at her, his eyes wide, and I remembered that no matter how well you know someone, seeing someone perform temporarily changes how you see them. I became very conscious of what I wanted to tell her. I'd read enough parenting books to know not to say what I'd heard as a kid from people who meant well: "You looked beautiful." Or, "You were perfect." Instead, I told her I loved seeing her perform. "You looked so happy up there."

My dad started in, praising Maxwell to the heavens. I

looked away. She and her friends headed back to her classroom, and Ace started pulling Eric to the door. They were going to throw around a football, and I was happy to cheer them on. But there was something else I had to do.

"Dad, come to the house," I said. "I'll ride with you."

He has this way of cocking his head when he is excited, a constant movement that shows all the energy inside him. "Of course," he said.

"I wanna play you some of my music."

As we made our way to the house, I could barely talk. I got Dad talking about the new car and his photography hobby and business, which he could talk about for hours. It was how I negotiated a lot of conversations with people at that time. I listened to every word, but only chimed in now and again to keep them going.

For the past year, I'd both dreaded and dreamt of letting my dad hear this music. As my manager, my father heard every demo I ever made. He knew all my music before it was even produced. But I hadn't told him I had been writing. And I had not just been making music about what I'd been through in life, there were songs about him.

We got to the house at about 9:30, and Dad had to navigate his Mercedes around the party rental trucks already lining up. That night I was set to host a Halloween party. Eric and I had become famous for our extravagant parties, especially on Halloween. Every year I posted a photo on my socials of the family in costume, and in 2011 I even announced my second pregnancy in a Halloween post of me holding my bump in a tight mummy costume. I put pressure on myself to make each year bigger and better than the last. My friend Stephanie, who

I've known since fifth grade, is an amazing event planner and I asked her to put together a Halloween party that would also celebrate our friend Koko's birthday. In our circle of friends, I have always treated every birthday as a sacred event. I always collected the candles they'd wished on, carefully placing them in a Ziploc bag to give to them to hold until the wish came true. My friends joked that they had drawers full of ungranted wishes, but if they refused to take them, I secretly held them for them. I couldn't give up on their wishes.

As soon as my dad and I got into the house, I got a new glittercup going. There was comfort in the weight of a full tumbler, the slosh of the ice as I took sips. Liquid courage to go downstairs to the recording studio. Ozzy Osbourne had it built when he lived there before me. He was so sweet, but let's just say we have a different design aesthetic. The studio was all black and scary when I moved in. I made it mine, lightening the room and overlapping pretty rugs to create a sound cocoon.

I took a rolly chair at the console, bending my leg to put one foot up on the chair as I absently swiveled back and forth. I kept catching eyes with the idols that I'd put up to inspire me. A blown-up Polaroid self-portrait by Stevie Nicks in the 1970s, wild-haired and wild-hearted, leaning into the camera to fix her lipstick. Keith Richards smirking at me in sunglasses, sitting on a private jet in L.A. with Ron Wood in 1979. An eight-by-ten of Led Zeppelin in 1970, the four of them just on the verge of becoming rock gods. What would they all make of a pop star afraid to even press play for her daddy?

He was quiet, as if he were afraid of changing my mind. In hindsight, I am sure I seemed petrified. I realized, within that year of writing, how much I went through without letting him know. His choice to leave my mother was like a bomb going off in my life, and I still found myself clinging to whatever I could hold on to. The feeling of displacement made my anxiety so much worse, and I drank more to quiet those thoughts. He didn't mean to hurt all of us so badly, but I knew for a fact that he had realized his decision would have consequences. I know he knew that because that's what he had taught me. But I had kept that from him. And now I needed him to hear that I was singing about him.

I cued up "Practice What You Preach," which I saw as a direct hit at him. I was standing in judgment of someone who I felt had compromised his values. As he listened, the blood drained from his face until it was ashen. *What have I done?* I thought. He nodded, and started crying, which got me crying.

"Jess, it's beautiful," he said. I thought he was bluffing. I played another song, "Rolling with the Punches," his story set to my music. Again, my voice filled the room as I said nothing. "I see a little kid crying in you," I sang on the track. "I see the little kid dressed in his Sunday best." I went right into "Party of One," which is about how abandoned I'd felt by him and my mother choosing the very moment I needed them most, becoming a mother, to go off and start their new lives. I'd never been brave enough to tell him I was mad at him. I watched his face as he listened, eyes closed. I don't know what I expected from him. Anger? That he would leave? He didn't. He got up and put his arms around me until I shook with tears.

"I am so proud of you," he said.

For the first time in my entire life, he was responding to something I created not as a manager, but as a father. "You're not mad?" I asked.

"No," he said. "I'm sad I'm not the one promoting it." I waited for him to start with a business plan, some pitch to lure me back in. Instead, he just said, "I love you."

A weight, one I didn't even know I was carrying, lifted. I'd gotten so used to it. The sense that my father wouldn't love me if he wasn't managing me. The certainty that I did something wrong. But instead of relief, I felt untethered. Who was I if I had no one to blame for my life but myself?

The edges of my memory begin to blur here. I know I led him upstairs, and he talked about coming back for the party later. "I'll see you tonight," he said.

I held it together until he was outside, then I leaned on the closed door. Slowly, I fell to a sitting position, put down my glittercup, and slumped down to lay on the cold, pale, white stone floor of my entryway. On my back, I looked up at the vaulted ceiling, focusing on the chandelier as tears fell. *I lost him,* I thought. Even though he loved and accepted it, I experienced the pain of him not being my manager for the first time. I had been so frustrated with him that I never mourned the loss of his guidance. How was I ever going to be successful without him? And why in the world would I ever be so judgmental of my father when I wasn't true to what *I* said in my life? Forget what *he* preached. *I* was a fraud. I took all the pressures in my head and blamed them on my relationships with other people. Instead of it being my relationship with myself.

I felt nekkid. Not naked, nekkid. Truly bare, with no one else to blame anymore but me.

I wasn't drunk. Trust me, two was not doing it at that point. All the feelings I had been suppressing washed over me in a rush, and I was drowning in them. My world was rotating around me so fast that I didn't have any clue as to how to control it. I tried to talk to God, because we had always worked things out together, no matter how lonely I felt in life. He would tell me, "Get up, Jessica," and give me the strength to do it.

Nothing. I heard nothing. I still knew He was in control, though. He was doing this to me so I understood I couldn't live like this anymore. That I had to change. And then a voice did come.

"Are you okay?"

It wasn't God, it was our house manager Randy. He was my dad's best friend when I was a kid. His wife, Beth, was my dance teacher in fifth grade, then my choreographer on tour, and now she helps run my clothing line. When I love you, I want you to stick around.

I didn't answer at first. It was a real question. In my entire life, whenever someone asked me if I was okay, the answer was a reflex: "Yes." Because, no matter what, I always wanted it to be true.

"I am *not* okay," I said, surprising myself. I said the words again, differently each time, like an actress trying to get hold of a line, seeing what it felt like to admit I needed help. "I am not *okay*. Randy, *I* am not okay."

He went to get other people. I don't know who. There's always a lot of people at my house. The entryway is a high-traffic area, and people literally had to walk over me to get the house ready for the party. I had always been the boss, always in control, so I guess they thought I just needed a minute.

There was a flurry of texts. My friends freaked out and called Eric. I always joked to them that I was a mess, but the girlfriend bat signal had gone up for real: "Jessica's not okay." I was ashamed, and more so because it was Halloween. I had to be a mom that night. I had to take my kids trick-or-treating. I had to be here for the eighty people who were coming over. And now I was stuck on the floor—

Ace would see me like this, I thought. At any moment he would walk in with Eric. That's what got me up. I needed to hide.

I got another glittercup. By then my close friends started arriving to check on me. I greeted everyone the same way: "I'm not okay." Not as an apology, but a baffled realization. I couldn't fix it. The car I drove at a hundred miles per hour was out of control with the steering wheel locked, and I could only turn to the passengers and say, "Well, this is bad."

Then the hair and makeup team arrived. A glam squad for a breakdown. The plan for my Halloween costume was to dress me up as Willie Nelson, my friend and spirit animal ever since we worked together in late 2004 on my first film, *The Dukes of Hazzard.* We still call each other by our character names, Daisy and Uncle Jesse. He and his wife are my role models for marriage. My own marriage was collapsing during that movie, and on set I hung out in his trailer, let him see through the happy face I put on for people. Now and then through the years, just when I needed it, he would text me a simple, "I love you, Daisy. Love, Uncle Jesse." I needed it every time.

Me dressing up as Willie was Eric's idea. We were in our study, where I have a big picture of Willie with his friend Waylon Jennings on a shelf, right below Eric's 49ers helmet. He looked at the photo and decided it would be hysterical if I went as Willie and Eric as Waylon.

I zoned out while the team went to work for hours, gluing a gray beard to my face and helping me into a wig of Willie's signature long braids and an American flag bandana. I stared at the mirror, relieved not to see me at all.

Eric came in and I made like I was in character. It saved me from being honest. He asked if I wanted to help the kids get ready. I didn't answer. I let it seem like I was too busy, when he knew that kind of stuff was always a joy for me. Maxwell was home, he said. I was terrified of letting her see me in that shape. She was going to be Belle from *Beauty and the Beast*, while Ace was going to be a cowboy. I am ashamed to say that I don't know who got them into their costumes that night. I was the mom who set the alarm an hour early if my daughter wanted a French braid for school. Usually, I would a hundred percent be there for a moment like a Halloween costume. I wasn't.

But I needed the picture to post. Eric and the kids didn't care, but people expected it, I told myself. Through the window I saw Eric, who in his black hat and vest looked more like Kevin Richardson from the Backstreet Boys than Waylon Jennings. My mom gathered Maxwell and Ace for the photo, and I finally joined them outside. People had already started to arrive, and there were so many kids. I strummed my guitar as Willie would, holding it out to keep people at arm's length as they laughed at my transformation. Ace looked uncertain, but I was relieved when I realized it was because he didn't know who I was in my beard and braids. *Perfect,* I thought. *This broken person is not your mother, my sweet son.* Nothing to see here.

So, I went through the motions and got the photos, like every mom does on special occasions. Just get the damn photo so we can create the memory. Then I can go back to real life.

Then I could go back inside and hide. In the photos, Eric has his hand on the small of my back. He is smiling, but I know he is scared for me.

As I turned to go inside, Eric announced we were all going trick-or-treating. All the kids at the party yelled in excitement, and I shrank. I forgot this had been the plan. We'd rented golf carts to take everyone out around the gated community where we live.

"Eric, I can't," I whispered.

"What do you mean, you can't?" he said. He had been shouldering much of the party hosting on his own that day. There was frustration in his voice. "We've got like twenty golf carts."

"I can't."

"Just get on the golf cart," he said. "We're going to go trick-or-treating."

"I'm just gonna sit down for a while."

I turned and went upstairs to my room. I could hear guests tooting golf-cart horns and kids laughing. I started peeling off the beard, but found it was stuck. I didn't care. I couldn't care. I didn't care if I had a house full of guests. I felt broken, undeserving of even being around them. I always put so much pressure on myself to have these parties. Now, it all felt so pointless. I would spend weeks choosing the perfect wrapping paper for people's presents, and it would be ripped up in a minute. Nobody expected this kind of extravagance, it was just me imagining that they did. Now it was worse than not being enough—I couldn't even show up for my own party.

I took an Ambien. Maybe two. It was a security pill to me—no matter how tired I was, I was terrified of being awake in bed. I knew exactly why I was always so afraid, but that didn't mean I was ever going to do anything about it.

My housekeeper, Evelyn, found me crying in my room. She had been with me fifteen years and was like a second mom to me. She sat next to me and held me. I felt like I swam for hours, and barely made it to shore. She laid me back, stroked my forehead lightly, and I was gone. I welcomed oblivion.

HERE I WOULD LIKE TO TELL YOU THAT I GOT UP EARLY THE NEXT DAY AND got my kids to school. I did not. I slept in, afraid to see them and hoping that Eric would tell them I wasn't feeling well. I had failed them. No matter how much of a mess I had been, I thought that I had always shown up for them. The fact that I wasn't present for them, even for just one night, was unacceptable.

I hid until they left, then drank. I felt emotionally hungover, and thought I needed it to recover. I needed to be normal for when my friends came over for our weekly meeting. There's a core three who help me take care of business: My publicist Lauren, who is way more my friend than my publicist to be honest; CaCee, my friend since I first signed with Columbia in 1997; and Koko, who is not just my assistant but one of my best friends.

Koko. I had bailed on Koko's party. I had a huge cake for her and everything. I wondered if they'd even brought it out. It was another failure.

That day was supposed to be special, because I'd flown my hair colorist Rita Hazan in from New York. She's an artist and has been doing my hair since 1999. She packs everything she might need into Burton snowboarding suitcases for an at-home process that takes about an hour. She is so chill and cool with her light Brooklyn accent that I never mind her hearing anything. The girls would be here while I had my hair done. Multitasking.

CaCee and Koko arrived first, finding me still in a panicked state as Rita readied her station in my home. Koko was obviously hurt, and I immediately started crying to her. I blubbered with apologies as Rita left the room to get something.

"I . . . missed . . . putting . . . the . . . candles . . . in . . . the . . . Ziploc . . . bag . . ."

"It's okay," Koko said meekly.

"But I feel awful."

Stephanie walked in. She was there to load out the party she had put so much work into and that I had missed. She took in the tension right away.

CaCee gave me a sharp, direct, "Why do think you feel awful?"

"Because I wasn't present?" I said, like I was guessing at a math problem.

"And why weren't you present?" she said.

I knew that one. "Because I probably drank too much?"

"Probably?" CaCee asked.

Stephanie, the good cop to CaCee's tough one, cut in with her sweet Texas lilt. "Jess, maybe you should—"

Rita came back in, and I was so relieved. She ran her hands through my hair, letting it catch the light to better examine it, and asked what look I was going for.

I sighed. "Bleach it," I mumbled. "Just completely bleach my hair and make me look like Andy Warhol." Suicide by hairstyle.

"What the hell are you talking about?" yelled CaCee, shaking her head "no" at Rita, her head of blonde curls swaying with her anger.

"I just want it all off," I said.

"*Jess*, why do you think you drank too much?" asked CaCee. "Do you think you've been drinking too much a lot of days?"

"Yes," I blurted. "I need to stop. *Something's* gotta stop. And if it's the alcohol that's doing this and making things worse, then I quit."

Stephanie sighed, as if CaCee had pulled the right plug to stop a time bomb at the last second.

But CaCee didn't relent. She grabbed my face, holding my chin in her palm. "You better not be lying."

The chin grab was CaCee's signature move. The first time I had to go onstage alone after leaving my husband Nick in 2005, I stood frozen backstage, convinced no one would accept me on my own again. She grabbed my chin, and said a firm, "*Get out there*."

"Jessica," she said, as Rita looked on. "This is your rock bottom. This is it. Do you want to change?"

"Yes!" I said. "Like, right now. Yes."

I know my limits, and I had gone beyond them. I was allowing myself to be taken away from moments that I should have been in. Now I needed to turn inward. To live in the moment and not live in the lie anymore.

I breathed in, breathed out, and looked around. "At least I can say my rock bottom had pretty pillows," I said. "A soft landing."

The girls gathered me up in a group hug, and from the center I called out to Eric.

He came in. "Babe, I'm gonna stop drinking," I said, just like that. As if I said, "I'm going to the store. Need anything?"

He looked right at me. "Then I will too," he said.

"Really?"

"Yeah. We're in this together."

"Okay, can you make me one last drink?" I asked.

"What?"

"Just the last one to say good-bye."

I know, I know. I hear the record scratch, too. But I said I'd be honest with you. I had one more glittercup.

But CaCee wasn't going to let me weasel out of my promise. She immediately texted Lauren, who was still on her way. "Dude get your people moving. She's ready."

And then, as Rita wrapped foils around my hair to dye it a sane color, Stephanie, CaCee, and Koko explained that they had been planning for this moment for more than six months. Lauren already had a doctor lined up, one who specialized in getting celebrities in-home treatment for addiction. It's a company town, after all. Lauren had pulled over and was already on the phone, getting a time for me to talk to the doctor, who would then dispatch a therapist specific to my needs depending on what I said on the call.

I had the nerve to be offended. "You were all talking behind my back?"

They each shared their intervention plans, making it clear they did so because they were afraid I was going to die. Stephanie, for one, had planned to talk to my mother.

"My *mother*?" I said. "Oh God, no. Steph, if my mom told me to stop drinking, I would drink more."

Another plan was to have Linda Perry talk to me. She's in

the Songwriters Hall of Fame, and I had recently been working with her creating music. Linda had already reprimanded me about writing under the influence. "I don't want that drunk stuff," she said. "I need sober writing."

"I would have been so insulted," I said. "She's known me three months."

"See?" Said CaCee. "We had to let you—"

"But why would you never just come to me?" I said, trying to stay still for Rita as she worked on my hair. "Say, 'This is too much, Jess. We're gonna have to take it to the next level.' Because I would do that to you guys. *For* you guys, I mean. Why would you be scared to talk to me? I'm not gonna be mad at you."

"Like now?" asked CaCee.

"I mean, I am out with all y'all in different places, ordering drinks and you're ordering drinks, too," I said, on the defensive. "Why wouldn't you just be like, 'Let's not drink tonight.'"

They were quiet. A long beat.

I broke the silence. "I mean, I would have probably laughed at you . . ."

Everyone laughed, even Rita. "But then I would have known it was worrying you." It didn't break my heart that I was such a mess that they wanted to intervene. It broke my heart that they felt they had to go behind my back. But they were right. I had deeper problems than alcohol, and I couldn't resolve the problem until I threw away the crutch.

"Guys, I think we should pray," said Stephanie. She has been with me since we were kids going to Heights Baptist in Texas. She knew what faith means to me.

I stood, foils still in my hair, and the four of us held hands.

"Lord, she's giving this burden to you," Stephanie said. Koko gripped my hand tight.

"I'm giving this to you," I said. "I am your humble servant and—"

A ding went off. Rita's timer.

"Okay, you gave it to God," Rita said. "We gotta wash that stuff out now. Or you *will* look like Andy Warhol."

She rinsed me out, just as Nikki and Riawna arrived to put in my extensions. They are the co-owners of Nine Zero One, a big salon in West Hollywood. I know, this story only gets more over-the-top, but so was my life. We were getting set up in the wooden chair in my study when Lauren came in.

I was crying, tears pouring from my eyes, and we just exchanged a look that said it was time. She told me she lined up the call with the doctor. "She's ready now. Are you?"

"Yes," I said, looking up at Nikki and Riawna. They nodded. I didn't hesitate for a second. I trusted them and I knew now was my time. Besides, I didn't care who heard my truth. I was tired of letting shame dictate my actions. And do you know how hard it is to schedule Nikki and Riawna?

Once I was on the phone with the doctor, I started in with a complete play-by-play of all my life's traumas. The sexual abuse I suffered in childhood, and the abusive, obsessive relationships I clung to in adulthood. I was crying, the women doing my extensions were crying, and my friends were a mess. Still, I reeled off everything in a matter-of-fact manner, connecting dots about why each event had contributed to my anxiety, finally ending with, "So this is why I need help and why I can't do this on my own."

I paused to breathe.

"Wow," the doctor said.

My eyebrows shot up. Was I that bad?

"First of all," she continued, "people don't know themselves that well. And the fact that you don't know *me*, and you're telling me all this on the phone tells me you are desperate."

I wasn't trying to get an A in breaking down. She said a lot of people who use alcohol as a temporary coping mechanism generally aren't aware of what they're covering up, so the abuse becomes permanent. Knowing what I had to face was a good sign for me.

She lined up a nurse and another therapist to come over that very night. In the meantime, we moved every drop of alcohol out of the house, but we didn't really need to bother. I had no craving for it. I was mad at it. I was starting to feel. Like, *Oh, this is what it felt like to be living.*

The therapist came and hesitated in the doorway like the exorcist coming to cast out the demons. The house was dark, and I led her to my study, right where I am writing to you now. I thought she was stiff at first and spoke so softly I could barely hear her, but she was just getting the lay of the land. Eric had the fireplace going for us, and we sat across from each other.

"So," she said, "let's talk about what's brought you to this point."

And the work began. To walk forward through my anxiety, I first had to look back to understand what pain I was running from, and what I was trying to hide.

2

SINGING MY LIFE

I don't remember the accident. I was a month shy of turning two years old, so I have to borrow the details of this memory from my mother.

She was driving near our home in Fort Worth. It was just us in Dad's heap of a car, a 1964 Chevy Nova with a rust paint job. It was so old there were no seatbelts in the back, and I would constantly shift across the cracked vinyl.

I wanted to go to McDonald's, and my mom didn't seem to understand how serious I was about this. I stood on the backseat and leaned so I could throw my arms around her, grabbing her face with both hands to yell, "McDonald's!"

"Jessica!" she screamed. She looked away from the road. How long? A second? Two? Enough to drive across the lane and hit a car coming toward us.

I flew headfirst at the windshield. I went halfway through it, cracking my skull on the way. The drag of the glass held me, and I fell back inside the car, landing on the floorboard on the passenger side. The shattered windshield then fell on me in a shower of glass. Mom had a bone sticking out of her broken leg. She had also broken her arm and collarbone. She couldn't get out of the driver's side, so she climbed over me to pull herself out. Sitting on the ground, she brushed glass off me, not sure if I was alive.

A good Samaritan ran over to help us. An ambulance came and rushed us to the hospital, and thankfully no one in the other car was injured.

Someone at the hospital called my dad and told him his wife was in the hospital. "Your baby is in critical condition." I had two purple-black eyes, and a very bad concussion. My mom stayed in the hospital for a week.

My stutter started soon after, and the doctors said it was from the head injury. My mom said that when I stuttered it looked like my brain and I were trying to say ten things at once. My voice just wouldn't work.

"You can't focus on the one idea you need to talk about," she told me. "Just say the one thing, Jess." She is the youngest of three—the Drew girls of McGregor, Texas—and her middle sister Connie was a speech therapist. Aunt Connie advised her to get me to calm down.

"Take a breath," my mother would say, getting down to my level to look me in the eye. That only worked so well. If you want someone to calm down, try telling them "calm down" and see where it gets you. But Connie had another idea, something that worked with other people who stuttered. Singing.

"What you're trying to say," Mom said to me one day, "sing it to me."

I turned the phrase over in my mind, smoothing the edges of its consonants and vowels until the words became the breaths of a song. A lyric I could control.

"I want Cheeeeeeri-ohhhhs," I sang. I can't describe that release. The rush of simply being understood.

"Yes, you can have Cheerios," my mother yelled. "You can have whatever you want! You sound so beautiful."

For the next two years, singing was the only time I didn't stutter. I sang for everything I wanted, like some Disney princess making a wish. Around four, the stutter became more pronounced and my parents took me to a therapist. He used art therapy and asked me to draw myself in the family. I drew my parents standing in front of our house, then put myself inside looking out from a window. He told my parents I had a fear of abandonment. Looking back, I know my parents never left me alone, and maybe I was even around them too much. But somehow, I still had a fear that they would leave me.

I kept going, and the stutter resolved. I stayed shy, though, and it didn't really help that our family was constantly moving. We would move eighteen times before I hit fifth grade. You move around a lot working in the Baptist church, but my father was especially restless. Even when he left the ministry for a few years when I was little to see what it would be like for us to actually have money, he kept accepting transfers from his job selling postage meters for Pitney Bowes.

He usually gave my mom and me one month's notice. "Say bye to your friends." The ones I had just made. Even with my shyness, I learned to adjust until change was maybe not easy but expected.

We were briefly living in Waco when my sister Ashlee was born in October 1984. I was four and had prayed for a sister. I stopped every single person I saw at the hospital to bring them to the nursery.

"That's my sister," I said, over and over again. I didn't care if you were a nurse or doctor who had somewhere to be. You were going to see this baby girl. That night, I had a temper tantrum when Nana and Papaw, my mother's parents, said they were taking me to stay the night at their house. I didn't want Ashlee to spend the night without me. She was my baby. When she came home, I kept putting a little pallet beneath her crib so I could sleep under her. When she was one, and we were living in Littleton, Colorado, Ashlee began to climb out of her crib and sneak into my room to sleep with me. Every morning, my mother would find us snuggled like two little puppies.

We moved to Littleton in September 1985, the only time we left Texas during my childhood. I think my dad was escaping something. His father, my Papa, had died suddenly in May of 1985 at age sixty-four. He had been a beloved Southern Baptist preacher after serving as a U.S. Army sergeant in World War II—the nicest man on the planet. I just remember he had massive hands and this great big belly laugh. He always sat on a recliner, and I would tickle his feet just to hear him laugh. He died while my parents were on a trip to Hawaii that they had saved up for and probably still couldn't afford. They left me with my mom's parents and Ashlee with dad's. Papa showed up two hours early to get Ashlee the morning of the trip, and the change in plans infuriated my dad. He didn't feel like entertaining his father. "I've got stuff to do," he yelled at Papa. They got on the plane and he never saw Papa again. He died of a heart attack while they were in Hawaii. One minute he was mowing the lawn, the next he was gone.

After that, my dad felt lost. We moved to Colorado and didn't even go to church. The irony is that my dad got a job selling to churches—supplies like choir robes and stained glass. I thought he sold BMWs because he drove one and it was all he talked about.

Littleton was magic to a Texas girl, so opposite to what I knew. I'd only seen snow in picture books about Santa Claus, so there was a magic to it. We moved just before I started kindergarten and I liked school, even if the day sort of peaked with The Pledge of Allegiance. I loved hearing our voices in unison with our hands on our hearts making this solemn vow that felt important. I was just never going to be the best student, because I didn't know yet that I was a different kind of learner. It was hard for me to focus in school, and as the teacher talked my mind wouldn't just wander off. It would take off running like a track star. By the time I realized I wasn't listening, I'd accidentally given my mind such a head start that I could never catch up. But if we went on a field trip, I could tell you all about where we went and what we learned. I told myself I was more of a life experience type, and I would rather travel to the place that we were talking about and form my own opinion than be told what was important.

The morning of January 28, 1986, we kindergarteners sat on the floor—criss-cross applesauce—to watch the Challenger space shuttle launch. Our class had spent a couple weeks learning about space and planets in preparation, because our school was one of the many in America that NASA TV had hooked up with a live viewing of the launch. NASA made a big deal about that flight because it was the first time a "normal" non-astronaut was going into space. Christa McAuliffe, a social studies teacher from Concord, New Hampshire, was picked from thousands of applicants in NASA's Teacher in Space Project. We were all excited, because when else did we get to watch TV in school?

At 9:38 a.m., we watched as the Challenger blew up in a ball of white smoke. At first, we thought it was the blastoff moment. I think even our teachers did. And then there was just nothing in the air. A teacher turned off the TV, but it was too late. A room full of five-year-olds had just watched seven people die and there was no hiding that fact. They were there, and then they were gone. Let's just say we had some questions.

When I got home, my parents let me watch President Ronald Reagan speak to the nation from the Oval Office at three o'clock our time. I didn't understand much of the speech, but I listened when it felt like he talked directly to me. "And I want to say something to the schoolchildren of America who were watching the live coverage of the shuttle's takeoff," he said. "I know it is hard to understand, but sometimes painful things like this happen. It's all part of the process of exploration and discovery. It's all part of taking a chance and expanding man's horizons. The future doesn't belong to the fainthearted; it belongs to the brave."

The future belonged to the brave. When I went to bed, I prayed for all the astronauts. For Christa McAuliffe and her family. President Reagan had talked about their sacrifice, and in my five-year-old mind, I decided the best way to honor that was to take on Christa McAuliffe's work and become an astronaut and teacher. Christa McAuliffe needed me to do it, and kids like me who had trouble following along in class needed a teacher who understood the way they learned.

I was so serious about becoming an astronaut after this tragedy that my parents let me attend space camp that summer. I was all in. They gave each of us a little NASA blue button-down shirt, so I was basically already an astronaut in my mind. They led us into the zero-gravity simulator, built to look like you were in a shuttle, and I took right to floating around, flying through the air just like I did in my dreams.

And then I hit the first roadblock on the race to space. Lunch. They served freeze-dried ice cream as a "treat."

"This is what they eat in space," one of the counselors said, cheerily passing out the foil-wrapped squares, each with chemical stripes of strawberry, vanilla, and chocolate. One small bite of that chalky excuse for dessert felt like a betrayal.

"Ugh," I said, spitting it into a napkin. "I can't be an astronaut. No way."

I hung up my NASA dreams right then and there.

BY THE END OF SUMMER, THINGS WERE TENSE AT HOME. MY PARENTS WERE fighting a lot, each accusing the other of overspending. They always stayed kind to each other in front of Ashlee and me, but sometimes one would have to storm off to keep from saying something nasty.

This made me think about money from a young age, even though we'd never had any, so I didn't know any different. Before I was born, Dad took out a two-thousand-dollar loan from the one bank in Cross Plains, Texas, and had them keep the money because he knew mom and he couldn't help but blow through it. Then that money went to pay the hospital when I was born. My dad paid the doctor who delivered me with the Canon 24-70mm lens on his camera. Dr. MacDonald admired it as dad photographed my arrival. "I tell you what, Dr. Mac-Donald, I will trade you this lens for your bill."

More and more, I heard them fight, and my dad saying, "We'll fly by this month. We'll be fine." I wanted to help, but didn't know how until the answer came to me, at where else but the mall? I remember walking by some kiosk that had these ornaments with everybody's name and its meaning. I saw mine and held it on the hook. "Jessica: The Wealthy One." It stayed with me. I walked around thinking, *I'm the wealthy one*, not realizing it meant rich in spirit. I just thought it was about money, and every time my parents seemed worried, I said, "I'm gonna be rich." I'd be the one to lift my parents out of their struggles. I'd be the one to end their fights, once and for all.

"Well, God provides," my dad said. "He'll always provide for you."

But we needed money *now*. There was no secret fortune for me to find and no cute barter stories about camera lenses to be had. My family declared bankruptcy to get out from under the weight of the bills. As part of what my mom called a "re-organization," my parents announced we were moving back to Texas. Dad called around and got a job as a youth minister in Burleson, a little town in the Fort Worth area. So, it was time to say good-bye to my friends again. Soon after we moved, I started first grade. I walked into a roomful of strangers who all seemed to know each other, and I did my best to fade into the background. I was relieved my seat was in the back, and I chose to sit in the back whenever I could at school.

We lived in a two-bedroom apartment, which my mom hated because she'd gotten used to living in a five-bedroom house in Littleton. We weren't there much, because our life revolved around church. When my dad returned to preaching, I thought we moved because God would tell my dad it was time to move. He studied to be an adolescent therapist, learning how to reach that brain. Because he was such a good storyteller, he could tug at the heart, too. He'd make people weep, holding up their hands as they listened to him share the Word in a way they had never heard. Even as a kid I could feel the energy of change in the room when my dad was working.

And I changed also. In the Baptist faith, you choose to be baptized when you are ready. It's for believers only, and it's up to you. You don't just baptize an infant and make the decision for them, which is kind of cool because for a religion that can be painted as so confining, individual choice is a fundamental part of being Baptist.

On a Sunday that had felt very normal up until that moment, I felt the Word and I made the choice. My dad was up front preaching, and he asked if anybody wanted to come down to be baptized in the name of Christ. I stood up in my white dress, hugged my mother, and stepped forward. As I approached, my father began to cry. He helped me into the baptismal pool, and I felt his hand on my back as he gently submerged me. The water washed over me, and I emerged new. Growing up, there would be kids who would get baptized a lot. I always kind of rolled my eyes at that, because a lot of them did it for attention. It's not a car wash, you know? The one time took for me.

Dad's youth minister salary was about $25,000 a year, so my mom was always looking for ways to supplement the income. This was the era of Jazzercise and she saw that *Jane Fonda's Workout* was becoming the highest-selling VHS tape of all time. She thought, *I can do that.* Since we were always at church, she decided to start teaching an aerobics class there. She had to go talk in front of the whole deacon board to get approval, and she brought us along. There was this old country man who kept staring at her as she talked about aerobics.

He finally interrupted her. "You gonna be doing acrobatics in the church chapel?"

"*Aerobics,*" she said, overenunciating every syllable. "Working out. Good for your heart."

The men looked at each other. It was bad enough my dad had an earring, and now his crazy wife wanted people dancing in the church.

Finally, she hit on the point: "I'm going to be helping women get their best bodies possible."

Again, the men looked at each other, but this time they were sold. She started the Heavenly Bodies company, and the class was called Jump for Jesus—

No, I will not shut my mouth. That is really what she called it. Let's continue.

Jump for Jesus was popular, and I went to almost every class, collecting all the checks made out to Heavenly Bodies. I sat in the back, with all these women jamming to Michael W. Smith and Amy Grant, the *cool* Christian singers at the time. "Stretch your arms towards the heavens," my mother would yell. "Lift those knees higher for Jesus!" Mom made her own workout video, which I also sold. If we went to any Baptist conferences, you bet we brought those tapes along.

Laugh, but she got what she wanted. We left the apartment and leased a two-story house as we continued to make payments on our debts. They still overspent, but not on extravagant things. They just wanted to be the parents who said yes when their daughters asked for Caboodles for Christmas. We opened a lot of credit cards, and thank God for layaway. It was part of their relentless positivity. They were in the business of changing lives. Mom and Dad were always taking people in. When parents threw their pregnant daughter out, she needed a place to sleep until they came to their senses. When a kid was trying not to do drugs, he needed to get away from parents who had their own issues with addiction. In the South, there are so many secrets, and my parents were there to give people a safe place. Even when my parents didn't physically take people in, they collected people to look after.

One day after Jump for Jesus, my mom took me across the street to a young woman's house. I will call her Jane to protect her privacy. Jane was probably nineteen, a heavyset girl with brown hair who had run away from Iowa to follow some dumb boy who liked her because she wasn't used to that. He got her pregnant, and he skipped town before the baby boy arrived. She was stranded in Burleson, broke with no support, and her parents thought she had made her bed so she could just stay there.

This was before anybody understood postpartum depression. When it was just women who could recognize it in each other and step in to say, "Let me help you." But Jane had nobody. That's why my mom had a heart for her.

So, when she hadn't seen her for a bit, she was concerned. She called the house from church and there was no answer. "Come on, Jess," she said. "Let's just check on her."

You could hear the baby crying before you even got to the door. Wailing. Mom knocked and there was no answer. "Jane?" she called. She looked at me for one second, and some mom instinct in her kicked in. The door was unlocked so she let herself in.

"Jane, it's Tina," she called out as she made her way to the room with the crib. There was no answer. The baby was left all alone in the house. He was on a plastic sheet, not even a real sheet, and he was covered in pee and poop. When mom went to lift him, she realized that he was literally stuck to the bed.

"Jess, go sit in the living room," she said.

I did as I was told as my mom ran to the bathroom and took every towel and washcloth she could find to run under warm water. She brought them to the crib and used the warm wet towels to unstick the poor baby. She lovingly cleaned him as we both cried. She went to the kitchen and made a bottle of formula just from the muscle memory of motherhood.

"You're okay," she whispered to him again and again, as he took hungry gulps. "You're okay."

When he was finally calm, she held him in the crook of her arm and went to the phone on the wall.

"Joe, I'm at Jane's," she said. "I'm bringing this baby home."

She left a note for Jane saying the baby was safe and asked her to come to our house. When she showed up, my parents didn't judge her. My parents were always good like that. They were just doing the best they could, too. Jane wasn't a bad person, she just needed help with her depression. She would not be equipped to parent until she could take care of herself. If she had a family, my mother explained to her, they would see how she was struggling and step in. Jane didn't have that, but she had us. That's the power of faith in action. It's not about talking and judging. It's about doing.

Jane's baby lived with us for six weeks, and I thought I had a new baby brother. I know my parents were prepared to formally adopt him if need be. As we cared for the baby, my father got Jane into therapy, and my parents helped her reconcile with her family. Soon, she was able to take the baby back to Iowa with her.

My mother tried to make it a joyous thing for us. Jane was going home to be reunited with her parents. "The baby is going to be where he needs to be," she said.

I felt a real loss, though. As I remember it, she just up and vanished with the baby, which of course isn't true. But tell it to a six-year-old. I loved him—the way he slept with his hands up, totally at peace as a little boy in Ashlee's hand-me-downs. The first morning after he left with Jane, I briefly forgot he was gone, and I felt that all-body disappointment that kids can experience. Your shoulders sink with your heart, and you think you'll never get over it.

I did. I had to. With the same fervor that my mom now flips houses, my parents fixed people throughout my childhood. We took in people who were sick or neglected, and it wasn't always fun. Sometimes it was a chore to share my parents with others. Our family time was always with others, whether they were there physically or talked about in our prayers. "To whom much is given, much is expected," was what I heard. I understood, but sometimes I didn't feel we had much to share.

NO MATTER WHERE WE MOVED, NANA AND PAPAW'S HOUSE IN MCGREGOR
was home base. The five of us cousins—the children of the
Drew girls, my mom and her two older sisters—would play
outside from the second my parents pulled into the driveway.
The oldest were Debbie's kids—Zeb and his younger sister
Sarah; then Connie's son Drew; then me and Ashlee bringing
up the rear. At six years old, I was exactly two years and three
days younger than Sarah, who I idolized as more of big sister
and best friend than a cousin. Sarah was already so effortlessly
cool that I loved anything she loved. She liked pigs, so I liked
pigs. When her family visited us in Colorado, we made snow
pigs instead of snow angels. She went horseback riding, and,
well, I tried.

Now that we were back in Texas, we made the hour-and-a-
half drive down to McGregor all the time. McGregor is a small
town next to Waco, the buckle of the Bible Belt. My grandparents lived on Leafy Hollow, named for all the tall skinny trees
that reached so high to the sky. The trees created clouds of white
flowers in the spring and a canopy of green throughout the summer. There were at least a dozen in the front yard alone.

We cousins played in the creek behind their house, and all
of us wore our McGregor Bulldogs T-shirts. Even Ashlee, about
to turn two, danced around in her size small T-shirt, swirling
in it like a princess dress. This was in tribute to Papaw, who
was the beloved line and strength coach at McGregor High.
Acy Drew was Ace to everyone when he made First Team All-
State as a quarterback in high school, then played football for
Baylor. But by the time I came along, everyone in town called
him "Coach," stepped aside for him when he passed and never
once thought about cussing in his presence for fear of what he

would do. Believe everything you've heard about the reverence for football in Texas. In the name of the Father, the Son and the Hail Mary pass . . .

He'd been a tough man, but he'd softened with age. Men don't normally change, I know, but they can. I like it when they do. The only thing he loved more than his Lord and Savior Jesus Christ was us kids, and he would casually patrol the creek while we were out there, keeping watch for snakes. If he spotted one, he'd pick it up and squeeze its neck, even the rattlesnakes.

My Nana, Dorothy Jane, was my prayer warrior. She held firm to her Christian faith and did all things through He who strengthened her. Her steadfastness was almost a response to her mother. Bertha Dee died a couple weeks after I was born, but she was a legend to me. "She was full-blooded Indian," I grew up hearing in whispers from cousins and my mother. My great-grandmother read people's fortunes and aligned her gardens with the stars. This was always said before a long, dramatic pause. Nana never wanted to talk about her. If I said anything about astrology or being a Cancer, my grandmother would go move quick to hush me.

I heard different stories about my great-grandmother, cautionary tales about what could happen if you leaned in hard on that intuition. I don't know the full story, but I also know that she was a card reader in Waco, Texas, at a time when that was not done. She was considered crazy by a lot of people in town. That buckle on the Bible Belt can come down hard and leave a mark.

But I'd stare in the mirror at my brown eyes and high cheekbones, convinced I was Native American. More than that, we Simpson girls, my mother included, all seemed a little witchy. A nicer word would be intuitive. We had a good sense of people from the get-go and we often knew what was going to happen before it happened. Sometimes we chalked it up to our faith that God would provide, sometimes to just paying attention. But often it felt like we knew what was destined to be. Everything that happened in my life just felt preordained. Still does.

If we weren't at Nana and Papaw's, the family usually met up at my cousin Sarah's house. Her dad, Uncle Boyd, put up a tire swing while I was in Colorado, and when I got back it was all me and Sarah wanted to do. Sarah loved the swing, and, like I said—I loved anything she loved.

Aunt Debbie, Sarah's mom, was even more of a devout Christian than my parents, and while Sarah and I ran outside, she would listen to one of her evangelist tapes. Sermons all the time, loud so everybody could hear. You'd dip in and out of a deep, solemn voice rolling across the yard as we played. "Now, I want you to turn with me to 2 Chronicles, the 33rd chaptah . . ."

It was spring, and I sat on the grass as Sarah swung in the twilight air. I watched the long curls of her brown hair trail behind her like a comet. It was just us, and I wanted to tell her something, because I could always talk to her about anything. But this time, I stayed quiet. Something had happened, twice now, and I was supposed to keep it secret.

The daughter of a family friend was abusing me when my parents brought us for overnight stays. It started the winter I was six, when I shared a bed with the girl. She was a year older than me. After lights out, I would feel her hands on me. It would start with tickling my back and then going into things that were extremely uncomfortable. Freezing became my defense mechanism, and to this day, when I panic, I freeze. We had an earthquake recently here in L.A., and instead of running for cover, I grabbed a bag of Cheetos and just stood there eating them.

The second time she abused me, it was during a spring visit, and Ashlee also shared the bed. I lay between them, fiercely protecting my sister from this monster. I didn't want her to feel as disgusting as I felt.

For six years, I was abused by this girl during our family's visits, which happened three times a year. Eventually it wasn't just nighttime. She would get me to go into a closet with her, or just find a way to linger until we were alone. It got to the point that she would sneak into the bathroom to watch me shower. I did not know how to get away from her.

She continued to try to sleep next to my little sister, and I would just scooch Ashlee over and get between them whenever she did. I never let her near Ashlee, but I also never screamed or told her to stop. I was confused, wondering if it was something that I wanted to keep going. *Why am I not telling anybody?* I would ask myself. Is it because it feels good? The irony is that I was protecting my abuser. I thought that if I named what she was doing, she would feel the shame I felt. And I wouldn't have wished that on anybody.

I never slept well again. Well, I could sleep, but it took forever to get there. Even at home in my own bed, there was a feeling that I had to stay up to keep watch. I stopped waiting for Ashlee to come to my room and started sleeping in her bed. I remember the humiliation of saying to my baby sister, four years younger than me, "Ashlee, can I share your room?" Even then, I would lie awake waiting for my brain to shut off. I wanted to keep us both safe, but I also wanted her protection, too. Ashlee was already becoming her own person. She always took good care of looking after herself, and I was terrified someone could take that courage from her.

Over the years of this family friend abusing me, I learned that she was being molested by an older boy. I can't play armchair psychiatrist and guess what her motives were for abusing me, but I can feel her pain and mine at the same time. She would describe her experiences in detail, and it was all so crazy because I was so young that I didn't know anything about sex or about my private parts. My parents never talked to me about this. I mean, they taught me my body was a temple of God, but that was in reference to some imaginary guy in the future. It was never about someone who's supposed to be a friend making you do things you don't want to. So, I came to understand sex and my body solely in terms of power, or in this case, lack of power. I was just gonna let her do whatever it was she wanted to do because I didn't want to hurt her feelings.

That's kind of how I was in many of my adult relationships, too. At first, I held myself back, refusing to have sex until I was married. I was afraid sex, and the need I had to give pleasure no matter what, would destroy me as I let men walk all over me.

I was right. But I am getting ahead of myself.

I only found the strength to tell my parents what was happening because I made a deal with God. I was twelve, and my family was in the car on the way out of the town where the girl lived. It was a four-hour ride, and my father would always stop at the gas station to fill up the car and buy two scratch-off lottery tickets, one for me and Ashlee. I won so often that it was like a family joke—"the wealthy one" at it again—and I always thought it was God looking out for me.

My dad handed us each a ticket and a quarter when he got back in the car. Usually, I scratched the ticket right away, but this time I stalled. First, I wanted to tell my parents what was happening to me. What had just happened *again* the night before. For me, this would be a confession, because I felt like I might be sinning by allowing her to continue to do these things to me. I was the victim, but somehow, I felt in the wrong.

I waited until we were on the road, when Ashlee would put her headphones on. She was eight, and I wanted to protect her from hearing what I had to say. But when she did put them on, I lost my nerve, and decided not to say anything. I rested my head against the window to feel the rhythm of the Texas road. Occasionally, I lifted my head, ready to speak. And then I didn't. It was like back when I stuttered. The words just wouldn't come.

I rubbed the quarter between my thumb and pointer finger. "In God we trust," it read. God and I were always in conversation. No matter what I did in life, He was there. *If I do this, my reward will be in this ticket,* I thought. He'll give me a prize for being honest.

I started with a quiet singsong of "Ummm, guys." Like I was tuning an instrument. My parents didn't hear me. I cleared my throat, and the worlds spilled out in a quiet rush.

"I feel like you guys might know that this has been going on," I said, "but if you don't know what's been going on, she's been touching me for years and it makes me really uncomfortable and I don't ever want to go back there."

I couldn't undo it. It was done.

My mother slapped my father's arm with the back of her hand. "I told you something was happening," she yelled at him.

Neither turned to look at me. Dad kept his eye on the road and said nothing, his shoulders sunken. It didn't surprise me that my mother knew. I already understood denial and how much it fueled the actions of families, especially Southern families. People want to paint the picture pretty, especially a minister's family. They were probably also shocked. These good people who did everything to help others hadn't been able to help their own daughter.

"Hello?" I said. I expected them to say something to me. I wasn't angry, I was just confused. I wouldn't be angry about their silence until much later.

I scratched off the ticket, knowing that I would win something. It was fifteen hundred dollars. I looked up to God. Then I brushed the ticket against my mother's shoulder, forcing her to look back at me. She took the ticket and screamed to my father.

"One *thousand* five hundred dollars," she said, drawing out the words. Dad pulled over, and Ashlee pulled off her headphones in confusion. They told her, so excited, and she looked at me with her eyes wide. She gave me a huge smile, and I took it so I could manage to give it back to her.

Dad did a U-turn to take us back to the gas station so we could collect our winnings. My parents clung to the happiness of that ticket, thrilled to be rescued with a change in subject. We never stayed at my parents' friends' house again, but we also didn't talk about what I had said.

Instead, we just went back to start. As if what I said happened to me happened to some other girl, in some other car, in some other life.

3

SAVED BY FAILURE

SPRING 1993

"I once was lost, but now am found," we all sang in unison. "Was blind but now I see."

There were seven hundred kids that last day of church camp, all from different schools in Texas. I was a seventh grader, twelve, and I had tagged along to so many church camps and vacation bible schools as a preacher's daughter that I was excited to be with kids and believers my own age. One of the best parts of every church camp stay was when we sang together. People who were once strangers sang hymns that felt they like were written for just that shared moment.

We were in a huge church, and as we paused between the choruses of "Amazing Grace," the pastor spoke on the mic. "There's somebody here that's going to use their voice to change the world," he said. "They will use their voice to minister to others."

We continued, and then I heard it: My own voice. "How precious did that grace appear," I sang. "The hour I first believed!" I have spent years trying to describe the feeling, and I still have trouble. I felt a light upon me, and then the certainty of a calling. *It's my voice, I thought.* And because I was twelve, I added, "*He is* totally *talking about me.*"

I realized I was walking forward down the aisle, the only person doing so. I felt wrapped in purpose. You have to understand how rare it was to just have one believer swept up at camp. Sometimes, peer pressure or a need for attention can make the front of the room a popular space. I reached the pastor just as we finished the song with, "And grace will lead us home."

He invited everyone to do silent prayer and looked at me. "I just heard myself sing," I whispered, "and I think that's the voice that God wants me to use."

"Well, let's pray," he said.

I felt like God had delivered me to myself, and I decided right there to give myself over to the ministry. I walked back, right past my friends, and went straight to the pay phone to call my dad at church. By then, Dad had been the youth minister for two years at the Heights Baptist Church in Richardson, a suburb of Dallas. We'd left Burleson after I finished third grade, then did a year at a church in Duncanville, which brought us closer to Dallas. But now my father had his dream job. It was a megachurch, so his salary doubled to $60,000, and being a pastor there was like being a rock star. Mom still taught aerobics and did as much work as my dad with all kinds of charity outreach.

I dialed Dad at work and the church secretary answered.

"Hi, it's Jessica," I blurted out. "Can I talk to my dad? It's really important."

"Hold on, Jess," she said.

I looked back at all the kids. A girl came up, waiting for the phone. I could tell she was shy and being with someone who was timid always made me less so. At lunch, I had started sitting with kids at school who sat alone. It wasn't that I felt sorry for them. I was grateful for the company. It's like when you're in line for a roller coaster and you find out your friend is even more scared than you—and you both feel stronger by joining hands. "I like your sneakers," I told her.

"Thanks," she said, smiling. She looked down at them as my dad came to the phone.

"Jessica?" he said. "What's wrong?" I held a finger to her to say, "hold on."

"God called me into the ministry, Dad."

"*Nooooooo*," he said. "No, no, no."

He said it so loud the girl heard him through the phone. Her eyes widened.

"I know," I said. I had grown up hearing about the politics of churches. In Richardson, we'd built up the youth group, but we did it by hosting dances and having cool events like lock-in sleepovers. Dad had studied to be an adolescent therapist, and his practice at the church didn't treat kids like sinners. He encouraged self-care and communication with parents, which had proven effective. But some of the church elders still preferred the brimstone. He fought the battles so the kids didn't have to, I guess, and he wanted something different for me.

"Jessica, you should think about this," he said. "There are ways to be of service without—"

I turned toward the pay phone for privacy. "Well, I don't think I'm gonna be a music minister or anything," I said. "But I know now I'm supposed to use my voice to change the world."

"We'll talk about it when you get home," he said. "But I'm really proud of—"

"I gotta go, someone's waiting," I said. I smiled at the girl and hung up. "I was called," I told her as I walked away. "I mean, I made the call just now. To my dad. But I was called." She laughed, so I laughed, and it felt good.

God was going to use my voice. It was weird, because I never really knew that I had a good singing voice. I just liked to sing. I'd sung solos in church since I was younger, and the one I remember loving most was "His Eye Is on the Sparrow." My mom had started to enter me into vocal competitions the year before. But I thought that was just because Beth Pliler, who ran the dance studio where Ashlee and I took lessons, could tell I was miserable dancing. I would go to competitions in a whole new outfit and come in seventh and it just didn't seem worth it. Beth was probably tired of trying to hide me in the corps when I wanted to stand out. One day I had been crying trying to get on point and Beth turned to my mother.

"Tina, they have all these vocal competitions when we do the dance competitions," she said loud so I could hear. "Maybe she could do both." I fell to the ground and gripped my poor toes. "Or, just," she added, "uh, sing?"

I looked at my mom and nodded, wiping away a tear. "That's a great idea."

"She *could* really shine," my mom said. So, the summer going into sixth grade, I did my first vocal competition, going to San Marcos, Texas, to sing "The Rose" in a big purple dress with giant sleeves. I won, and we kept on entering around the region, and I kept winning. Mom and I would go thrift shopping for stage outfits. Then, she started buying clothes at Dillard's and leaving the tags in so we could return them. I know how that sounds, but she was trying to make me happy and we couldn't really afford all those outfits. I've met my share of stage moms in my career, and she was not one of them. She pushed me to be excellent at whatever I chose to do, but she didn't tell me what to do.

Two weeks after my "Amazing Grace" moment at camp, my mom was at church when one of her girlfriends, Cindy Caves, came up to her with a cutout from the *Dallas Morning News*.

"Jessica's really talented and you should take her to this," she said.

The producers of the *The All-New Mickey Mouse Club* had placed ads around the country looking for new talent for its third season. There would be an open-call audition at the Dallas Hyatt the following week. Mom knew Ashlee and I watched it all the time, singing and dancing along with Keri Russell and JC Chasez onscreen as Mouseketeers. The show was a weekly afterschool Disney Channel variety show with comedy skits and kid-friendly versions of popular songs. The producers specialized in finding talented kids who were also relatable, which was why they held open-call auditions for 50,000 kids around the country instead of just in Los Angeles, where kids got agents in kindergarten.

My mom brought the ad to Beth at the dance studio to see if she thought it was legit.

"Well, why don't you take everyone?" asked Beth. "Everyone should have a chance."

Beth and my mom drove the whole dance troupe to the auditions. It looked to me like a couple thousand kids had shown up. We were in line for hours, and everyone got a Mickey Mouse T-shirt, which I still have today, thank you. As I approached the table of casting agents, they started talking about me.

"Cindy Crawford!" one said.

"*Young* Cindy Crawford," said another. Cindy was twenty-six at the time.

I knew I had to sing, and I chose "Amazing Grace" because it was comfortable for me. Then they just randomly played music and you were supposed to dance around. The song was Vanilla Ice's "Ice Ice Baby" so I can only imagine how I looked. At the end of the day, only ten people were invited back for the second day of auditions—and I was one of them. Matt Casella, the head casting director, told me I had real promise. My mom kept saying, "Do you believe it?" And I did. It wasn't that I was stuck up, it was that God told me to use my voice and here I was.

The next morning I went in for the callback, and this time they took video of me. At the end, they kept just three of us from Dallas, a boy named George, a girl named Audrey, and me. Matt Casella told us that they were holding a casting camp in Orlando in a month, a sort of entertainment boot camp. "It's going be two weeks in Disney World," he said. "We'll fly your family out there and put you up. We'll see if you make the cut!"

"There's just one thing, Jessica," one of the agents added. "You need to work on your acting. We're going to send you to Chuck Norris."

Yes, *the* Chuck Norris. Look, I was twelve, so for years I told people I went to the Chuck Norris Acting School. Honestly it was probably just some school he was affiliated with, since he shot *Walker, Texas Ranger* in the Dallas-Fort Worth area.

My mom dropped me off at Chuck Norris and it felt like I was the only kid in class. I think that's why I was given David Joyner as my scene partner. He was nearly twenty years older than me, but he had recently landed a gig playing Barney the Dinosaur on PBS. Chuck Norris was there, as intense and chest-puffed as you're picturing. I couldn't wait for my mom to come back for me.

The first day Chuck didn't say much to me, but the next time I went he had some notes. He stopped me in the middle of my one-on-one with him. "You have too much expression," he said as he trained his eyes on me in a squint. "Do you know who the most powerful actor in the world is?"

I wasn't sure if I was supposed to say Chuck Norris.

"Denzel Washington," he said.

"Oh," I said. Every person in the room nodded in agreement, which is what people did whenever Chuck spoke.

"Do you know why?" he asked. This time he didn't wait for me to answer, he just turned and grabbed a green roll of Scotch tape. "Denzel can say anything without moving his eyebrows," he said. "So, Jessica, I'd like to try something."

He pulled out a long strand of tape and stuck it across my eyebrows to tape them down tight.

"Okay, let's do the scene again," he said. Now, anybody who's seen me sing or even tell a joke knows I have the facial expressions of Jim Carrey. That tape was working overtime. I can't remember what the scene was, but everyone acted like this was very normal. The Chuck Norris Method.

From then on, I had to do all my scenes with my eyebrows taped down. I already hated going, but now I *really* did. It wasn't torture, it was just embarrassing.

"I don't wanna go in there," I said in the parking lot on the third visit, sinking down so nobody would see me crying in the front seat of our minivan.

"You have to," my mom said. "If you wanna do this thing, you have to go in there and do these classes." She had to drag me out of that minivan in tears, but that third time was the last time. I don't want to make a big deal about it, and I wish Chuck Norris and Barney the best, but I will say the experience ruined every single Denzel movie I've ever seen since. I just watch his eyebrows the whole time, waiting for them to move.

When my family flew to Orlando for the casting camp, there was no question that we would also pull Ashlee out of school for the two weeks. Our family was a package deal. The first event was a pool party with the finalists. I am sure we were already wide-eyed from the opulence of a Disney industry party, but the very first two people I saw were Keri and JC from the show. So, I about died right there. It was the first time I'd ever seen stars in real life. I watched them meet people and do that dance of "I know you know who I am, but I am going to introduce myself to you anyway." They were already pros.

There was one boy running around the pool, completely "on" like he knew the audition finals had already started. He kept doing backflips into the pool, totally grabbing everyone's attention. He eventually came over to where I was standing.

"Hi, I'm Justin Timberlake," he said, the Memphis accent stronger than it is now. Right away, another boy appeared. He was there with his mom, all the way from Canada. I liked Ryan Gosling *very* much. I decided he was definitely the cutest there.

Then there was Christina Aguilera, this timid, frankly kind of mousy girl in glasses from Pittsburgh. She was known for singing "The Star-Spangled Banner" before the Penguins and Pirates games and had a local reputation as the little girl with the big voice. Her mother had tried to get her on the show when she was ten, and the casting director, Matt Casella, said she had to wait. He kept in touch with her because she was so talented. She was just so tiny that I didn't really get how she could possibly get on television.

The parents were all hanging out, trading stories about what their kids had already done in show business. My mother gravitated to Lynn Harless, Justin's mom, who was so sweet. She had a whole portfolio about Justin, with studio head shots, and photos from pageants and talent shows. "He just did *Star Search*," said Lynn.

"Wow," said my mom.

"Well, what's Jessica done?" she asked in her Tennessee twang. "Because she's so beautiful."

My portfolio was a manila folder my mom brought. "Uh, well, here's her school picture. And a Polaroid." I'm surprised she didn't have my report card. "You can see her B+ in English."

The casting agents had said to bring a headshot, and the Polaroid *was* of my head, so. . . .

We were just so green. Everyone at Disney was sweet and helpful, and booked time for me at a photo studio so I could get an actual headshot by a photographer. "Give him this," a casting agent said, handing me a headshot of Cindy Crawford posing with her hair swept over to the side. "This is the look you want."

When I got there, it was definitely different than Olan Mills. The photographer had specific poses in mind, none of which made sense to me. "Okay, now look off into nowhere," he said.

I did, trying to look thoughtful.

"And enjoy it."

I smiled. I looked crazy. The main direction of the day was "smile bigger!" At one point he handed me a huge fake flower, just comically big. *This is the biggest flower I have ever seen,* I thought. *How is this going to land me my deal with The Mickey Mouse Club?*

"Smile bigger." Now I know how to get through photo shoots, because I know every angle they need. I do this super weird thing for my friends where I just slightly move my face to do a speed round of each red carpet pose and photo shoot I've done. The big smile, eyes up and then down, the Mona Lisa, the chin-down-lips-parted, the "Oh hi!" . . . My friends scream because I look like a robot model shorting out. But let me tell you, it makes it easy on the photographers.

Once I had my new photos, we Mouseketeer wannabes went into the two weeks of bonding and learning as we prepared for the final auditions. There was a music class, lessons from the vocal coach from *The All-New Mickey Mouse Club*, and I worked with an acting coach who didn't tape my eyebrows down. I mentioned that and people thought I was joking. I liked getting that laugh. Ashlee was in entertainer mode, too, coming along to do cartwheels for the talent agents. "Come back in four years," they told her.

Justin and Ryan were huge flirts, and I was the girl they focused on. Ryan was my first hard crush. He tried so hard to sound tough, a voice like Marlon Brando but with this squeaky-clean face. He did that same thing he does in movies: He leans forward like you're drawing him in, he lowers his chin, and then opens his eyes to look up at you. I don't know what old movie he saw that move in, but it stuck. I was in love. Before anybody knew how hot Ryan Gosling was going to become, I had a vision.

There were eleven of us, and the term "Top Eight" became the Holy Grail. Throughout my time at camp, my parents kept hearing, "She's gonna make it. She's our Top Eight." At one point, Matt Casella came up to me and my parents. "Jessica, it looks really positive," he said. "I can't tell you one hundred percent, but you all need to start looking for an apartment in Orlando." It was one thing for my parents to think I had talent, but these professionals were now telling them their daughter had the potential to be a star.

That night I overheard my parents talking quietly about what that would mean. There was Ashlee. Would they just uproot her? And what about my dad's job? I'd get a *Mickey Mouse Club* paycheck, but not enough for everybody to live on.

The final day came, and I wore an outfit my mom and I put together from the $5 rack at a discount store. I had a

Blossom-style derby hat, denim jacket, and a tie with pigs on it. (Remember, my cousin Sarah loved pigs, so I loved pigs.) It all made sense in 1993. The finals were held on the actual *Star Search* stage at the Disney Hollywood Studios theater. Christina came in, ready to go on right before me, and I almost didn't recognize her. One of the casting people had taken her to the mall for a full makeover and contact lenses. She still seemed so little, but Disney had done a full Cinderella on her.

And then another girl walked into the theater.

She had these big beautiful eyes, brown like mine. I heard her talk and she was Southern, like me. I heard an "oh my goodness" come out of her and I knew she had to be a Baptist choir girl, too. We had such a similar look. Nobody else in the competition had looked like me, and here was this last-minute—

"Hi, Britney," said Matt, the casting director.

"Hello, sir," she said, and he laughed.

My mom got the lowdown from another parent. Britney Spears had first tried out when she was eight, and Matt had said she was too young but hooked her up with an agent. She had missed the camp because she was appearing in a play in New York. "*Off*-Broadway," someone emphasized to my mother, though neither of us knew what that meant. All I knew was that I seemed like less of a shoo-in than I had ten minutes before.

Christina was slated to go on right ahead of me, and they put me in the green room so I could watch her on the monitor. Not out of competition, but because we'd really all become close. We were pulling for each other and I did a little "yay" clap watching her cross to the center of the stage. And then this sweet little girl opened her mouth. She was so extraordinary that we all, even my parents, gasped. I knew she was good, but she must have been holding back slightly all week and knew this was the time to go for it. The visual just didn't match what I was hearing.

"How is that even possible?" whispered my mother.

My nerves started setting in. I had to follow *that*. Just typing this to you now, I am like, "Here we go. Cue the crash."

I have blocked out some details, so bear with me. I sang my two songs—Amy Grant's "Good for Me Baby" and a Christian song by Crystal Lewis—and I did fine. But singing is where I should have been able to play to my strengths. As I was beating myself up about that, I just froze. My choreography was completely off, and then I couldn't remember lines from my monologue. I stared at the camera, and knew I'd blown it completely. The theater was silent.

"Thank you," I said, trying not to cry. I walked off the stage and tried not to even look at Justin, who was about to go on.

"Ooooooooooh," Justin said, his eyes so wide, his mouth open like a slack-jawed cartoon. "What did you just *do*?"

That started the tears. Oh, I cried. I cried big heaving sobs. My parents came to me, asking again and again, "What happened? What happened?" All those questions and scenarios they had gamed out about me being a Mouseketeer—Do we all just move to Florida? Do they homeschool me *and* Ashlee?— all of that was gone because I choked. I crashed down to earth, landing right on top of them.

When Britney got out there and did her full-on, out-of-the-box dance routine like a machine, I knew it was over for me. They told us all that the higher-ups would look at the videos and make the final selection. We would get a letter in a few weeks. I had grown so close to these people, and I thought we were all going to be on an adventure together.

My family were all so deflated on the way to the airport. We were caught between the world where I was a regular kid and one where we were in show business. I had missed this opportunity that could bring an end to all the family fights about money and keep the peace for good. I sat with my mom on the plane, and finally she was able to see past her own disappointment to try to make me feel better.

"Jessica, you have to know something," she said. "You're gonna have to face this again."

I whimpered.

"No, I have a really strong feeling that you're gonna see these girls again," she said. "Somewhere down the road, you're gonna cross paths again. So, you better get ready."

She was right, and I would also see Justin and Ryan again. This story is strictly for the Mouseketeer Clubhouse diehards, but Justin and I met up years later, after my divorce. We were both single, and we got to talking about the old times, leaning more and more into each other until, suddenly, we shared a nostalgic kiss. As soon as the kiss was over, he pulled away and got out his phone.

"I gotta call Gosling," he said.

"What?"

"We made a bet at the casting camp," he said. "Who was going to kiss you first. I win!"

"Well then tell Ryan you won big," I said as he dialed. "'Cause the odds were definitely in his favor."

BACK HOME IN TEXAS, THE KIDS I'D TOLD ABOUT THE CASTING CAMP couldn't understand why I didn't know yet if I was on the show. People, especially girls, kept asking leading questions that showed they thought I'd made the whole thing up. Things people said would remind me of something sweet Christina said, or a song Justin danced to, and I would miss my new friends all over again. "They're going to send a letter," I told people. "They said it would take a few weeks. We'll see." The girls smirked.

Every day I came home from school and checked the mail like I'd spelled out HELP on a deserted isle. I felt marooned, still stuck between being a regular kid and being someone on TV. On a Saturday afternoon, my family and I went to see a matinee of *My Father the Hero* with Katherine Heigl. We looked alike, and as I leaned back in my seat I watched her and put myself into her life. One of the acting coaches from the camp talked about the importance of "choices," so I followed the character during the movie, but also Katherine. Why had she lifted her chin when she laughed? Was that her or her character? I wanted to be in the movies, to be that big and important on the screen.

We came home and I knew the letter would be there. It just felt like it was time. I admit I thought that every other day, too, so I am not *that* psychic. But I wasn't surprised to see a skinny little envelope from Disney, certain it would be a rejection. I still had the hope to pray, though. I opened it in front of my parents in the living room.

It was a no.

I started crying as soon as I realized. I handed it to my

mother and ran to my room. As I remember, the letter amounted to "Not you." But here's the thing: It was a nice letter. I only know because I just now called my mom. I knew she would still have it.

"It was addressed to us, first of all, Jessica," she said. "It said your daughter has a ton of talent, she's amazing. 'Keep doing what you're doing. I know we're gonna see you again someday.'"

I had to sit with that for a minute. For over twenty years, I just remembered the "We don't want you."

"Well, everyone got in but me and one other person," I said.

"Jess, that's not true."

"It was just me that got cut?"

"Honey, no," she said. "They were choosing eight but instead they chose seven." She paused, realizing that I messed up my final audition so bad that they lowered the final head count to seven to exclude me. "You were gonna be the eight. There were twelve of y'all there, so five people didn't make it."

When I got the letter, something shifted in me. That afternoon I had imagined what it would be like to be on the screen, big and in front. And now I shrunk from it. I never wanted to sing again. Not if it could lead to me feeling that forsaken. I cried for days. I know people say things like, "I cried for days" and you kinda think, *Well, didja really?* Well, I can assure you, I cried for days. I cried eating cereal, I cried peeing, I cried praying at church . . . the sense of loss and missed opportunity was suffocating.

It scared my parents, but they differed on what to do next. Every parent thinks their kid has a gift, or at least they should. But Matt Casella's words stayed with them. I had talent. I had been so close. What if I got that close again and, oh I don't know, didn't blow it? My mother acted like we'd touched a flame, and now we knew better. She didn't know that we could handle something that devastating again. My father, on the other hand, was mesmerized by the flame. They had told him his daughter was a star, and it was his responsibility to make that happen for me. And, yes, for us. They had huge fights about it, when they thought I couldn't hear them. When my father would start in on some new plan to launch me—saying maybe he should call one of the casting agents or look into getting me my own agent—she would stop him. That summer I was in the bathroom, staring at my reflection so long in the mirror they probably forgot I was even home.

Dad's new idea was that he'd found a pastor named Buster Soaries who had started a gospel record label. Dad was planning a vacation bible school in the Destin area of Florida. He would invite him as a speaker, and then have me perform.

"It's gonna happen now," my father said. "This is it."

"Why can't she just be a regular girl?" my mom yelled.

"Tina, she can *be* a regular girl," he yelled. "She can be that girl. She can be that girl *and* be a star."

I came out of the bathroom. "I want to do it."

My dad grinned, but my mom just said, "Are you sure?"

I nodded. "I want to be that girl."

MY PARENTS LOOKED FOR A VOCAL COACH IN THE AREA, AND MY DAD took me to Linda Septien. A former opera singer with a Texas twang, Linda was blonde and just gave off an air of being well-to-do and professional, even though her place sat at the end of a strip mall on the edge of Dallas. She asked me to talk about myself, and I looked at my dad, who ran through the whole tragedy of the *Mickey Mouse Club* audition. She asked me to sing, so I did "Amazing Grace."

"You have a beautiful voice," she told me. "You just got squelched and you have to get past it." She told me I seemed shy and that I sang "churchy." Linda saw the potential there, if I worked on getting more control of my vocal cords. As we worked together, she tested my octave range by having me sing notes. Notes go on a scale of one to eight, and I learned that I have a vocal range spanning four-and-a-half octaves.

"Is that good?" I asked.

"Well Mariah is a five," she said. She could do lower notes like me but go even further up the scale to the highest notes. That was why I couldn't do the high-pitched whistle she did when I sang along to "Emotions."

Linda gave me the confidence I needed when I tried to impress Buster Soaries at the church camp my dad organized for that summer. Rev. Dr. DeForest B. Soaries was the stately, if a little flashy, lead pastor of one of the largest African American congregations in New Jersey. More important to my dad, he was starting a small gospel record label, Proclaim Records. He was there to discuss one of his favorite subjects, teen abstinence, and I was there to sing as an intro to warm up the crowd. I chose "I Will Always Love You," telling the crowd it was about true love waiting.

Afterward, Buster came over to me. "You remind me of Nippy," he said.

"Nippy?" I said, looking at the splotch of gray on top of his otherwise jet-black hair.

"Whitney Houston," he said. He told me he knew her

when she was around my age, and that he would slip into her church in Newark during choir rehearsal just to hear Nippy sing. I admitted to him that was why I chose that song, because my dad had told me he was friends with her family. He smiled and right there, that day, he signed me to the label.

Dad and I went up to New Jersey to go to a recording studio he'd booked, only to find that his plan was for me to record with a full gospel choir crammed into the room. They seemed to be just as surprised to see me as I was to see them. Like, *Who is this little girl?* We recorded an absolutely abysmal song that I gave my all to, because now everything seemed like an audition and I was not going to blow it. The song was "God Says Wait" and it was about—guess what?—not having sex. I will spare you the lyrics, but it was basically a call to arms-length love.

Buster got me gigs on the gospel circuit. When the travel got tough or I seemed too nervous to sleep, I would drink some NyQuil. I realized it knocked me out when I was sick, so I took it when I was healthy, too. Then I started taking Tylenol PM. It was a godsend after years of lying awake with fears of being alone. I took each pill like it was a magic potion, because it freed me. I was able to sleep in my own bed, or a bed on the road, without needing Ashlee. I didn't think I was dependent. In fact, those pills actually helped me feel independent.

Near the end of summer, Buster wanted me to come back to New Jersey to record. The choir thing did not go over very well with the crowds, and I was really interested in doing solo stuff anyway. My mother wanted me to take a break and just focus on school for a bit.

"Just be an eighth grader," she said. "Try being a cheerleader."

Be a cheerleader, they said. It will be fun, they said.

4

CHEERLEADER BLUES

"Hey, Jessica," said a bright voice behind me.

I was between classes at North Richardson Middle School, walking from eighth-grade English, which I loved, to Pre-Algebra, which I hated. It was a guillotine walk every day, so I turned quickly in hope of rescue or at least distraction. It was a blond boy, smiling with four other boys. They were ninth graders, and they were all cute.

"Hi," I said.

"You know," the blond boy said, "you'll make more friends if you jump up and down."

"Really?"

"It's a trick, but it totally works," he said.

I jumped up and down, once. A short hop.

"No, no," he said. "Keep going."

I did it some more, higher, and the boys seemed mesmerized.

"There you go," he said, smirking.

A girl walked by, hissing at me, not them. "Ugh," she said. "They just want to see your boobs bounce."

"No, they—" They laughed, and I knew it was true. But I laughed along with them.

"You *know* that," she said, sneering at me as the boys ran to class. I tried to talk to her, but she kept moving. Honestly, I'd come to trust the intentions of boys over girls after the way some girls had treated me. I had a core group of girlfriends who I loved, but they were all from youth group at church. They went to other schools, and it was like when I saw them, I was Dorothy when life turned technicolor. If boys were nicer to me because of my breasts, well, at least they were nice to me.

Ugh, my breasts were so annoying to me. In the eighth grade, they were already a D-cup. I hated them when I started developing in the fifth grade. As they were growing, I started wearing baggier and baggier T-shirts, thinking I could hide them because no one else had them. By the end of fifth grade I was a B-cup, but I thought I had mastered magician-level skills of sleight of hand, crossing my arms over my chest and constantly pulling at my shirt. I didn't like how they made older kids and men look at me differently, but they also just made me feel like I was getting fat. I couldn't wear what other kids wore. My daughter wears a blazer uniform for school and I just thank God that I didn't have to. I could *not* have pulled off that look.

Finally, my mother confronted me, and bought me a sports bra. She tried so hard to make me feel okay about it. "It's how

God made you and God loves you," she told me again and again.

Not everyone was so nice. In seventh grade the pastor at our church nearly grabbed my mother after I performed at the service.

"Jessica can't sing in front of the church because—" he paused. "You could see her breasts."

"Her breasts?"

"Her nipples!" he said, trying not to yell for all to hear.

"Well, why the hell are you looking?" my mother asked. She was always that tiger mom. She had her own resentment about putting so much into the church and not getting credit. Any slight to her family gave her the release valve of anger.

"She will make men lust!"

"She's thirteen!"

Mom had to explain the nipple controversy and I thought I'd done something wrong. "I'm just catching the spirit of the Lord," I said. The compromise was big vests for summer and roomy blazers for winter. Anytime I sang, I had to cover myself. I got my revenge in little ways. I would intentionally laugh loud during church. Any odd thing that happened, I would let it rip, and the pastor would shush me in front of five hundred people. My dad hated it, but my mom would laugh, too.

It wasn't just my pastor. When I performed at abstinence rallies, people were especially hard on me. I would be wearing the exact same shorts and T-shirts other girls my age wore and get yelled at for dressing sexy. When I did a big Southern Baptist youth conference, singing in front of nearly 20,000 people at Reunion Arena, I wore flowery Doc Martens, black leggings, a T-shirt, and a white button-up vest. To be safe, my mom even put a second denim vest over me. I wanted to look exactly like Rebecca St. James, who was also on the bill. She was a huge Christian singer at the time, beloved in that same outfit.

Right before I went on, the guy who was leading the music for the conference approached me and my mom. He looked at me a long time, and then turned to my mother. "You know that she is an abomination to the Lord," he said quietly, deliberately emphasizing each word to maximize my shame and my mother's complicity.

"Excuse me?"

"Yes," he said, pointing a meaty finger at me. "Dressed like that. People are going to look at her. And they are only going to see what she is wearing."

"What is she wearing that's wrong?" my mother asked. She was genuinely confused, and so was I. He walked away as they announced my name from the stage.

"I'm sorry, baby," she said. "You are beautiful."

I went out there, smiled, and sang my heart out for my allotted two songs. My heart was pounding, but it was the start of that feeling I get when I'm performing: Once I get going, I don't want to leave the stage. But sure enough, I got slammed for my outfit. Even though I dressed exactly like Rebecca, I was dancing around up there so I guess things were bouncing.

Being a preacher's daughter, I was used to being looked at and held to a higher standard. But having people focus on something completely different than what I was trying to do was strange. "Wait," I wanted to say. "I'm singing to God right now. God's using me right now. Let Him sing through me and stop looking at the vessel." All that judgment, and it was constant, toughened me up for what would come when the crowds got bigger, I know. But then, I was just thirteen, singing to the Lord and trying to do what He called me to do.

My mom recently joked that middle school was when her life became all about covering my breasts. "Those boobs definitely ruled our planet," she said. "What were we gonna do, tape them down?"

"Which we did," I said.

"Well, that was to play Tiny Tim in the seventh-grade pageant."

"Tim wasn't so tiny, Mom."

"Heck no," she said proudly. "That took a lotta Ace bandages."

AT LEAST I HAD MY NEW CHEERLEADER FRIENDS. EIGHTH GRADE WAS MY first year putting on the sleeveless green-and-gold-striped uniform to cheer for the Vikings, and I was excited at the idea of being part of a squad. I liked wearing the uniform on game days and I felt like I belonged, which I'd only truly felt at youth group. There were about twenty girls, and they were all popular. I admit that I thought they would be good to recruit to youth group. I was always helping bring people in, not just to "sell it" but because I was rigid in the thought that accepting Christ would save their souls.

There was a girl on the squad who I'll call Beetlejuice. I call her that because I don't want to call her by the name of someone you might know or meet in real life. What she did to me was so awful that you might tell that person off out of reflex and I honestly don't want anybody to get hurt. Beetlejuice and I had sleepovers, and we would camp out in her backyard until the fall Texas air chilled to the point that we would run inside laughing, dragging our sleeping bags into her living room. I still had trouble sleeping, but I would bring a Tylenol PM just in case.

Beetlejuice and I became like best friends, and we discussed kid stuff like teachers we couldn't stand and boys we liked. She talked a lot about her obsession with a boy named Mark who was in our English class. If he looked at her, even to ask her to move aside to get through a door, she reviewed it with a play-by-play. We traded so many small confidences that we built enough trust to get to the big stuff. Beetlejuice confided something to me that rang true for me as well. She shared a secret: someone she knew had been molested. I worried it might still be going on, so I immediately said that person should tell an adult she trusted.

"It happened to me," I said. I said it out loud, brave because I thought she and whoever this was needed it. I had only ever told my parents about what happened.

"Really?" she asked.

"I didn't say anything," I said. "It was a girl and I let her do it for too long." I shared about the girl who had abused me. When I finished, Beetlejuice didn't hug me. My story hung there in the dark.

About two days or so later, we were at the start of English class. We were midway through a unit on *To Kill a Mockingbird*, which I read in the back of my mom's Jump for Jesus aerobics class or sitting outside my dad's counseling office at church. I liked the escape of reading, and it didn't feel like homework. I was in the back of class as usual, so I could see when ahead of me some guys were talking to Mark and then looking back at me. When they caught my eye, it was like they'd hooked a fish. They pulled back, full strength, to reel me in.

"Mark loves Jessica," they chanted. He didn't deny it, and instead smiled at me. I rolled my eyes and reflexively smiled back. Then I looked over at Beetlejuice, who looked down in anger. At the bell, Beetlejuice ran out of the class. Mark lingered and I walked right past him to try to catch up with her. I didn't, but I knew we had cheer practice that afternoon. I would just clear it up then.

But the girls were all whispering when I went in the gym. I took a seat on the end of a bleacher with them, waiting for the coach, and each moved over to leave two feet of space between me and them.

"We know what you did," said the girl closest to me.

"I don't like Mark," I said loudly to Beetlejuice, who had moved even farther down the line.

"Of course you don't," she said. "You don't even like boys, lezzie."

"What's 'lezzie?'" I asked.

The whole squad alternated between this look of disbelief and disgust. Beetlejuice stood up. "I told them what you did to me."

"What?" I asked.

"How you tried to have sex with me at my house," she said. "Touching on me and stuff."

I jumped up and yelled that it wasn't true. I ran out of the gym to a pay phone and called the church, asking them to find my mom. Beetlejuice had taken my story of abuse and told everyone on the squad that I had done this to her on one of the sleepovers. This started some chain reaction thing where three other girls—and I remember their names, too—then claimed that I had done the same thing to them. I'd never even been alone with some of them, let alone at their houses. But I was the town witch, and torches were going cheap.

When my mom picked me up, I was a blubbering mess in the car. I didn't even know how to explain what they said about me. I got home and ran to my room.

That night our house got egged. I think my parents thought it was just a prank, but I knew. I told my parents I was sick and couldn't go to school. The next morning, Mom tried to convince me to go, but a neighbor called us and told us we better look outside at the front of our house.

In the night, someone scrawled DIE BITCH in black shoe polish huge across our home. I felt so bad for Ashlee, who was nine and so confused. Dad took a hose to it, but it wouldn't come out until he scrubbed it with something from the hardware store. From the window, I watched him work at the stain, and I felt ashamed. I had brought this on our family, and I was petrified of going back to school. If they were doing that to our house, what would they do to me?

For two weeks, I refused to go to school. My mom tried to talk me into going back and facing them. I thought she was naïve. She called the school and they were actually very nice to her, promising they would protect me if I came back. My absence didn't help. Someone found a stack of anti-gay flyers and threw them all over our yard. Dad started staying up to watch, but we'd still get egged by cars racing past. People I didn't even know were backstabbing me, tormenting our family. And I'd handed Beetlejuice the knife by telling her my story.

Finally, my mom made me go back to face them. It was School Picture Day, and the worst part was that my outfit was already set: My cheerleader uniform, because we were taking the team photo. There was also a basketball game that night that my squad was supposed to cheer.

"We've got to do this, Jessica," she said.

Later, that emphatic "we" would mean *me* going onstage no matter how I felt or doing an interview with someone when I didn't want to talk about my personal life. That "we" meant "you." But this time, I took the "we" seriously, and made her walk in with me. And I am glad I did because it was exactly the cheesy horror movie I knew it would be. Picture me walking in, and the hustle of a junior high morning freeze-framing to a still while people took in the big scene. They'd had two weeks to turn me into some creation of their darkest fears and fantasies, and here I was, the lesbian cheerleader holding her mommy's hand.

I kept my head down walking to my locker. I could tell from the clogged vents of my locker that it was full of junk. People had slipped garbage in, literal garbage, but also the trash of the same anti-gay pamphlets that littered our yard. The contents spilled out onto the floor, and I cried, not sure what to do with my backpack, which now seemed so pointless because clearly I could never come back there.

Mom took me to the office, where they assured her I would be safe. When I asked her to take me home, she looked at my uniform and reminded me that I needed to face the girls on my squad. Still, I hid most of the day in the library or the bathroom. I stood facing the bathroom mirror, running the water and washing my hands when anybody came in to cover that I was hiding. I smoothed the green flare skirt of my uniform again and again, trying to look perfect. I knew the pose for the photo from looking at last year's yearbook. I practiced my smile, placing my fists on my hips, making ninety-degree angles of my arms.

"You can do this," I said to the mirror. And I shrugged.

At picture time, I smiled for my solo shot, and then hung in the back when they gathered the cheerleaders for the group photo. One girl, Lesa, said hi. "I missed you," she whispered. It was this small little beacon of kindness, a tiny light in the distance that said to keep floating and don't sink. As they took their places, I stayed off to the side, taking a floor spot and hitting that ninety-degree arms look. I stole glances at Beetlejuice, but she didn't seem able to look at me.

I got through it, so I felt obligated to cheer at that night's basketball game. I didn't want to let anybody down, while at the same time I didn't feel welcome. Things started off okay, just people in the crowd staring at me during the first half. Then I saw one of the girls, one of the accusers, run over to the opposing side. I saw her whisper to a cheerleader for the other team, who then whispered to another and pointed. Down the line like a sick game of Telephone.

After a huddle, that squad had a new chant, aiming pom-poms at me. "Les-bi-*an*, Les-bi-*an*."

Again, I ran, my parents running after me. At home in our kitchen, I wondered if this was who I was now. I didn't understand what it was to be gay. If I was touched sexually by a girl, and didn't stop her, did that experience make me gay for life? Did it define me, even if I didn't want it to happen? I honestly didn't know if that was how it worked.

Mom asked what I wanted to do, and I said we should pray for all those people who called me names. It was surprising to me, too. It just seemed like if I prayed for them, they would stop. "If you forgive them," my mom said, "God will forgive them, too."

"Okay," I said.

"Look at the big picture, Jess," my mom said, something she would say to me on a regular basis throughout my life. "Where are they going in life?"

Maybe because the bullying was so public and noticeable to the spectators at the basketball game, the school brought in outside counselors to talk to the kids. Dad made me go back and the girls all ended up recanting and apologizing to me. I still quit the cheerleading team. It wasn't my dream to be a cheerleader, but what if it was? We talk about bullying as a harassment issue, but it's also about limiting opportunities and potential. I had to work hard to make up for missing two weeks of school. I really wanted to talk about *To Kill a Mockingbird*.

When I started high school in tenth grade, when all the junior highs were coming together, I would walk by people and hear, "That's the lesbian." By then I was such a heavy-duty Christian recruiter that nobody could conceive I could pull off being gay. People moved on, but the scar remained. I had opened up to someone and look what it got me.

I actually know where those girls went in life. One of them became a Hooters waitress and then went on to be a preacher's wife. I don't point that out to be petty—I love a Hooters girl— I just really love the idea that life gave her options and she tried out both. I also really hope she met her husband at Hooters.

I don't hold any ill will. When I was so sick during my

pregnancy with my daughter Birdie, I told Eric, "I wouldn't wish this on my worst enemy." And then I remembered, I don't have any enemies, let alone a worst one. No, the people I want to focus on are Lesa, who was kind to me and went on to become a successful therapist, and you. If you are being bullied, whether it's because you're gay or someone decides they don't like something about you, let me be the Lesa who says, "I see you." You are perfectly made.

AFTER SCHOOL, I USUALLY WENT RIGHT TO CHURCH, WHERE MY PARENTS always were. Dad's therapy office was right over the church gym, which might sound crazy if you've never been to a megachurch. They often have a big basketball court with hoops that can be raised when they need the space for praise and worship. It was one of the reasons our church was so successful bringing in young people.

I'd do my homework sitting outside my dad's office as he counseled kids who were written off as troubled. Often, he would talk to the whole family, including parents who would not be there if there had been some way to sweep this under the rug. Things that we are used to talking about now, they thought they were the only parents in the world dealing with. A kid who couldn't stop cutting herself, another boy who would find alcohol like it was a 24/7 job. And some kids were just written off as bad. It made me afraid of drugs, not because of what it did to the kids, but because of the faces of those parents when they left the office. Broken. It was a great way to raise me, because it was everything I did not want to be.

And yet. There's always a boy, isn't there? Jason was a "bad boy" who came through my father's counseling a better person. He was a few years older than me and was on the wrestling team. He was one of the guys who used to cause trouble and then tried to do lots of good works to make up for it. Eventually, he would be my dad's intern at church, but back then he would look after the younger boys in the youth group, playing ball with the shy ones and taking the rougher ones to things like Car Day, where he taught them how to care for cars in the hopes that it might be a trade for them.

We started "dating" when I was in the eighth grade, but our time together was always chaperoned. Dad would even listen in on my phone calls, and my mom would scream at him to stop. I liked that he was kind to my friends from youth group, like Stephanie. Before Stephanie became my go-to event and intervention planner in Hollywood, she was a tomboy soccer star who never jibed with other girls. We bonded when she told me she dreaded the retreats and sleepovers because she felt like the girls spoke a language of makeup that she didn't understand.

"It's not like French," I said.

"You speak French?" she asked.

"Sí," I said, laughing. "No, but I do speak makeup." I always did her makeup, applying MAC spice lip liner on her and telling her about the Bath and Body Works body sprays that my cousin Sarah introduced me to. To this day, she remembers that the first time I did her makeup I told her that she had pretty eyes, and that small compliment changed how she saw herself. It is so easy to notice things about people and tell them. I don't know why people don't just give out compliments every single day.

Stephanie and I went to a weekend discipleship retreat, Firefall, in the beginning of February, and all I could talk about was what Jason and I were going to do for Valentine's Day.

"Do you think he is going to kiss you?" she asked as I applied a light blush. The look I was going for was sexy but saved. Come hither but leave room for the Lord.

I nearly dropped the makeup brush. "You think?"

"Jessica, of course Jason is going to kiss you."

"Stephanie," I said. "*Jason is going to kiss me.*" We even prayed on it! I know it seems so innocent, but believe me, a first kiss was a huge deal to a girl who had already decided sex was so sacred that she was going to be a virgin on her wedding night.

On Valentine's Day, my parents agreed to let Jason have dinner at my house, with my parents, of course. The plan was that I was going to cook for him. My mom suggested that we make this peppermint ice cream pie we'd never made before.

"I was thinking brownies," I said.

"Let's just try this," she said. I went ahead and just let her do it. I am not a cook now, so I was definitely not a cook then. Dad was very anxious, and once Jason came over the whole dinner was weird. He was like so into this peppermint ice cream pie, and my mom put extra peppermints on the table. I stared at Jason, who was just chewing on all this peppermint candy and seeming so nervous.

At the end, my mother started yawning in this very fake way, telling my dad it was time to go to bed. I walked Jason to the front door, and he sort of ushered me outside under the porch light. The temperature was in the 50s, but we were both shivering.

"Jessica—" he said, and then he didn't finish the sentence. He kissed me, and I had all these thoughts going through my head. The main one was "I love him," but there was also this weird feeling that everyone but me knew this was going to happen.

But it felt good, and I wanted to do it again. He went to his car, looking back like he wanted to kiss me again, too, but didn't dare. I ran inside to tell my parents what they already knew. They were actually pretending to be asleep. I turned on the light.

"I had my first kiss," I said. My mom tried to pretend to be shocked at the admission, but all that fake yawning had exhausted her acting abilities. "You knew that was gonna happen," I said. "All the peppermints."

My dad told me Jason had asked permission to kiss me the week before. "I told him it was just for tonight," he said.

"Just tonight?" I asked.

"Just tonight," he answered, as my mom rolled her eyes.

I went to the bathroom to see if I looked different. I turned my face in the mirror to see what Jason saw. I leaned forward and kissed my own reflection.

5

AGAINST ALL DISCOURAGEMENT

THANKSGIVING 1995

My cousin Sarah and I sat near the middle of the theater waiting for the movie to start. I was stewing with an empty seat next to me, and every few minutes I turned back to give a hurt look at Jason. He'd sat in the back with my boy cousins, Drew and Zeb, instead of with me.

It was Thanksgiving night, and we cousins had all gone out to see Jim Carrey in *Ace Ventura: Pet Detective*. I was back in Texas after being in Nashville all week, recording a gospel album for Buster. He and my parents decided that was what I needed to jump-start my career at age fifteen. I'd been missing a lot of sophomore year—and time with Jason—putting in eight to ten hours a day in the studio, singing up-tempo secular-sounding songs with lyrics like God being a "sure thing." We flew home to Texas that morning because the fare was cheap, and we drove straight to Sarah's house. Her mom, my Aunt Debbie, was hosting that year. Jason showed up after I'd eaten a ton of turkey and dressing, but he seemed more interested in hanging out with my cousins than me. He Jet-Skied with Drew and Zeb even though it was cold on the lake, and so it was Sarah who had to hear all my stories about recording my music, not the boy I had pretty much decided I was going to marry.

"It really hurts me," I whispered to Sarah. "He can be so—"

"Jessica, you've got to relax," she whispered back, passing me the popcorn. I put my head on her shoulder, breathing in the cucumber-melon of the soap she loved. She was always telling me to relax. Because, well, I needed to hear it. I was working so hard to be a rigid version of "godly" that I judged so many people. I held myself to an insane standard, and while I beat myself up about always falling short, I definitely held it against the people who I thought weren't trying.

I didn't know how Sarah managed to be just as devout a Christian as me—if not more so—and still be cool. I always started talking about someone at school who went to a party and drank, and she would shrug and cross the red cowboy boots she loved. She was a girl who would turn up the car radio when Mötley Crüe's "Smokin' in the Boys Room" came on but who could also counsel people about faith. She talked to my little sister, Ashlee, who was already so smart and questioning everything at eleven years old. Ashlee did what worked for Ashlee, and if she didn't feel like volunteering at church that day, she didn't. I didn't even know you could say no. But when Sarah talked about Christ, Ashlee listened. With Sarah, God could be cool.

After the movie, I sulked in the car, sticking my lower lip out in a pout. Sarah rolled her eyes at me, and I'm not sure Jason even noticed. He was going to spend the whole weekend with the boys, so they could Jet Ski. I would spend it doing vocal exercises. Sophomore year was such a weird time for me. I had this thing that I was afraid to call a career because it seemed so make-believe, so I just called it "my music." I never felt like I was doing enough to make it happen, and it didn't help that no one at my school thought it was real. Me and my mom would go to Nashville periodically to record, sleeping in the one bed in some smoke-stale hotel room to save money. Buster would come in and out of our lives, making promises about my future and his belief in me, and then he would be back in New Jersey, while we just ran on faith.

I was getting used to planes, and the Tylenol PM I took before a flight or to come down from a recording session or concert. I was doing more appearances and handing out more headshots to audiences at Bible camps and revivals. I wished we had an album to hand out or, better for my family, sell.

When I was home, I clung to normal things, like the church lock-ins and pancake breakfasts. Our Sunday school teacher, Carol Vanderslice, was especially kind to me. She both welcomed the fact that I'd recruited so many boys to come to youth group and joked that it was a full-time job keeping them from falling all over me. More than a few times, I heard her remind some guys where my eyes were.

Carol was so sweet, and when we had sleepovers, we girls could talk her into anything. She knew our faith set us apart at school. We didn't go to parties where there'd be drinking or anything "sinful," so in many ways we were isolated. When we spent the night at her house, we would convince her to help us do things that we thought were wild, like pool hopping. Six or eight of us girls would climb into her SUV at one in the morning on a Friday night, and she'd drive us around to the houses of the boys in the youth group. I should specify, the cute boys. She'd park down the street a bit, and we'd get out, climb the fence, and all six of us would go to their pools, jump off the diving board, and then move on to the next house. Innocent pranks helped us feel less alone in a world that called us uncool.

Carol started to become a second mother to me, one who really just wanted me to be a kid. My mom wanted that, too, but she was also invested in the promise of me. She had to think big picture, like she always said.

I fell further and further behind in school, so that gave me license to give up on algebra. It just seemed so useless if I was going to be a singer. But I kept up with my reading for English, always packing books on my trips. We did a Shakespeare unit first semester, so I remember reading *Romeo and Juliet* in an airport, *Hamlet* on breaks in the recording studio. It all seemed so romantic, even though *Hamlet* was tragic. The next semester we read my favorite, *Great Expectations*, a book I have returned to again and again. It was even the theme of my wedding to Eric. Just the title alone grabbed me. "To whom much is given, much is expected" was something my parents had always told me. So the expectation to be great, that was everything to me. I'd only had these dreams of making it as a singer for a couple of years, but time moves so slowly when you're that age that it felt like a long time. My dreams felt grand but worn down, just like old, jilted Miss Havisham, still wearing her wedding dress in the dusty but still-gilded mansion of Satis House. But I kept trying to make them happen, because I felt called to music. Waiting for my life to really begin, I underlined a passage in chapter 29 of my paperback copy: "I loved her against reason, against promise, against peace, against hope, against happiness, against all discouragement that could be."

That quote has stayed with me. Sometimes through the years, it was about a man who I wished could love me as much as I loved him. But more often it was about my determination to make good on the expectations placed on me. By God, by my parents, by me. No matter what.

FROM THE MOMENT MY MOTHER WALKED IN THE DOOR OF THE HOTEL, SHE was pulling my outfits out of suitcases to drape them around the room. We were in Nashville, and I was about to have a photo shoot for my album. It was finally something tangible for my mother to help with, and she seized the moment. She preferred being behind the scenes while my dad did all the talking as my manager. But this she could do. My mom moved quickly around the room, arranging the "looks," as she now called them. She'd put different tops with the jeans, and then stand back like a painter judging a canvas.

She made me anxious, so I told her I was going to take a bath to get rid of that plane feeling. It was May 3, three months after Buster had reappeared at a concert I did in Atlanta. I had been sick, and I talked about it with the audience, telling them I had prayed to God to help me. I asked them to help me, too. We all really connected, and afterward Buster said he would book more time in the studio to finish the album.

Now the album was about done, and we needed a cover. I filled the tub, absently singing to myself. I wish I could remember what it was, because this moment would always be the Before in our family.

The hotel phone rang, an angry buzz I had grown to hate from morning wakeup calls before going to the studio. I heard my mother answer, putting on the professional voice she always used at the hotel and studio. "Hello," like she was just doing something important but was willing to give you her undivided attention.

There was a silence, then a loud, "What do you mean, *died?*"

I stepped out of the bathroom and saw my mother crumple. She screamed, holding the receiver to her chest, and it was as if that scream had just left her hollow. I stood there dumbly in the threshold, not even saying "What?" or "Who?" because I had never in my life seen her like this.

"Oh God, Connie," she said. "Oh God."

Aunt Connie, I thought. What was this about? When she hung up, she tried to gather herself, talking through her body seizing with this sudden grief, hitting like a heart attack.

"It's Sarah," she managed to say. "Baby, there was an accident."

It felt like someone had passed me something hot, and my hands leaped up to drop it. My knees buckled, and I knelt. I curled my body as my mother covered me with hers, not saying anything. Now there were two worlds: One where Sarah was alive, and a completely insane one where God had taken her. And the only person I could think of who would help me understand that was Sarah.

I heard the pounding of the water filling the tub. I crawled away from my mother, unable to walk. I reached up to turn the faucet off just as the water was about to overflow. It felt like I had stopped something bad from happening. And yet the worst had already happened to us. I leaned against the tub, listening to the drip of the water. I looked out to see my mother still on the floor. Past her, my outfits now seemed strewn about the room, meaningless in this new world.

SARAH AND HER BOYFRIEND HAD BEEN DRIVING HOME FROM OUR NANA'S house. They were seniors on the edge of graduation, and each was getting ready to go to college. Sarah was accepted at Baylor and Howard Payne University, both in Texas. Sarah's mom, Aunt Debbie, planned a big party at her house in conjunction with the Senior Party. Sarah wanted to get rid of kid stuff and make a little money for a trip to New York, so she had gathered things to sell at the annual Harris Creek garage sale in Nana's neighborhood.

That Friday, Sarah and her parents went with her boyfriend to get it set up for the following morning. Then they headed back, and Sarah got in her boyfriend's pickup for the fifteen-minute drive home. Aunt Debbie and Uncle Boyd were about five minutes behind them.

There was a rodeo going on in McGregor, and there was a horse named Gracious Will, likely getting its name from the eleventh chapter of Matthew. Jesus marvels to God that children like Sarah can see what matters in life better than the supposedly wise. "Yes, Father, for such was your gracious will."

Gracious Will did not perform well that day, and the kid in charge of the horse was angry. So angry he hit the animal, and so hard the horse took off running.

The horse made it to the highway, narrowly missing two cars as it galloped against traffic. It stopped and stood in a ditch on the side of the road. As the pickup was about to pass, the horse suddenly leaped in front of it, going through the windshield and landing on top of Sarah.

My aunt and uncle drove up, and first saw the horse, dead on the road. Then the pickup in a ditch. Sarah's boyfriend was outside of the truck, in shock. He had one small scratch on his face.

My uncle Boyd was a Texas highway patrolman, so he'd worked wrecks his whole life. He'd seen all kinds of stuff, shepherded so many people at the worst moments in their lives, and here was his Sarah. My Aunt Debbie, she had such a strong faith that she believed God would heal her daughter if she prayed enough. He would bring her back.

The ambulance came, and they all followed it to the hospital. Sarah was pronounced dead when she got there. She was gone. I know there are families who have had tragedies. But we were always somehow spared. There's a comfort you slip into as good Christians. *God's got his angels over me,* you think. I was taught—and generations before me believed—that we were protected. Without that blind faith, what did we have?

Mom and I got on the next flight home. I was in shock, I realize now, thinking if we did everything right, we would somehow undo the reality. Maybe like Aunt Debbie's prayers. I thought we would go up in the air and then touch down on a world where this hadn't happened. Going through the clouds, I put my head down on my mother's lap.

I don't know if I fell asleep, but I had a dream that I had fallen asleep, if that makes sense. Whether it was a dream or a vision, Sarah came to me. She had her long curly hair again. She had gotten her hair cut shorter a few weeks before and told me she hated it. But there it was. "I'm okay," she said, giving me that smile she gave me every time she gently shook her head and told me to relax. "Please tell my mom I'm okay. Please give her a hug for me."

Mom stroked my hair, and I sat up. "Sarah just came to me in a dream," I told her, adding what she'd said about her mom.

"Well, you should let Aunt Debbie know," she said. "She needs to hear that."

Once we were home, my mom was my aunt's lifeline and naturally set aside everything to focus solely on getting her big sister through this. Aunt Debbie summoned such grace to surrender all that pain and put it in His hands. I learned so much about strength and vulnerability walking hand in hand during those days. Our faith had not protected the very best of us, Sarah, the most precious and kindest member of our family, but there was also no way to get through this without faith.

When we arrived at Aunt Debbie's house, she asked my dad if he would do the service.

"Of course," he said.

She had been reading through Sarah's journals and shared them with my parents. I didn't even know Sarah kept diaries. They were so moving that my father asked permission to take them home to pull things from them for the service. He wove together passages of her writing, along with scripture and songs of praise that she highlighted. He told me how mature she was for her age, and how much she trusted God's will. Her last entry was about her upcoming graduation, and she wrote that it was not nearly as important as her faith. "Since I know God and Jesus," she wrote, "when I die, I will graduate."

"Jess, there's something else," he said. "When Sarah prayed

for people, she wrote their name down and what she asked God to give them." He handed a journal to me, and I opened it to see the bubbles of her handwriting. Again and again, leafing through it, I saw my name. "Sarah prayed for you every day," he said. "Every single day, she put your name down."

Even now, I burst into tears. I had grown up so lonely. Not always alone, but always lonely. And that whole time, Sarah had thought of me with love every day, possibly at the very moments when I felt the most lost. That realization—that I was never truly alone all that time—changed how I thought about heaven, it wasn't some place in the sky. It was with Sarah, and Sarah was with me. What had seemed like blind faith when we lost Sarah, the naive thought that we were protected, was real. I was never alone, and everything was going to be okay.

I stayed up late to read through the journals, seeing for myself how Sarah was always thinking of ways to help people and be of service. As I read, I began to feel an overwhelming sense of purpose, and I realized that I had inherited Sarah's. I would keep her work alive through my life. *Those are pretty big shoes to fill,* I remember thinking. Just as quickly, I pushed away my fears: *Well, they're the only ones you've got.*

Sarah's funeral was held at her home church, First Baptist Church, Woodway. The service was exactly what she would have wanted. In her journals, she mentioned a song she particularly loved, "How Beautiful," which she hoped to play when she eventually married. Dad asked me to sing it, and I was afraid to. But I knew it would be what Sarah wanted, so I just asked her to help me through it. It was the only time I didn't cry at the funeral.

I recently talked to Aunt Debbie to get her blessing to share

Sarah's story. She told me many people, young and old, later said that the service inspired them to accept Christ and to go into ministry or mission work. A day or so after the service, the letters started arriving. Sarah had written notes to every single member of her graduating class, telling them about Jesus and saying she was praying for them. She wasn't preachy, just saying that in times of trouble she had found comfort in prayer and she wanted everyone to know they could come talk to her if they needed that support of Christ. She had mailed them a few days before she died, wishing everyone a great future. It was a powerful lesson in creating a legacy by choosing your words with intention. We are on this earth such a short time, cruelly short in Sarah's case. What message did I want to leave behind?

I wasn't the only person Sarah visited after her death. She came to Aunt Debbie and her boyfriend in dreams as well. She told him that she was okay, and he saw many kids around her that she was teaching. A girlfriend of Sarah's told Aunt Debbie she saw Sarah in heaven, living in this big mansion, with white pillars . . . Aunt Debbie told me she nearly fainted, because what this young woman described was something Sarah had told her father about a week before her death. They were driving to check out Howard Payne, because she had been offered a scholarship there and had never visited. She was so excited on the two-hour ride. "I have this vision," she told her dad, "that I'll live in this huge house. With a big balcony and huge colonial pillars."

"Well, you better marry someone rich out here," Uncle Boyd joked.

"Or someone who loves you a lot," Aunt Debbie recalled saying quickly. She told me: "I did not want her dreams crushed. If she wanted a mansion, I wanted her to have that dream."

My aunt has extended that loving heart to so many. That poor boy who hit the horse, who set Gracious Will into motion, later reached out to her. He was just thirteen, a little kid, and his mom called and said, "My son's gotta tell you something." Aunt Debbie had to make a choice: Make this kid feel more terrible than he already did or tell this boy that he was okay and all was forgiven. She chose the latter, refusing to be bitter. Sarah's boyfriend went on to be the great man that Sarah saw in him. He became an EMT. Another friend of hers named his daughter after Sarah. "I recently saw her, and she is such a beautiful, kind young woman," Aunt Debbie told me.

Shortly after Sarah died, I started reevaluating what I was spending time on. The push-and-pull games with Jason now seemed childish, and I felt like God wanted me to make space for bigger things. Jason stayed very active in my dad's church and went on to become a pastor.

I started journaling when I saw how Sarah could express herself so beautifully on the page. On May 13, 1996, I wrote: "I am starting a prayer journal. Sarah dying taught me how much I take for granted. God, help me keep this promise and please keep me accountable."

God and Sarah began to keep me accountable, so I stuck with it. I listed the people I prayed for and the things that scared me. And as I wrote, I started to get to know myself better, readying myself for what was before me.

part two

6

TAKING FLIGHT

The Casa Hogar Elim orphanage was about a dozen miles from the Texas border town of Laredo and a world away for us kids from church youth group. There were about a hundred of us that first time I went. On the bus from the airport in San Antonio, we leafed through magazines, showing each other a Ford Mustang convertible we had to have and the red, white, and blue Tommy Hilfiger ad for the white polo that was different from every polo we already had because this one was *Tommy Hilfiger*. I had begun to picture myself not just wearing the clothes in the magazines but being *in* the magazines.

It felt like I was getting closer. I was sixteen, just a few days from turning seventeen. On my birthday, July 10, I was going to fly to New York for meetings with record labels. I had plateaued on the Christian circuit and needed to go mainstream.

Buster came to us shortly after Sarah died and told us the label was folding, so it seemed like all that work producing my gospel album would never see the light of day. My Nanny, one of my biggest champions, came to my rescue and gave my father $7,500 to do a pressing of the record so we could make CDs and tapes to sell ourselves at concerts. We named the album *Jessica*, and used one of my black-and-white *Mickey Mouse Club* audition headshots as the cover, giving it a sepia tint to make it look arty. I dedicated it to Sarah, and just as I had done with the Jump for Jesus videos, I was relentless, selling those CDs every chance I got.

Dad treated it like a business card, and he was effective. My vocal coach, Linda Septien, got us hooked up with Tom Hicks as a potential investor in my career. He was a near billionaire who had recently bought the Dallas Stars hockey team. I used to joke that my dad called 1-800-ENTERTAINMENT LAWYER, to find Tim Mandelbaum, but now I know it was from talking with Linda. Tim was in New York, where all the music labels were, and he shopped my CD around to drum up interest.

And there was. After the trip to the orphanage, we were flying straight to New York to meet with eight labels. Tim had lined up the meetings over a couple days, and I would basically be auditioning at each one, with my dad pitching me as my manager.

But first, there was the weeklong mission trip to the orphanage. When we drove up to the two-story complex of sun-bleached stone, everyone got quiet. Now we weren't a bunch of pampered extras from *Clueless*. We'd seen poverty up close on mission trips before. As a group, we traveled to the Bowery mission in New York to sing and serve at the soup kitchen. And we'd done vacation bible school in Belize, where our van broke down during a rainstorm in the middle of the jungle. We were stranded, and I made everyone get out and pray in a circle around the bus. You know, to heal the van, I guess. Maybe it worked because a busload of soldiers, all with rifles on their laps, happened by. No one said a word the whole way back to the city limits. When we finally got back to the hotel, Carol Vanderslice, my Sunday school teacher, told me she thought, *Great, I'm going to get the pastor's daughter killed.*

But there was something humbling about the trip to the orphanage, knowing all the kids who surrounded us had no one but each other and Mama Lupita, the woman who ran the organization. There were about eighty kids of all ages milling around in worn hand-me-down T-shirts with slogans and out-dated video game characters. The orphanage had no running water or electricity, and since it was not state-owned, it relied solely on donations and the work of church groups like ours cycling through. Mama Lupita—Guadalupe Carmona was her real name—started the orphanage in 1986 when she took in four kids whose father couldn't care for them after their mother died. My dad told me Mama Lupita also visited prisons to pray with people, and the women there often asked her to take in their kids, too. It just grew from there.

We spent our week doing odd jobs to fix up the place, cook-ing meals to serve to the kids, and doing lots of babysitting. We all got so attached to the children that we kept walking into town to buy them stuff because we had it to give. There was a new baby who had been found in a dumpster and brought to the orphanage the morning we arrived. I pretty much decided it was my job to hold her. I distinctly remember worrying that I was going to confuse her by speaking English, so I called over to one of the smarter kids in youth group.

"How do you say 'I love you' in Spanish?" I asked.

"*Te amo*, Jessica," he said with googly eyes, and laughed.

I smiled back and turned my face to the baby. "*Te amo*," I said, over and over again, meaning it. I wanted her to know she was loved. I wanted it to be a familiar feeling, so that when unconditional love came into her life, she would recognize it.

A few days into the trip, I was holding her when someone came looking for my dad. There was someone on the line for him, on the one phone in the whole place. When he came back, he told me it was Teresa LaBarbera Whites, a Dallas-based A&R rep for Columbia under Sony. A&R means Artist and Repertoire, so they're supposed to scout the talent and then match them with the right material.

"How did she get the album?" I asked. The baby was sleeping, so I kept my voice down.

"No," my dad said, knowing I wouldn't like the answer. "She heard the demos."

"What," I whisper-yelled. "How?" The demos were three secular songs I'd recorded at a studio in Dallas and hated. I only did them because it seemed smart to record "regular" music so I could show the labels I was meeting with what I could do besides gospel. I sang the Céline Dion song "Seduces Me" and Whitney Houston's "Run to You" and "I Have Nothing." I had the nerve to be upset that I didn't sound like Céline or Whitney on the playback. When the sound engineer, Chuck Webster, said they were fine, I said I was a perfectionist and asked him to just trash the tapes. If I was going to do mainstream music, I didn't want it to sound like okay karaoke.

"Well, Chuck played the demos for Teresa," my dad said.

"What part of 'Never play this for anybody under any circumstances' didn't he understand?"

Dad shrugged and said Teresa was anxious to meet me in person to see if I could really sing. She was upset that I wasn't going back to Dallas before New York. "She says she has to see you," he said. "When we leave here, she's willing to come down to San Antonio to see us before the flight."

I looked down at the baby and sighed. *Well,* I thought, *what difference could it make?* "Might as well," I said.

DAD AND I ARRANGED TO MEET TERESA AT A HOTEL IN SAN ANTONIO. THE first thing I noticed was that she was very pregnant. She later told me she was eight months pregnant, and had brought her maternity records with her, just in case she went into labor. This was that important to her.

"You drove all the way down here to see me?" I asked. Now I know that being that pregnant on the four-hour drive down I-35 would mean hitting the bathroom at every single rest stop.

She smiled. "I flew," she said. "Forty-five minutes in the air. I know we don't have a lot of time, and I had to get down here," she said. When she spoke, she was incredibly serene, with long black hair that hung loose around her shoulders. She looked more like a cool art teacher than a music rep. She told me she loved my voice on the tape but wanted to make sure I matched it in real life.

"I'm me," I said. "We match."

We made some small talk, which was very small on my end because I was so nervous. Teresa talked with her hands, and I was kind of mesmerized by the languid movement of these long fingers. Her hands seemed to glide and dip with her accent, which was deeper Southern than ours but still Texas. Teresa told me about her history with Sony and Columbia, how she prided herself on being what she called "an artist's advocate," nurturing young talent and putting them with the right songwriters and developing them as songwriters themselves. She had signed a Houston girl group, led by a singer she had known since she was nine. "She's sixteen now, amazingly talented," she said. "Her name is Beyoncé Knowles."

I nodded. Dad said, "We'll have to remember that name."

Finally, I couldn't stall any longer. "Should I just sing?" I asked. She nodded, and then seemed surprised when I started singing a capella. I did two songs, "I Will Always Love You" and "Amazing Grace."

She stayed perfectly still as I sang, only speaking when I stopped.

"Okay, I'm going to New York," she said. "I will get you a meeting, and you do exactly what you just did. We need to sign you."

"We're already meeting with Epic," my dad said, playing it cool. Epic was also under Sony, and where Céline Dion signed when she came to America. "We have eight meetings lined up actually—"

"I can get you straight to Tommy Mottola," Teresa said. As green as we were, I definitely knew who Tommy Mottola was. He was the head of Sony, but more important to my mind was that he had just separated from my idol Mariah Carey and had signed her to Columbia in the first place.

"I'm really blown away," Teresa said, looking right at me, as if she were trying to convince just me. "How old are you again?"

"Seventeen," I said, getting used to the idea. "Today."

"Well, happy birthday," she said.

Dad and I flew to New York that night to start the rounds of auditions. Through the two days in New York, I was fortunate to meet with the heads of many record labels, going into boardrooms and corner offices. There were so few women in the offices, and I'd never felt so Southern, standing there with my long pink nails and hair so high to be nearer my God to thee.

I would sing a capella or listen as they nodded through a song off my tape. Dad talked a lot, getting better and better with each meeting. A preacher hitting a groove. I kept saying the same thing, remembering why God had even put me in those rooms in the first place: "I will only go with you if you believe that I can change the world."

Sometimes they would cock their heads at that, like they were weighing a sales angle. But other times I felt a real connection, particularly at the Mercury offices. It was such an innocent way of thinking, and I'm sure some of them thought it was a childlike faith. But they couldn't say it wasn't real.

When I sang "I Will Always Love You" at Jive, they were direct with me. "We *just* signed a girl who's just like you and sang that same song," someone in a suit said. "This girl Britney Spears."

"Oh, I know her," I said, my stomach flipping.

"Small world," he said.

"Yeah," I said, defeated all over again. Then at RCA I got the same story, as if the girl had just been in the same boardroom and ink was still drying on the contract. She had apparently nailed a song on a Disney soundtrack, and they were going to sign her.

"Christina Aga-something," said the guy, looking around the room for someone to give him the right name. "Aguilar?"

"Aguilera," I said, holding back a sigh. "She's really talented."

My mother had been right about running into those girls in the future. I didn't expect they'd be taking my spot again this soon.

When I got to Columbia in the Sony building in midtown, Teresa told me she lined up the meeting on the strength of her ear alone. "I didn't play them anything," she said, leading us through an incredible lobby that made me feel tiny. "You just have to let them see you sing."

We got there at 11:45, and I remember first meeting someone who acted very important, talking about having to leave for a label lunch. "Well, can you just sit down and listen for a minute?" I said, and I started singing. He sat down.

"Oh my God, you can't leave," he said. "I have to go to this thing. Um, let me sit you in the Sony Club, okay? Have lunch. *Don't leave*."

"We're not," said my dad. Teresa smiled. The Sony Club was in the top of the building, with executive meeting rooms, then all marble and mahogany, but the real draw was the view of Manhattan. You could see the whole city below us. He came back quickly, bringing in a bunch of people. I'd go into one office after another, until finally they led us to a secret elevator down to Tommy Mottola's office on the thirty-second floor.

"He listened to Mariah sing in the shower, Dad," I said, as the elevator went down. When I get nervous, most people can't tell. On the outside, I seem very calm, but inside there's a tornado. The doubts and fears swirl and I keep trying to grab them to compartmentalize them. In the elevator, I started to pray. *God use me*, I thought, *I am here for Your will. If this moment is right, it will be the right one.* I knew that I had prepared as much as I could. This was not the Mickey Mouse Club. Back then, I didn't even know what preparation meant.

And there he was, Tommy Mottola, sitting at his desk in jeans and a black button-down, his hair slicked back. Don Ienner, the president of Columbia Records, was also in the office. "So, what do you want to do in life?" asked Tommy.

I knew the answer to this one, because I'd just written it in my journal the night before. "I want to be an example to girls all over the world," I said, "that you don't have to compromise your values to be successful."

I don't think it was the answer he was expecting. Don piped up. "I've never heard that from anybody in here before. I want to hear you sing."

I was so scared, and I asked God and Sarah to help me. I stood in the center of the room to sing "Amazing Grace." When I finished, I waited a beat before I was about to start "I Will Always Love You," but Tommy put up his hand.

"That's enough," he said, getting up from his desk. It was over. I didn't know what I did wrong. How had I blown it? I stood there, trying to fight back tears, and he said, in that same flat voice, "Okay, you can have a seat."

My shoulders started to sink, but I held them up high. I sat down, and he walked over to stand in front of me. "As far as I'm concerned," he said, "because I still have to talk to Donnie, I would sign you today. Your music is fantastic how it is."

I had this tremor of relief go through me. I didn't blow it. And before I could even get to my speech about why I wanted to make music, Tommy started in. "I believe that your voice—and who you are as a person and what you stand for—can change the world."

I was like, *Sold.*

We received offers from two other labels. There was Mercury, who had Bon Jovi, and Atlantic, who was putting so much behind new artists like Tori Amos but also had an incredible history with Aretha Franklin and the Rolling Stones. I went back to Dallas torn.

My parents pressured me to decide, and I was afraid to commit and make the wrong choice for my future. I drove myself to a voice lesson with Linda, and on the way over, I started praying, asking God for a sign. Whenever I asked Him for guidance, He came through. Just as I did so, a black bird flew into my windshield. I screamed, and I bet it screamed, too, because it flew straight up. At the next stoplight, I lingered because I was shaken up.

"God, what did that mean?" I asked out loud, alone in the car. "There's no Bird records."

And I looked over to my right, and I saw the sign. COLUMBIA HOSPITAL. How many times over years of going to voice lessons had I rolled through this intersection and never noticed there was a hospital there?

"Columbia," I said. "Okay. Columbia."

As I moved forward, another black bird—or maybe the same determined one—swooped down at my windshield a second time. "Okay, I hear you, God," I said, loud so He and the bird could hear me. "I get the message. Thanks, God." I didn't want any more birds getting hurt.

MY WHOLE FAMILY FLEW BACK TO NEW YORK TO SIGN THE COLUMBIA contract in Tommy Mottola's office at Sony. Right after we all took a picture, Tommy looked me up and down.

"Okay, you gotta lose fifteen pounds," Tommy told me.

"What?" I said, not really understanding. I was five-foot-three and weighed 118 pounds. And I was seventeen.

"I think you're going to have to lose fifteen pounds," he said. "Maybe ten. Because that's the image you want to have. That's what it will take to be Jessica Simpson." He spoke clinically, the way a plastic surgeon would take a black marker to show you all the flaws that could be magically erased. I looked at my parents. They said nothing.

Neither did I. I thought I had the job, and now I had to change myself to be "Jessica Simpson." It was as if he tied my value as an artist to my weight right there, like a rock, and then threw it out the window of the thirty-second floor of the Sony building. Maybe Tommy was being realistic about the times, and he knew what it would take for me to be successful. He believed in me, and he would be a beautiful part of my career, but it was hard to hear what was required to be a star.

I immediately went on an extremely strict diet, and started taking diet pills, which I would do for the next twenty years. It's important that I say this now, if only for my daughter, whenever she reads this: You are perfect as you are. But at the time, this is what we thought we had to do. I say "we" because I was about to become the family business, and there was a lot of pressure to be what the label needed me to be. And my dad didn't know when to say no. We were Podunk, coming to the big time from nowhere. Any industry room we walked into, whoever was in there had more experience. "This is how it's done" was all we needed to hear. We didn't know if things were being done the right way or if we were being mistreated. We were just glad to be in the room.

I only went to my senior year in high school for a month. It felt like a waste of time. We had to leave Dallas so I could start working on my album. Tom Hicks, the hockey-team-owner friend of my vocal coach, gave my dad $275,000 in exchange for a percentage on the start of my career. I think it was points on my first album, but I never asked. I don't know if my father asked much about it either. That money was more than four times what he made in a year with church and his odd jobs, so he could retire from that career and move us out to Los Angeles. Looking back, I realize that investment money was just for me, but it was the start of the "my money is your money" mentality that seemed very natural to me.

When my dad told everyone at church we were leaving, I felt responsible for the uncertainty I saw at the Heights. A pastor becomes a father, a shepherd to the flock, and when they leave, people can feel lost. Dad's youth ministry was at an all-time high, with a record number of kids coming to events and church on Sunday.

My Sunday school teacher Carol, a very important person in my life by now, hosted a goodbye party for our family. Each of us had four members of the church assigned to write us a goodbye letter. I was such a crying mess that I can only remember that Beth, my dance teacher, read hers to my mom and Carol read hers to me. "I know the responsibility you feel," Carol said, "and we are always here praying for you, Jessica."

"I wish I could bring you to L.A. with me," I told her after.

"I'll visit," she promised.

Our move to Los Angeles was set for October 2, the day before Ashlee's thirteenth birthday. I bought a used red BMW convertible with some of my signing money, and I drove it all the way from Dallas, with my parents caravanning in another car. I have always loved driving, and loved that trip, singing along to the radio as the country-rock stations of Texas gave way to the pop DJs of the west.

We moved into a home that was for sale in Hacienda Heights, but, no, we didn't buy it. My mom was a talented decorator, so realtors would let us live in homes and stage them until it was sold. It was the first of many places where we lived the first year because my parents were always working some angle to make money.

To say that Hacienda Heights, an hour's drive to the Sony Music headquarters in the usual traffic, was not conveniently located would be an understatement. But we dived into L.A. life, driving around on the hunt for celebrities. The first big sighting was Garth Brooks, which was a huge deal for us. On a day off from the studio, the whole family went to visit *The Bodyguard* mansion in Beverly Hills so I could be Whitney for a moment, then on to Rodeo Drive so we could have our *Pretty Woman* moment. We didn't have the money to buy anything, but we touched the fabrics like we were seriously giving it a thought. I doubted they would have the same friendly keep-the-tags-on return policy as back home.

One of the first things I did in Hacienda Heights was take Ashlee to the nail salon for a girls' day. I was getting my acrylics in that late-90s French manicure when I looked up and saw a headshot of Fergie. This was before the Black Eyed Peas, so I knew her as Stacy Ferguson from her years on *Kids Incorporated*. "Love you guys!" she wrote in red with a big heart.

"She came here?" I asked the nail tech, pointing at the photo.

"Oh sure," she said. "Many times."

I sat up straighter, turning to my little sister. "Ashlee," I said. "We've made it."

TERESA HAD HER SISTER COME TO TAKE CARE OF HER NEW BABY GIRL, and three weeks after giving birth, she took me around to meet songwriters and producers. "Everybody says, 'Oh, I've got a girl that can sing,'" she told me. "But I need people to meet you so they see you're the real deal." We didn't have demos we wanted to play for people, so she would just set up meetings and I'd sing. Teresa didn't want me to do anything that wasn't authentic to my experience. She knew I was inexperienced, so when I recorded love songs, we had to put up pictures of boys I was fascinated with—actors and singers—just so I could emote that longing.

I worked hard on my album, but Columbia always had some reason to delay. Well, two. Jive was pushing Britney Spears's album to press, which then made RCA really rush Christina Aguilera's album. As the label argued over calling me

Jessica Simpson or just Jessica, there was a sense that I would get lost among the invasion of the teen blondes. I could not believe these two girls were getting in front of me again. The process was also slow because Tommy Mottola had taken such a personal interest in my album. He was picky about every single song, getting involved in the mixes of each one. He would come to the studio, displaying an ear that I completely respected. There was a reason he was who he was. He liked a song I had written, called "Heart of Innocence," pulling lyrics from my journal to sing about holding on to my virginity until marriage. I am sure he partially liked it because of the marketing angle. I recorded a strong ballad "Did You Ever Love Somebody" that Columbia was able to get on an episode of *Dawson's Creek* in November. I watched it with my family, and I jumped off the couch when the show turned up the volume of my voice as Pacey leaned in to kiss Andie. (Yes, I loved Pacey Witter, too, so you diehard *Creek* fans understand what a big deal this was for me.)

Teresa continued to guide me, always acting as my buffer, wanting me to truly be an artist. If I mentioned worrying about sales or my look, she would remind me to just focus on the work. She sent me amazing tracks and paired me with songwriters who would showcase my voice. Her office also made sure I was working to get my GED and assigned a junior Sony staffer in her office, CaCee Cobb, to constantly call me to make sure I was doing my homework and turning it in on time. CaCee was two and a half years older than me and soon took a big-sister interest in my life. Schoolwork was definitely not a priority for my parents, but CaCee took her job seriously, and she's the only reason I got my GED. When we finally met in person—she was my assigned minder at an event in Atlanta—her gorgeous hair reminded me of Sarah's, and I was immediately at ease. Whoever was paying for the trip only booked one room with one bed, and CaCee's response was like, *Uh, nope.* She was a real professional, and I know she thought of me as a kid. But I felt like Sarah had sent CaCee to me, so I was just excited to hang out with her. She had gone to Baylor and understood the business far more than I did. I could ask her real questions about what the label expected of me, because I was confused from mixed messages I seemed to be getting.

It had started when Britney was first out of the gate, with her ". . . Baby One More Time" single hitting in October. She premiered the video on MTV on Thanksgiving Day, and my job had gotten a lot harder. I got word there was a halt on my album and the label decided I didn't have the right songs and needed more Britney-type songs. I had been signed for my voice, but I had to now contort myself into this mold of a dancer.

My answer was "Whatever you want." I just wanted to have my song on the radio.

The weekend after Britney's Thanksgiving premiere, I was supposed to meet with someone who might co-manage with my dad. His name was Paris D'jon, pronounced like the mustard, but hold the I for reasons I never knew. He was going to be at the Hollywood Christmas Parade, looking after a boy band he managed. The band was going to be on a float, and their album was performing well. It spoke well of Paris, who was this tough bulldog of a guy who seemed like he could make things happen just on force alone.

And just behind him was the most adorable guy I'd ever

laid eyes on. It was the smallest moment, two people locking eyes. At eighteen, my usual move was to be coy and look away, but I didn't. He came over, walking in a more casual version of the onstage boy-band saunter I'd come to see him do time and again, but still purposeful.

"Hi, I'm Nick," he said.

Hello, my life, I thought.

7

ROMEO AND JULIET

The thing about falling in love with someone in a boyband is that you're not alone. There were a lot of girls out there who had already compiled all the details on Nick Lachey. The night after I met him at the parade, I went home and researched him and his group 98 Degrees. I learned Nick was a Scorpio, loved the Bengals, home team of his adopted hometown of Cincinnati, and he liked dogs. *Aww.* He was twenty-five, seven years older than me, and had the look of a bad boy. He'd formed the band in 1995, and I read that he and his younger brother, Drew, who was also in the group, saw 98 Degrees as more of a tougher, working-class version of Boyz II Men than a boy band like 'N Sync or Backstreet Boys, who had been put together by talent scouts.

The next time we saw each other was at a *Teen People* party for a cosmetics convention in Boca Raton. This was not what I'd pictured from reading *Romeo and Juliet*, but it would have to do. He brought his mom, and part of the fairy tale was that he said to her, "Mom, your mission for tonight is to get me in good with this girl."

He was wearing red overalls with the left strap off, and a cream turtleneck. He kept trying to catch my eye all night, and eventually just came over to me. We talked schedules—"It's been crazy" was always the answer—and I wasn't really listening because not only did I think he was so attractive, I loved his voice and the way he said "Jessica." He got my number, and I swear I said to my mom, who was also at the party, "That's the man I'm going to marry." I immediately felt safe.

When he called soon after, Nick told me he had broken up with the makeup artist he had been seeing. We arranged to meet when he was in L.A. for the American Music Awards. It was weird to just meet in a hotel room, so Nick suggested we go up on the roof, where we talked for several hours. Nick was much more than what I'd found researching him. He'd started singing in barbershop quartets, making money in high school doing cheesy a capella songs at a theme park in Ohio. He was incredibly passionate about his work. Whereas I counted on God and destiny to make my dreams come true, he was methodical, making it clear he had a five-year plan for success. We talked about our families and how his parents divorced when he was young but his dad never lived more than two miles away from wherever he lived with his mom. It made him grow up fast, becoming the kind of kid who did his own laundry at eight years old. I may have been the breadwinner of our family, but I couldn't work a washing machine to save my life.

As we talked, he reached over to put his hand on mine. It was like an electric shock, so I pulled back.

"There's something I need you to know right away," I said.

"What?"

"I'm a virgin."

"Okay."

"And I don't want to have sex until it's with the man I've married."

He paused, taking it in. I thought, *Well, Jessica, this dreamboat has sailed. See ya.*

"I respect that," he said. "Thank you for telling me."

I didn't tell him what I already knew in my heart. He was the man I was meant to marry.

Nick went back to touring, and we had three-hour phone calls from his bus or his hotel room after the show. That was it for me, we were totally dating, at least over the phone. I wrote about him in my journal, calling him Nicholas because it made me feel older and closer to his age.

I traveled to see him on tour, so all our first dates were at hotels. I would go to his room to hang out, and he remained respectful of the boundaries I placed on us. We had a first kiss in a car, but that was it—he wasn't getting anywhere near my body. Still, I was this good girl with a potty mouth, and I would "accidentally" make double entendres but dismiss it as Southern charm or ditziness, which he seemed to love. Just being around him tested my own commitment to virginity for sure. I had always been a sensual person, but I'd never had someone draw it out of me like Nick. One time, he hugged me, and I thought I was just going to burst into flames. I had to push him away, not because I didn't trust him, but because I was teetering on the edge of just giving in. Suddenly, I completely understood why my mom got married at eighteen. Her mother had at least made it to twenty.

Our seven-year age difference worried my dad. I also thought my father might just be jealous because he heard a lot of "Well, I asked Nick and he said . . ." More and more, I went to Nick with career questions. My mom can be guarded and tough on people, but she liked Nick because Nick seemed like a more sarcastic version of the good old boys she grew up around.

When I was asked to open for 98 Degrees on their North American tour starting in March, I immediately said yes. We asked my dance teacher Beth if she wanted to come be the choreographer for the show, and she agreed. My parents were not going to send me out on the road alone, but what would that mean for Ashlee? She was fourteen and had been studying at the School of American Ballet. Mom asked if she wanted to come be a backup dancer for me.

"It's not ballet," my mom said. "It's more hip-hop."

"I can dance hip-hop," she said.

It's okay to chuckle. We were going for this urban cowgirl direction, which in hindsight is ludicrous, but we just wanted to get onstage. I say "we" because Ashlee is a born performer. As much as she and I are opposites—Ash is more edgy than me and pushes limits while I think out every possible risk and outcome before I do something—each of us thinks of the stage as home, a comfortable place. Back then, I was so focused on doing whatever I was told I was supposed to be doing that I didn't think about how those actions might affect her. I know now that for every time I say, "I'm glad I got to have a somewhat normal high school life," she didn't. I have felt guilty about that for a long time. And as she danced behind me then, I didn't get to see how well she interacted with audiences. It wouldn't take long, though, for her to take the microphone herself.

So, at the time, to me it just felt like fun to do this as a family. I had been locked in recording studios so long working on my album that I just wanted to see people react to me singing, period. I didn't care if the dancing didn't really jibe with the tone of the songs.

Nick and I decided to do a duet for my album, "Where You Are." It was about loss and feeling someone is always with you even after death. Of course, in my mind, it was all about Sarah. The week before Nick and I recorded the song in New York on March 15, I did my first-ever press interview and talked about losing someone. "I wanted the people close to me who have experienced death to feel encouraged," I said. "I wanted the song to minister to a lot of people's hearts."

This was with a teen magazine, so the guy's response was, "Oh, cool." Even so, I knew my words mattered.

When Nick and I sang together, it just fit. I liked how he took the lead in the studio, and how if he decided he needed a break, he just took a break. If I wasn't already in love with him, I would have decided then. Two days later, I started the tour with 98 in Ottawa.

The girls all booed.

Okay, not all of them, but enough up front that I could see them. They came to see 98 Degrees, each with a sign saying "Marry Me, Nick" or "I love you, Drew!" Every girl in that arena thought they had a chance with their favorite, and who was this girl they'd never heard of? At first, I thought it was my singing, but I had a better sense of what was going on when Nick and I would go on "dates" to the local mall. We'd be at Abercrombie & Fitch and he'd get mobbed, and the girls would roll their eyes at me. Teen assassins in Wet Seal.

While I got used to the girls giving me the dirty looks, Nick had to get used to all of us Baptists being on tour with him. The Texas crew never drank, and the 98 guys were used to having beers at the end of the night. Beth, my old dance teacher, confronted Nick about it. "Oh my gosh, why are you drinking a beer?" she said it just like that: "*A* beer," because surely this was an isolated sin, and who would dare have more than one? She let him have it, going on about how I was around, and didn't he know he was supposed to be a role model for young people?

Poor Nick went to my parents' hotel room with this hang-dog face. "I apologize if I disrespected you or the family," he said. "For me, drinking a beer isn't wrong, but I really love Jessica, and, again, I'm sorry if I disrespected the family."

My mother told me the story and I cringed. We must have seemed so country. Still, I had to ask, "He told you he loved me?"

He did. I'd be on a tour bus leaning back on Nick, watching the world go by as he sang "You Are My Sunshine" in my ear. *This is easy,* I thought. *This is forever.* We both thought that. He had a different perspective because he was older and interested in something more real. And at eighteen, I was still such a sheltered baby that it didn't seem far-fetched to me that I had already found that person.

He stayed patient, and how the relationship progressed physically was always up to me. He was the first guy who ever touched my breasts, and it was such a big deal to me that I made my mom take me bra shopping for the occasion. I spent an hour in a Victoria's Secret before I settled on a purple one.

"First boob touch," I said, handing the bra to the girl at the checkout. "Tonight's the night." She laughed, thinking I was kidding.

MY CAREER STARTED PICKING UP IN APRIL, WHEN THE *DAWSON'S CREEK* soundtrack that included my song came out. I played track thirteen over and over again, imagining people all over the world playing it, too. Nick's 98 album went platinum, so his record company threw them a party after our show at the Beacon Theatre in New York. Someone took my picture, and the next day the photo was in the *New York Post*.

I screamed when I saw it, focused only on how I looked and hoping I looked skinny enough for Columbia. My mom read the caption. "*Jennifer* Simpson," she said. "Hunh." I didn't care, it was exciting enough to be in the newspaper.

I booked teen-focused summer tour gigs like Nickelodeon concerts, and Columbia started to get excited about the album. They booked a packed summer tour of radio events—seeming to add new ones every day—to build support for a late-August launch of my first single and a Thanksgiving week release of the album. Britney and Christina had gone with dance singles, so they wanted me to come in contrasting with a power ballad, "I Wanna Love You Forever."

It's an amazing song—the very first time I heard it, I knew it was a hit—but it is a punishing song to sing live. It just asks a lot of you physically and emotionally. And I had to go to as many radio stations as there were in the country to sing it over and over. Back then, radio was *the* way to get heard. Now we stream any song we want, but back then DJs and promoters had all the power. You had to go to every single one, do a showcase, show them your talent, and make them like you. You waited to hear, "We're going to put you in rotation." Columbia's vice president for promotion was Charlie Walk, a Boston guy who'd become a label wiz at thirty. It meant a lot that he believed in me. He didn't seem to sleep, so why should anybody else? I went wherever Charlie told me to go.

The schedule was so packed it just didn't seem manageable, but my dad and I never said no. I wasn't looking at the schedule and saying, "That's a lot." It was Nick who would question how things were being set up. My dad would then get annoyed, because he wanted me out there working and meeting people.

There was so much pressure, and much of the focus was on how I looked. The label was constantly telling me, "Let's show more skin, Jessica. Let's get comfortable with this." It was so strange for me, because I was still shy about my body, so used to being covered up at church. The orders that I show my stomach while singing a ballad at showcases just seemed off to me, especially since the proper technique my vocal coach had taught me meant that I actually stuck out my stomach during the big notes. And "I Wanna Love You Forever" was full of them.

But I tried to do both things. I did events for radio stations all over the country, going into clubs where I was too young to drink even if I had wanted to. Detroit, Boston, New York, back to Dallas . . . wherever they needed me. The audiences were mostly men, some obviously there for the free food and open bar. I remember they always had to announce that the open bar was closed while I sang so the guys would pay attention to me.

There were usually Sony staffers in the crowd, always cheering the high notes. As I hit them, I fluttered my hand around my stomach to hide it sticking out. My dad and I would stay to shake every hand, knowing each person might have the power to make my dreams come true.

In August I started feeling pain in my abdomen. I ignored the cramps in the beginning. There was too much to do. When I was briefly back in L.A., the cramping started to become excruciating, and I couldn't mask it with aspirin anymore. My mom took me to a hospital in Encino, where they told me I just had an enlarged bladder, a misdiagnosis. They pumped me full of fluids to flush me out and sent me home. My mom commented that I was so swollen I looked like the Michelin man.

The pain remained, but we had to fly to Boston to do a showcase for people who worked in radio. I writhed on the plane, but a deal's a deal. Backstage, behind a black curtain, I was in such pain I started throwing up. I made it to the bathroom, and I continued throwing up, even peeing myself, delirious from the cramping.

We had been trained to go to the label with everything. Charlie Walk from Sony had a friend, a girl from Boston, who gave us the number of her OB/GYN. We called, and they said to come right over. Mom got me in some borrowed blue Adidas track pants, and we took a taxi. I had my head out the window puking the whole ride over, my dad holding me to keep me from falling out.

The doctor opened the clinic just for me, and immediately placed a catheter in me and set up an ultrasound. There was no fluid coming out of me, so he panicked.

"The bad news is that I think you are going to need surgery," he said. "The good news is that I am probably one of the best surgeons for this in Boston. You're going to be okay."

Through heaves of pain, I said this: "Please don't give me a scar." I felt like I was going to die, but I was still worried that the label needed me to show my stomach.

He put me in his Mercedes, and we drove right to Brigham and Women's Hospital. Right before the surgery, he explained that I had a cyst in my right fallopian tube. They would have to remove that fallopian tube.

"I want to have babies," I said. "Please don't take them from me."

He gently explained that this would mean that from then on, I could likely only get pregnant every other month. Because he was so experienced, he could do the emergency surgery laparoscopically, going through my belly button. They removed the tube and the cyst, first draining it of two and a half liters of fluid. I think if I had been at any other hospital, at the stage I was at, there would have been no time, and they just would have cut me open.

I had to do a showcase the next day. But I wouldn't trade it, because all that work paid off with this moment: a few days later I was with my parents in a cab in Times Square when I heard "I Wanna Love You Forever" on the radio for the first time. We went nuts, there is no other word for it. Even the driver was going nuts—he had no idea who I was and then, all of a sudden, he was blasting the song with all the windows down. We started screaming to people in other cars, telling them to turn on Z-100. I looked so frantic, one old guy driving by put his window *up*.

"These poor people think I'm crazy, Mom," I said, laughing. "They're all worried they have flat tires or something."

All those years I had waited to hear my voice on the radio. I remember exhaling, like I had finally done it. It was, without question, one of the greatest moments of my professional life. When the single came out, it slowly moved up the *Billboard* Hot 100 chart until it stayed at number three for weeks. When we showed the video for "I Wanna Love You Forever" to Tommy Mottola, I couldn't wait to hear what he'd have to say. The setup was me singing at a photo shoot, dressed in what the audience would relate to, a series of jean jackets and tank tops. We shot behind-the-scenes footage of me and Ashlee hanging out with my friends in my trailer on the set. I was continually asked to hike up my shirts higher throughout the shoot to show my belly button, but the video ended with me on a stage, and I felt like the whole thing established me as a real singer.

"This video is great," he said. "but you can do better."

Immediately, I went over a mental checklist of possible flaws. Did I look awkward singing? Had I just not sold it?

"I want a six-pack for the next video," he said. "Janet Jackson abs."

8

EYESHADOW ABS

OCTOBER 1999

"Hello, New York!" I yelled to the crowd, one of the biggest I'd ever sung for. I was at Madison Square Garden, opening for Ricky Martin on the North American leg of his world tour. I'd already been learning so much watching Ricky perform and connect with his fans. There were twenty thousand people coming, night after night. His movements were so big, like he wanted the very last row to see him without the JumboTron.

That night I was inspired by Ricky to really go for it, too. I went out there dancing and singing "I Think I'm in Love with You." It was a dance-pop song with the John Mellencamp riff from "Jack and Diane," but there were still big notes for me to hit. So, center stage at MSG, I went to nail a high note, crouching down in a squat so I could really deliver.

My pants split. Right in front of all those people. When

I stood and walked, they started falling off me. I froze as the musicians tried to keep the song going, and then I just slowly walked backwards until I was backstage.

I started crying, and my mom ran over to me, frantic.

"What am I gonna do?" I said. My mom stood there a second, nodded her head, and kicked off her shoes. She stepped back and pulled off her jeans right there.

"You're putting these on and getting back out there is what you're gonna do," she said.

I put them on, and she leaned back to get a good look. "Take my shoes," she said. "You need a higher heel with that jean."

The absurdity of it came over me, and I laughed as I marched out, literally in mom jeans. I smiled a real, genuine smile as the crowd welcomed me, the girl who split her pants and got back up.

"Alright," I said into the mic. "I don't know who saw my booty, but I'm still gonna sing it off. So, here's my next song."

I got one of the biggest cheers of the tour. When people saw the real me, they wanted me to succeed. It was a fleeting thought, and I wish I had caught it and internalized it. I still thought people expected perfection.

I certainly wasn't hearing otherwise from my label. After all, Tommy wanted those Janet Jackson abs. Columbia got me a trainer, one who made me run on the treadmill and sing my scales or my songs. It was helpful, because I learned how to maintain my breath throughout an entire song while doing heavy-duty choreography.

I just wasn't getting that cut stomach. But I will tell you a secret: I faked them. Right before a concert, I would draw a six-pack on myself with my eyeshadow pencil. I thought, *I'm on stage, it's dark. People will be like, "Oh, wow, she's ripped."* Then I saw any picture taken with a flash and it would be like, "Oh, girl."

I HELD THE ADVANCE CD OF *SWEET KISSES*, **TURNING IT OVER AND OVER** to look at it fresh.

Remember this, I told myself. *Remember this.* I wanted to be still just for a moment and hold on to this feeling of happiness and pride. I had gotten so hung up on superficial stuff, but the music was what mattered to me, and now it was going to be out in the world. Someone who I would never meet in my life could press play, and they would feel what was in my heart. How many times had I set aside my shyness because that need to connect was the only thing bigger than my fear?

Columbia expected it to sell huge because my single had done so well. I did, too. Though it would eventually go double platinum, that first week it sold sixty-five thousand copies, landing with a thud at number sixty-five on the *Billboard* chart. Many critics, mostly men, seemed to review who they thought I was rather than the actual work. I would get used to that, but it was a shock to me then. One called me an aspiring trophy wife, and another wrote that I should leave because my mom was waiting for me in a station wagon. I still don't get that one—a convertible, maybe.

But it was only the numbers that mattered to Columbia and Sony, and I didn't know how I could have done more to sell that album. I was barely able to keep up with myself with all that I was doing.

"Britney sold almost twice as much her first week," I reminded my dad, though I knew he knew the exact number. We were in another hotel room. I was now someone who knew enough about the industry that I could throw around numbers, but not so much that I knew how to get them.

"But you're a better singer, baby," he said.

"Then why won't God let me have that success?" I asked. "I don't understand what He wants from me."

At the mention of God, my dad slipped into preacher mode. "He is allowing you to go through this struggle so that He can build a strong foundation in you," he said quietly. "So that when it comes time for you to have that success, you will appreciate it. And know how much work it takes. 'If you remain in me and my words remain in you—'"

"Ask whatever you wish, and it will be given to you," I said, finishing John 15:7 for him. You can take the girl out of youth group, but you can't take youth group out of the girl.

"That's a beautiful promise, isn't it?" he said.

"Yes," I sighed. The verse did minister to me, though I also knew my dad didn't really think fulfillment resided solely in sticking to scripture. Otherwise we'd still be in Richardson, and I wouldn't have to be working so hard to prove my worth.

I started to hear voices when I was alone at night, waiting for the sleeping pill to kick in. Half asleep, I would examine myself for flaws in the mirror, and a mental chorus would weigh in. They were intrusive and so mean that I was really convinced Satan was behind them.

"You're never going to be good enough, Jessica. Look who your competition is."

"Could your zits be any bigger?"

"What happened to your hair? It used to be so much thicker and longer."

"Do more sit-ups, fat ass."

These thoughts derailed me just as I had to work harder to sell the album. It should have been no different than back when I stood next to the stage at a small Texas rodeo, selling my very first album. Back then, I knew if I just kept at it, people would respond. But now I was running on fumes, then beating myself up for that, too. I was fully aware that I was being unreasonable with myself—I would even beat myself up over beating myself up—but like a lot of times in my life, just because I could name the problem didn't mean I was ready to do anything to fix it. Looking back, I see how my anxiety amplified the very real pressures on me, but I didn't have that perspective then.

So I doubled my efforts with radio, and when my tour with Ricky Martin was done, I went back on tour with Nick and 98 again. By then, the girls knew what was happening with me and Nick. A lot of them were just blatant with their hatred, literally throwing garbage at me and saving their bras for Nick and the guys.

I was working nonstop on the tour and promoting the album, but at a December tour stop in Madison, Wisconsin, my body again humbled me and told me I needed a break. I got a terrible kidney infection, and I spent nine days recovering on the fourth floor of St. Mary's Hospital. Nick's tour with 98 had to continue without me, and only my mom stayed behind to hold my hand. We watched the snow fall and complained about hospital food to fill the days.

I had to cancel so many showcases and fan events, and I'm

sure I cried on the phone to Charlie Walk about how bad I felt about letting everybody down. I don't know if it was him or Tommy, but someone arranged another call to make me feel better.

A few days into my stay, I was alone in my hospital room, watching *Family Feud*. This was comfort viewing from when I was a kid and loved game shows. The phone rang, and I picked it up, assuming it was Nick or my mother, who had gone out to run errands.

"Hi, Jessica," said a chipper voice. I had learned that this kind of voice at the other end was usually an assistant, and no matter how cheery the girls sounded, it didn't necessarily mean the actual news was going to be good. "There's someone who would like to speak with you."

I thought it was Tommy Mottola firing me. "Okay," I said, turning off the TV as I tried to sit up. Then this bright, beautiful voice came on, one I recognized immediately.

"Jessica, it's Céline Dion."

"Oh my gosh," I said. "I love you."

"I hear you are not feeling well," she said in her French-Canadian accent, rushing her words. "I just wanted you to know how much I love 'I Wanna Love You Forever.'"

"That means so much to me—"

Céline started *singing* my song. "I wanna looooove you forrrreeevvvveeer." She just nailed the line—full-throttle out of nowhere—and I was laughing because I was so happy.

"You just made my life," I said, meaning it.

"Jessica, I am so excited for you," she said. "You have so much ahead of you, and I want you to remember one thing I have learned: The best competition is always our own selves."

"Thank you," I said, crying.

We hung up, and soon after, a nurse came in to check my vitals and saw my tears.

"You okay, hon?" she asked.

By then I knew all the nurses on the floor. "Nanette, Céline Dion just called and sang to me."

"*Really,*" Nanette said, casually checking my forehead for a fever that might be causing hallucinations.

The best competition is always our own selves, I thought. Who knows who Celine was told she had to be when she started out, and later, even with all her success, who she was told she had to be to stay at the top? I looked at the window at the snow falling. A red bird had perched itself on the ledge of my hospital window.

"You see that?" I said.

Nanette was on her way out and stopped to look. "Pretty guy," she said.

"Don't you know to fly south for winter?" I said to the bird. "What are you doing in all this cold?"

"Nah, that's a cardinal," she said, leaving. "They're crazy enough to stick it out."

Me too, I thought.

NICK AND I HAD A RULE ABOUT NEVER GOING MORE THAN TWO WEEKS without seeing each other, and generally the way we spent time together was through work. We helped host MTV's New Year's Eve party to welcome 2000 and even did the countdown in Times Square. The ball dropped to a blizzard of confetti and fireworks, and Nick kissed me at midnight. *People* ran a photo, which helped us break out of the teen market a bit. After that, when I went to events with 98 Degrees, photographers would ask the other guys to move to the side so they could just get a shot of Nick and me. We started getting hosting gigs, and Nick was a natural. He could talk to anybody, answering the same interview question for the fifteenth time that day and act like his answer was something that just occurred to him. I've always said that if he wasn't a singer, he should have been a politician because he was so personable. I was always fumbling, saying something I didn't realize was funny until everyone laughed. It was interesting to me that MTV kept inviting me back when they seemed so reluctant to play my actual music videos. I had to beg my fans to call in to *Total Request Live* to get my video played. God bless 'em, because they did.

The label thought that we could bump up my sales by releasing my duet with Nick, "Where You Are," as my second single. I was happy because it meant that we would be together on the promotional tour and it wouldn't be just me on the dog and pony show. Around the release of the single, I did an interview with *Teen People* where they asked me about being a virgin. I said I wanted to wait until I got married. "I don't judge people who do have sex before marriage," I said. "And I'm not trying to make anyone think that I'm such a good girl or such a holy person. I'm a regular girl."

I didn't realize this statement was going to get so much attention, but the magazine got the most letters it had ever received about a story. Young people, an awful lot of "regular girls," talked about the pressure they were under to be sexual before they even really knew what sex was. I also didn't realize I'd just handed every daytime show a news hook for having us on. They asked Nick and me about my virginity at every appearance, and my take was that it wasn't so much about "saving myself" but building up anticipation. I was nineteen and still sheltered, so it was kind of bizarre to me that people felt free to ask, "How have you not had sex yet?" The interviewer would always start with me and then turn to Nick, who was twenty-six and a man. This situation did not compute for them.

"And you're okay with this, Nick?" they'd ask. He always handled it well, since we both knew the question amounted to "You're cool with dating a girl who doesn't put out?"

"I really respect everything that she cares about and everything that's important to her," he said on *The View*. "And she talked about this from the very beginning, and so I knew going in that that was an issue with her and that was cool with me."

It gave America a story line to follow. The sexy virgin and the long-suffering, but still understanding, hot prince. Barbie and Ken didn't have sex either, right? Nick loved the fact that I was so strong in my faith and that I had this wide-eyed innocent approach to life. He didn't share it, though. I would get so frustrated, asking God to take the blindfold from his eyes and help him find a spiritual center. And then I would hear Sarah telling me to relax and to just accept him for who he was.

Our duet, "Where You Are," sold okay numbers and didn't push the album higher on the charts, so Tommy Mottola was determined that I make good on showing my abs in the video for the next single. When discussing the concept for "I Think I'm in Love With You," the label kept using the phrase "MTV friendly"—which meant big smiles and skin. We shot over three days at the Santa Monica Pier, and it was freezing, but you would never know it. I wore a white blouse tied under my bustline, but where the ties of the shirt didn't cover, I made sure to keep "feeling the music" by placing my hands around my stomach. I was just so uncomfortable showing that much of my body and jumping around. *Nothing to see here, folks, buy my album.*

I had been on the covers of a bunch of teen magazines, and then Nick and I started appearing on magazine covers together. When we got the cover of the very first issue of *Teen Vogue*, it was a huge deal for us. Herb Ritts shot the cover on the beach in Malibu, and when I heard about the location, I got scared that this was going to be another "let's show some skin" situation. Herb had shot Janet Jackson's "Love Will Never Do (Without You)" video, which introduced the world to the abs Tommy Mottola thought I should have, too.

I didn't need to worry, because Herb immediately put me at ease. They didn't want me too done up, so there was very little makeup. He was so focused on the light of the sunset on our faces and capturing the real sweetness of two people who were genuinely crazy about each other. I wore J. Crew jeans and a baggy cream sweater from DKNY Jeans; Nick was in a Banana Republic sweater and Dockers khakis. Mall clothes people could see themselves in. I held the sleeves in my fists just like, well, a real girl on a date with her cute boyfriend. I swear, it seemed like he only took ten shots before announcing he had it. He was right. It was one of the first covers that I didn't pick apart for a flaw.

Condé Nast did a huge media push behind *Teen Vogue*, mailing their first ever issue to everyone who was subscribed to regular *Vogue*. This was incredible exposure for us and a chance to establish ourselves outside the teen market. The cover line was "Pop's New Princess" and then "Jessica Simpson" huge in red. And then beneath, smaller and in black, "& Nick Too." I was so proud, but I also recognized that I had entered the relationship as Nick's plus-one. Whenever I felt self-conscious about the increased attention I was getting from the media and how it might affect our relationship, I would tell myself, *He sells more records.* And he did. 98 Degrees had a single come out that June, "Give Me Just One Night (Una Noche)," which reached number two on the *Billboard* Hot 100. You were only as big as your last hit, and he'd just had his biggest one yet.

I didn't want to outshine him, because that just wasn't what I knew. He seemed so much older than me, my guide in everything. I wanted him to feel like he could show me all that he knew—about the business, about the world.

He was there for so many of my firsts, even my first taste of alcohol when we went to Hawaii. At twenty, I had never had a drink before, and I turned to Nick like a father, asking if it was okay. "You're on vacation," he said.

I immediately felt the effect, and Nick thought it was hysterical. I realized I liked the woozy feeling. "If we get in the hot tub," Nick said, "you'll feel it more."

"Oh!" I said. "Then let's go to the hot tub!"

I pinballed down the hallway, talking to everybody we passed. After I told an elderly woman she was beautiful, I whispered to Nick, "Was that weird?"

"No, just keep going," he said.

He was right about the hot tub. We kissed, and I stopped worrying about everything. "Okay, so what kind of drink can we have tomorrow?" I asked.

He brought two wine coolers to my room at the hotel, because of course we had separate rooms. These were the starter drinks the kids in my high school drank at the parties I avoided. I drank two, loving the feeling of calm it gave me, the closeness to Nick it gave me. I felt grown up, closer to his age.

"Ohhh, it's so pretty outside," I said, getting up to go to the balcony. I walked right into the screen door, knocking it off its hinge. It crashed to the ground, and I laughed because Nick laughed. He called down to the front desk to have it fixed, and I stood behind him when they sent someone up to fix it.

"Relax, baby," he said. And I did, feeling like maybe I was growing up after all.

We were all changing in my family, and in a real way we were all growing up together. We were having experiences we would have shunned years before. I am not sure when my parents started to drink alcohol, but they took to it. The lines are so blurred in the music industry—there's a need to be in the mix, and so many meetings and events are at bars and restaurants. They wanted to fit in. There were parts of us that were still *so* country, but we were all trying on these new lives. We didn't go to church, and I noticed my dad dropping f-bombs on the phone as he advocated for me.

As we changed, my parents' marriage had devolved from a friendship to a business arrangement. They fought more than ever, always nitpicking and blaming each other if some plan with my career didn't work out. When Tom Hicks, who gave us the money to move to California, came to get a return on his investment, my dad didn't want to pay him.

"It's pennies to him," he said, over and over. "He's a gazillionaire."

"Dad, you signed a contract," I said. "*We* signed a contract." I had to pay him a huge sum of money, and this was out of my income after taxes. He wasn't the last person I had to pay off because of a promise my dad made on my behalf. But I didn't ask questions. I just missed the days when we only had to save up to tithe.

SONY AND COLUMBIA DECIDED TO MAKE A PUSH FOR ME IN THE YOUTH market, so during graduation season, I did Disney Grad Nites in Orlando with Destiny's Child. Disney World would shut down the park certain nights and only allow high school seniors to attend. We would perform at the end, and I just loved it. It gave me more time to bond with Beyoncé and Kelly Rowland (this was pre-Michelle), and besides having Teresa in common, these were Texas girls who hadn't forgotten where they came from. Beyoncé and I had similar family dynamics, so I think we understood each other well. Her father had left his business—in his case, Xerox, not Jesus—and her mother, Tina, became the group's stylist. Our younger sisters, Ashlee and Solange, were both our backup dancers, and they, too, became friends. We shared failure stories to buck each other up. Hers was *Star Search*, back when the group was known as Girl's Tyme, mine was the *Mickey Mouse Club* disaster.

Destiny's Child were just really nice people, and I was so used to being one of the only girls on a tour with guys that I loved being with them. It was also ironic that here we were, two singers who'd left school to be the family business and never had a graduation day, celebrating all these other kids who did.

On one of the Grad Nites, we were all backstage just before a concert when a security guard came up to me.

"There's a girl who says her friend is a huge fan," he said, "and her dream is to meet you."

"Tell her I will absolutely be hanging around after," I said.

"Cool, cool," he said. He started to turn back and then added, "Just so you know, her friend is blind."

"Go get her now," I said. He nodded, smiling.

He brought back two girls. "This is Lauren," said the friend, who led her to me. Lauren was nineteen, my age, and wearing her school's baggy white Class of 2000 T-shirt.

"Hi, Lauren," I said, and I asked if I could hold her hands. She nodded, saying, "You sound like you."

"Well, I hope so."

"I've listened to your album like a *million* times," she said. "I know all the words." She told me she loved "I Wanna Love You Forever," but her real favorite was "Your Faith in Me."

"I listen to it when I'm down," she said. "You sing from the heart, I can tell."

"Your Faith in Me" is about going through something alone but getting through it knowing that someone who isn't even there believes in you. Her friend started to cry, I guess because she saw how happy Lauren was. It almost made me start, but I fought it because I didn't want Lauren to think I was sad about her situation. She was a beautiful, happy girl, and I was blessed to meet her. She cared about how I made her feel, not what I looked like.

"We all get down sometimes," I said. "Can't appreciate the ups without the downs. Life's like an elevator, I guess."

I had this whole plan to bring her onstage to sing with me on "I Wanna Love You Forever," but security wouldn't allow it. So instead, I promised to dedicate the song to her.

"Now, when you hear me say your name, I want you to yell

so I can see you, okay?" I said. "Don't leave me up there all on my lonesome."

During the concert, she yelled her heart out, and I asked everyone to give her a cheer.

"I don't normally do 'Your Faith in Me,' but I don't want to disappoint you, Lauren." I said. "Thank you for reminding me why I do what I do. You can lose track sometimes. This song is for people like Lauren, and any of you who feel connected to me through my music. If you feel it, I feel it, too, and you all inspire me to keep on keepin' on."

I did a few verses of the song a capella, and I was touched that so many people in the audience knew it well enough to sing along. "Your faith in me, it pulls me through," we sang into the night air. "When there's nothing around to hold on to."

AROUND THAT TIME, I TAPED A DISNEY SPECIAL WITH NICK, AND LOOKING back, I can see the beginning of the "roles" we would later play on our reality show. They filmed us at the beach in L.A., walking with his arm around me. "This is where I like to take Jessica on all our hot dates," he said. "I'm a real big spender. Three dollars to park." A wave came in and almost got our feet, so I screamed. We were just goofy and fun.

They set up a thing where some tween girls were sitting with me out on the beach, having girl talk. I remember this little cutie with a sweet face straight up asked me, "Do you think that less guys come to your concerts and stuff because they know that you have a boyfriend?"

I was a little taken aback by such a marketing-focused question from a kid. *Who taught you to think that way?* I wondered. *Sony?*

"That's a good question," I said, stalling. "I don't think that every guy is coming to my concert because they think they can be my boyfriend. I think that they come because they like to watch the show and they want to have a lot of fun. You know?"

Tommy Mottola disagreed. I had to look like somebody the boys wanted to be with. In a word, hotter. In July, we started work on my next album, and Tommy wanted to go all in on making me a combo of Britney and Mariah. He said he would be even more involved this time and said I needed to be doing more dance pop over the ballads I loved. I also had to get even skinnier. I started the Atkins diet hardcore, envying and resenting anybody who could just eat. Off the diet, I obsessed over how I looked 24/7; on the diet, I was also hyperfocused on food. It made me nervous. My anxiety had something to hold on to, and instead of examining my emotions, I could just block them out by focusing on carb counts and waist sizes. If I focused on controlling my outward appearance, I could avoid thinking about my emotions and fears.

My mother sometimes, with the best of intentions, fed into it. Her aerobics-teacher past would kick in, seeing a problem to fix and giving a solution she thought would help. When she urged me to exercise or told me she was going for a long walk and maybe I should come along, I knew what she meant. We ended up doing the Atkins diet together.

I was still out there promoting the first album, and in so many interviews I ended up talking about food and my diet. I had no filter and would say whatever was on my mind or slipped out of my mouth, whether it was about my strict diet or how irritating it was to be constantly compared to Britney and Christina. The marketing department thought it was too much of a peek behind the curtain on what it was really like to be a pop star. The label finally decided I needed media training after I did an interview with the *CBS Early Show* at the Arthur Ashe Kids' Day, a concert that kicks off the U.S. Open every year in August. I have to admit that I did not know who Arthur Ashe was. *Now* I know he was one of the greatest tennis players in the world and the first African American man to win Wimbledon. When he came out as HIV positive in 1992, he created an impact that lasted long beyond his death a year later. But back then, I just showed up and sang where people told me to. 98 Degrees was going to perform, so I was excited to sing with Nick again. I barely knew who any of the tennis players were, even Pete Sampras and Andre Agassi.

During the interview before the concert, the tennis players and us singers stood off-stage, and we were each asked what it meant to be there to celebrate Arthur Ashe's impact. "I'm just so proud to be here and to give back," I said, and then turned to Andre Agassi. "This is such a great event you put on."

Andre's eyes widened in a look of "I don't know what you're talking about." Everyone, including the news crew, realized I thought Andre was Arthur Ashe. The *late* Arthur Ashe.

That was the last straw for Columbia, and they made me do media training. It was awful. Imagine *My Fair Lady*, where they fire questions at you, completely random ones. I had to learn how to manipulate the conversation back to music, the reason you're doing forty-five interviews a day in the first place. It felt false to me, but I couldn't deny that I would lose the thread on every interview and spill my guts. An innocent question from a teen mag about Christmas plans would lead to me talking about my family missing Sarah and how we were all still grieving so the holidays were hard on us. Merry Christmas, kids! Or a journalist would point out that Britney and Christina seemed to be struggling with fame, and I would just take that bait and say that I thought Britney was the nicest girl but maybe Christina didn't need to have her security clear an entire hallway of staff and talent just so she could walk through it alone. I was too honest to play the game.

As you know, media training never really worked on me. Thank God. Part of it was that I was just so sheltered. I was trying everything to get on MTV, a channel that was forbidden to me as a kid. Then, as I grew up, I kept my head down working, so I didn't understand the most basic things about pop culture.

I grew closer to CaCee Cobb, the woman in Teresa's office who'd always hounded me about the homework for my GED. Our relationship was mostly on the phone. She also had to keep calling to track us down because we'd once again moved into another staged home or because Teresa needed to send potential tracks to wherever we'd landed. I was one to procrastinate, and CaCee's "you have to" was nonnegotiable. Still, when she called, I would always find reasons to have small talk with her, stalling whatever task she was going to give me.

"What did you do this weekend?" I asked her.

"I had some friends over to watch *Sex and the City*," CaCee said.

"What's that?"

"*Sex and the City*?"

"Is that like a dirty movie?" I asked.

"Jessica, it's a huge show," she said. "You never heard of it?"

"No."

"Okay, we need to fix that," she said. She said it was crazy that I was supposed to be making music and trying to be a star and I didn't even know about the show that was landing with the very same people I was trying to reach.

CaCee sent me tapes so I could catch up, and I devoured every episode.

"Oh my God, I love it," I told CaCee. "I'm totally a Carrie."

She laughed. "Okay, Charlotte."

9

WARNING: CONTENTS UNDER PRESSURE

Nick and I danced to one more song before we finally sat down. I took off my shoes, placing my legs up on his. We were at his little brother Drew's wedding reception, and it had been the most beautiful day. Drew and Lea were childhood sweethearts, friends since the fifth grade who were truly good people who belonged together. We had spent the whole week celebrating them in Cincinnati, Nick's adopted hometown, and every single person at the wedding knew we were witnessing something that was meant to be. Being included in such an important day, I officially felt part of his family.

Nick ran his hand on my leg, humming along to "Ribbon

in the Sky" by Stevie Wonder. I knew what he was thinking, because the conversation had been happening more and more. He was a month shy of twenty-seven, ready to settle down and get married—and he was stuck with this twenty-year-old. My father forbade me to even think about getting engaged until I was twenty-one.

"I'm not telling you not to marry him," my dad would say. "I'm telling you to wait. You're just too young. You have no idea who you will become in the next few years." I never knew if my dad meant that I would change emotionally, or if I would be too big a star to be tied down. Nick was the one thing my dad and I fought over. He never said no to the label, as much as he groused about how they were marketing me. But my relationship with Nick, that he could control.

I knew Nick was at a crossroads, and I was terrified of losing him. His 98 album *Revelation* had come out the month before and sold 275,000 the first week. That put them at number two on the charts, which would have been a huge week for me, but he moped about it. His competition was not me, he would remind me, but people like 'N Sync, who had set a record as the first to sell over two *million* the first week.

The week in Cincinnati was one of the longest stretches of time we'd spent together, but Nick was getting ready to leave me to tour Asia. "Are you gonna call me every night?"

"I promise," he said.

"I love you," I said in my sad puppy voice, almost as an apology.

He looked past me and sighed, tipping back another beer. "I love you, too, Jessica."

"That'll be us someday," I said, following his eye to his brother and his new sister-in-law dancing.

He got up to go to bar. "Yeah," he said.

I watched him walk away and it felt like I was running out the clock on a promise. But I knew myself well enough that if I committed to marriage this early, there was no way I could keep a singular focus on using my voice to lift others. The very thing I felt called to do. It seemed like an impossible situation: If I didn't marry him soon, I'd lose him. If I married him, I could lose me.

Not that I knew who that "me" was anymore. I was working hard on my album, which felt less and less like something that was mine as we headed to the summer 2001 release. I did most of the recording at the Sony Music studios in New York's Hell's Kitchen, close enough for Tommy to drop by whenever he wanted to check in, which was often. I'd wanted to do so much with this album, but Tommy was picking the most random songs, trying to turn me into a sexpot virgin. I had been able to pull off sexy virgin, but acting like a woman who loved sex but had never actually done it was a math problem I could not quite figure out. I didn't think it would make sense to my fans either. Teresa was completely pushed out, slowly having less and less say on what worked for me and my album. I missed her guidance. She was the only person in my life with the experience and strength to say no to the label.

In March, Don Ienner, the head of Columbia under Tommy and Sony, wanted to have a meeting with me to discuss the future. Don had a reputation for screaming, which he defended as being "passionate," so I was scared. I sat down with him and he looked at me for an uncomfortable beat.

"Who are you?" he asked.

"Excuse me?"

"What makes Jessica Simpson, Jessica Simpson?" he said. "As an artist? As a person?"

I stammered, my old stutter returning, but I had no words to sing. I didn't know. I was mortified. I had been trying to be whichever artist everybody asked me to be like that day. Britney, Mariah, Céline. But what about Jessica?

"This album is very important for you," Don said. "These days, if an artist doesn't have a hit single out of the box, the album tanks. When the album sales slip, there goes ticket sales. Less tickets sold means less people coming to your concerts, which means less people buying T-shirts. Add all those losses up, and it's a lot. The stakes are high."

I nodded. Without confidence in myself, people couldn't believe in me as an artist. And I had none. Everyone had been telling me who to be—"edgier," and "more mature"—whatever the word was that day, it always seemed to mean "skinnier."

By the time we got to the April release of the first single, "Irresistible," I had managed to get myself down to 103 pounds. Everyone went on about how great I looked, but I couldn't enjoy it because I was so freaking hungry. I envied people who could eat whatever they wanted, while I had to microwave slices of turkey with Velveeta cheese on top and call it a meal. But when I ate *anything*, I yelled at myself, asking why I was getting in my own way and why I hadn't gone to the gym.

I taped the video for the first single, "Irresistible," over three days in L.A. starting April 7. Each day I had a different outfit for the video, leaving more and more skin showing. In between the shots, I had a giant, baggy white bathrobe that I wrapped around me. The last day of shooting, we did a rooftop scene on a helipad at night, and I kept saying I was freezing just so I could keep a blanket over me to cover my body. When you're doing a shoot, there's always a hope that you can save it on the last day. I hadn't been happy with any of it, and I blamed myself for never quite getting the shot that I envisioned. Midway through the rooftop shoot, I almost walked off the set because I messed up a dance move. My mind was destroyed from exhaustion, and those voices started in my head again, telling me I was wasting everyone's time.

The video's choreographer, my backup dancer Dan Karaty, called for a break and took me aside. "Stop," he said. "Look at me. You are incredibly sexy. You have to see that yourself to make other people see it. Just feel the way you look, and it will come through."

I stared into Dan's calming eyes and relaxed. He had been on tour with Britney Spears and was a master at giving artists confidence. "I wish I could see what you see," I said.

"It's crazy you can't," he said. For the briefest moment, I felt something. A small flicker of what I felt with Nick, but it was there. It was the first time I ever thought there could be a man in my life besides Nick.

We were already starting to have problems. Nick and I each got condo apartments in the same building in Los Angeles. It was our way of "living together," but we were never there anyway. We were both always on the road performing or doing press tours, so our relationship took place mostly on the phone. We would both be exhausted, and I was—surprise!—terrible at the math of figuring out time zones. It was another thing that seemed to set him off. My childishness, which seemed so cute and sweet when I was first with him, seemed to annoy him. Now everything I said seemed to annoy him. We were both concerned about our careers, and our anxieties just seemed to feed off each other. So I stopped calling him as often, even though hearing his voice had become something I came to count on to help me feel safe enough to fall asleep.

I prayed on it constantly, and I decided that he was a good man who deserved a wife. I was two months from turning twenty-one, and I still felt like a child, going from doing everything to please my dad to then doing whatever it was I thought would make Nick happy. I was too dependent on him, and I would never become the independent woman he needed if I kept turning to him for everything. Nick needed a grown-up woman, one who would be willing to start a family soon. That flicker of a feeling with Dan made me wonder if I should take the time to date other guys before committing to forever. Also, I wanted to see who I was, without using another person's love for me as a measurement of my value. If I put all my attention on a guy, that meant less focus on my career.

"When someone special comes into your life at eighteen years old, your whole world changes," I wrote in my journal. "For a while, I was so caught up in the puppy love, I could only see perfection. I wanted to take the easy way out and just get married. Thank you, God, for providing me a way to step back and reevaluate my needs. These past couple of weeks, I have found myself. I can do it. People don't have to do it for me."

I told him we needed to take a break from each other, just to see what would happen if we both focused solely on work. It wasn't much of a break because we still talked constantly, which I know frustrated him, and even when interviewers brought

Nick up on the press tour for my album *Irresistible*, I said I was single but still hopelessly in love with him.

I kept telling myself that now I could focus on my career. That seemed like a very grown-up thing to say, and there was a lot to do. On June 4, Columbia threw me a huge record release party at the Water Club in New York City. I arrived on a yacht, and there was a red carpet just for me. Don Ienner and Tommy Mottola were there, flanking me as they gave me a triple-platinum record for *Sweet Kisses*. There were fifteen minutes of fireworks, and I finally felt like a real star. Ten days later, my *Irresistible* album came out and would sell 120,000 copies the first week, nearly double what *Sweet Kisses* did when it debuted.

Nick sent me flowers. "I'm very proud of you and with what you're doing in your life," the card read. "I'm happy I can be a part of it. I love you." I called him that week and started the conversation already angry at him for his absence when I was the one who pushed him away. Nick had this calm, paternal way of talking to me when he had to catch up on a conversation that in my mind was already in progress. He gently reminded me that I had broken up with him. "Our situation is yours to deal with," he said. "I'm just playing off whatever you give me."

"Well, what do you want from me?" I fired back.

That made him angry. "There is one thing in life I want to be, Jessica," he told me. "A good man. A good father. I can't help it that I fell in love with someone seven years younger than me. I just can't."

"I just want to make you happy."

"Being with *you* makes me happy," he said. "I loved us. I don't have that right now, and it's something I'm trying to deal with."

I was certain that one way he was dealing with it was seeing a lot of women, an accusation he said he refused to dignify with a response. I started hanging out with Dan, but that quickly fizzled even though he helped my dancing and on-stage confidence tremendously. I think my dad even preferred me dating Nick to Dan. I would tell myself I had no right to be jealous if Nick had a life of his own, and for the rest of that summer—as I toured with Destiny's Child on the *TRL* tour, and then began my own Dreamchaser solo tour—we would go through times of calling and not calling each other. I would congratulate myself when I didn't call him, and then he would call from some stop in Asia, and the cycle would begin again.

I knew Nick was excited about the Michael Jackson tribute concert he was doing at Madison Square Garden on September 10. It was the last night of a three-day tribute to Michael's thirty years in show business. Nick performed "Man in the Mirror" with 98, Usher, and Luther Vandross, and I knew how much that meant to him. I thought he would call me after, and I told myself not to be jealous that he was invited to do this major event while I sat alone at home nearly three thousand miles away in Los Angeles.

I fell asleep waiting for the call, and when the phone did ring, it was early in the morning. It was Nick, and there was a fear and a rush in his voice I'd never heard. He told me to turn on the news. Planes had hit the World Trade Center, and the towers had already collapsed. I just couldn't make any sense of the violence. I couldn't imagine how many people were killed.

"I only want to be with you," he said.

"Come home to me," I said. I couldn't imagine what it would be like to lose him. I knew in that instant I wanted to marry him.

All planes were grounded, so the band was trying to hire a van to get them out of the city. Again and again, I told Nick I loved him, and when I hung up the phone, I got down on my knees next to my bed. It felt indecent that God had put this love in my life, and I had the audacity to take it for granted when so many people had just lost those they loved the most.

WHEN NICK AND I GOT BACK TOGETHER, IT WAS SIMPLY UNDERSTOOD that we would marry. We kept it our secret, because my father was already angry that Nick was back in my life. In October, Dad's mother, my Nanny, got very sick. She had been fighting breast cancer, and now it had gone into her lymph nodes. She had been a nurse, and she knew her hour was near. She wanted to go on her terms, and a wonderful hospice team came to her home.

Nick came with me to see her one last time, and he was my rock. My father couldn't bear to go into her room, but Nick came in with me. She was beautiful, so sick but still radiating the grace she brought to the demands of being a pastor's wife. I realized that everything that was good in my life, I had because of her. Nanny had paid to press my first album. She was the reason I had a career at all and the reason I met Nick.

I smoothed her hair back as I told her I was there. She squeezed my hand.

"Nick is here, too, Nanny," I whispered. "I want you to know we're back together. I'm gonna marry him, Nanny. Just like you wanted." She squeezed my hand again. "We're going to have a beautiful wedding," I said, "and you'll always be with me. You'll be right there."

She had asked to have my version of "His Eye Is on the Sparrow," the last song off my second album, on repeat as she passed. As she took her last breath, surrounded by love and her family, my voice filled the room, saying, "His eye is on the sparrow, and I know He watches me." It's a celebration of faith and gratitude that no matter how insignificant we may feel, God is looking out for us.

At her funeral at First Baptist Church of Leander, Nick was a pallbearer and helped to carry her home. I will always be grateful to him for that. She was reunited in heaven with my late grandfather, to whom she had been married for forty-one years. I wanted that forever love for Nick and me, too.

In the airport, the television screens showed scenes of the war in Afghanistan, which had started a couple of weeks before. There was all this talk about anthrax attacks, airstrikes, and questions about when the U.S. would be deploying more troops. They said "troops," but I knew they were real men and women, many of them probably scared.

I asked God to help me figure out a way to be of use. And then He showed me.

10

FLIGHT SUITS AND WEDDING GOWNS

My husband, Eric, has a joke he likes to say: "Ask Jessica to sing about Jesus or America, and she'll be there. Super Bowl, backyard cookout, whatever you got, she's coming to sing 'God Bless America.'" And he's right. Growing up in Texas, I sang that song over and over. From Memorial Day parades to Veteran's Day pancake breakfasts—I was your girl. When I sang it at the East Room of the White House, I finally found out I had been flubbing the lyrics all those years. I was there to kick off the USO holiday tour for troops fighting in Afghanistan. It was the first time they let celebrities in after 9/11, because, well, they were busy. It was surreal to hear President Bush speak, thanking the chairman of the Joint Chiefs of Staff for his service, the transportation secretary for keeping the airlines safe. And then he added, "I want to thank Rob Schneider and Jessica Simpson as well."

They asked me to sing "God Bless America," and I gave it my all. President Bush was in the front row, right next to Laura, and I watched him quietly sing along, his mouth moving along with mine. Something went wrong after we got to the mountains, though. I said, "to the rivers," just like I always did, and, well, he knew it was "the prairies." I was so embarrassed that I apologized to him and Mrs. Bush after.

"I swear all this time I thought it was rivers!" I said.

"That's okay, Jessica," he said. "God blessed the rivers, too."

Two weeks later, my father and I got on a military cargo transport plane to start the USO tour with six Dallas Cowboy cheerleaders, Schneider, and a country singer named Neal McCoy. Every seat on the plane had a little card that read "C-17 Globemaster III: Airlifter of Choice," which cracked me up. "We know you have a choice when you pick a military airlift," I told my dad. "And we appreciate your business." He was so excited to play war and reminded me again he had been too young to go to Vietnam. He had made all this possible, reaching out to the USO as soon as I expressed an interest in helping support service members in any way I could.

Soon we were at Camp Eagle, a U.S. military base near Tuzla in Bosnia. The Tuzla airstrip was in constant use, sending planes to bomb the Taliban. As I talked to the service members there, I learned that before Camp Eagle had mostly been a peacekeeping mission to keep the Bosnian War from being reignited. They talked about having to be careful of landmines left behind.

"I'm staying put with you guys then," I said. I was mortified that before I came there, I had never even heard of Bosnia, and certainly didn't know that American troops were there. When I'd reached out to the USO to volunteer to perform for service members, I'd had a vision of these sorts of big brothers and sisters in the military coming in to save the day. I was gonna put on this big show for them, high-octane with lots of red, white, and blue peekaboo clothes that I felt I had to wear for them. I even had a bikini top made from parachute material to go with army pants. But when I met actual service members, I wasn't prepared for them to be so young. They were all my age or even younger.

I did "God Bless America" as my last song at each stop, a capella, and Bosnia is where things changed. It was right at that first "stand beside her and guide her." These men and women started to sing along with me, and I noticed they were just bawling their eyes out, so of course I did, too, and I knew that this was more than a song. It was a prayer. They just wanted to be with the people they loved, in the prairies, the mountains, and, yes, the rivers. I was so privileged to share in that moment. I have done a lot of singing at bases and aircraft carriers since, and every time I do "God Bless America," I ask everyone to sing along. "I don't care if you think you can't sing," I say. "I want to hear you."

After the Thanksgiving USO tour, I went to Afghanistan for a weeklong Christmas tour on the frontline. Between the two tours, I still had to do two radio-show concerts—the Jingle Jam in Kansas and the Jingle Ball in San Jose—and they felt surreal. The people attending those shows were the same age as the service members I'd entertained.

It might sound silly, but I was afraid I was going to die in

Afghanistan, because the military made it clear to me that they could not guarantee my safety. I think I hugged Nick a thousand times before I left Andrews Air Force Base, and he kept telling me I was going to be perfectly fine because I was going to have the world's strongest military to keep me safe. I told him the hiding spot where I had placed a pile of my journals in case something happens to me.

"Don't read 'em unless I'm dead, okay?" I said.

He looked at me like I was crazy, but he hugged me harder.

On that tour, we had to land on the USS *Theodore Roosevelt*, a nuclear-powered aircraft carrier. Now, I am not one of those cool girls who goes on a roller coaster and throws up her hands. I scrunch my eyes tight, white-knuckling whatever—or whoever—I can hold on to. You think an aircraft carrier just parks, but they are always moving, so the pilot must land the plane on the deck just right and then has a matter of seconds to bring the plane to a stop. There are wires that catch you, and you feel like you're going to get whiplash. But it's worth the tough landing because aircraft carriers always have the best audiences. The *Roosevelt* had been deployed in the North Arabian Sea since early October and had a crew of about 5,500 people. It felt like every one of them was at the concert. By then I understood it wasn't about a pretty girl in a bikini. I could just be me with them. Put on a Santa suit to get laughs and sang Christmas songs. I tried to meet as many troops as possible, and a lot of men and women would give me challenge coins or take patches off for me to keep. I still have them all.

When I got home, I could tell Nick was proud of me.

"Promise you'll do one with me, babe," I said. He swore he would, and he kept his word.

AT THE START OF 2002, I KNEW NICK WAS GOING TO PROPOSE. SO DID MY dad. He talked to each of us separately, constantly urging us to wait. He was convinced that Nick didn't understand commitment, which I didn't think was fair. "Marriage is about hanging in there," he said.

I know he accused Nick of making me dependent on him for everything, which is the pot calling up the kettle to have a long talk about being black. My mom loved Nick, but right or wrong, my parents had spent my life making me think that I couldn't do anything without them. At twenty-one years old, I was still very much a child. I didn't know how to write a check, but, somehow, I was paying for everything. I knew that I was making money, but I didn't think of myself as the family breadwinner. I just thought my money was their money. Honestly, what I knew for sure was that it stopped my family from having as many fights, so I felt lucky that I could be the one to help keep the peace.

I was already on to my next album, determined to make it mine this time. I constantly tried to write my own songs, with recurring themes of freedom and taking flight. I didn't want to have to work to find myself in the songs, I just wanted them to come direct from my heart. When I worried what Tommy would think, I would murmur Colossians 3:23 to remind myself why I wanted to make music in the first place. "Whatever you do, work at with all your heart, as for the Lord and not for men." I had been called to do this.

That year, the NFL invited me to perform at the halftime show at the February 9 Pro Bowl game in Honolulu. The Pro Bowl brings the best of the best in football together, and Nick tagged along because it was a dream for him to be on the sidelines seeing all the all-stars up close. He was acting weird during the game, and I thought he was just star-struck by athletes.

The next day he told me he'd chartered a sailboat for a six o'clock sunset cruise on the Pacific. That whole day he drove me crazy, asking me the same questions over again because he was distracted, shaking even. When we were finally on the water, I leaned back in his arms, mainly to stay warm. I was chilly, even in my gray Arthur Ashe Kids' Day hoodie sweatshirt and the USS *Detroit* ball cap a sailor had given me. The captain gave me a blanket to cover me, but Nick was shivering, too.

"Do you need more of this blanket?" I asked.

He didn't answer.

"Nick."

"What?"

"What is *wrong* with you?"

"Nothing's wrong," he said, sounding hurt. "I'm just happy to be with you is all."

"Great," I yelled. The boat was rocking so much, and when water splashed in, I couldn't help but scream for fear of getting wet and even colder. Nick kept turning back to look west, checking the sun as it dipped to the horizon. And then something clicked in him.

"Jessica," he said, "you mean so much to me." I wish I could remember exactly what he said because I know it was beautiful. I was too busy trying to figure out why he was being so sappy.

Finally, he pulled out a little box, opening it to a reveal a ring with a pear-shaped diamond. "Will you marry me?" he asked.

"Yes!" I yelled. On some instinct, we asked the captain to take our camera to capture the moment on video. "I'm engaged!" I said. "Right here in Hawaii."

"*Nick*," I said. "If I'd known you were gonna propose, I'd have dressed up."

"You're perfect," he said.

I believed him. We kissed, and I leaned further back into him as the boat continued to sail through the rough waters. But I was happy.

WE DECIDED ON AN OCTOBER WEDDING, THROWING OURSELVES INTO wedding planning. I was that girl, and Nick wanted to come to every meeting with our planner, Mindy Weiss, to keep the budget in check. I didn't think about cost, and I just wanted the whole thing to be epic.

This obviously scared Nick, who was coming into the marriage with much more money than me. As we got closer to the wedding, he casually mentioned that maybe we should talk about getting a prenup. Part of the tabloid mythology of our marriage is that my dad played hardball and refused. No, this was an intimate discussion between a man and his soon-to-be wife. Which is to say that I exploded.

"What are you talking about?" I said. "For when you want to get a divorce?"

"No, of course not," he said.

"You're already thinking about how you're going to leave me?"

"My advisers say it's for the best."

"Well, then marry *them*," I said, and stormed off.

He dropped it. To his credit, he respected my feelings and probably got a lot of flak about it from his "advisers." They had no inkling that I was going to leave our marriage with much more earnings than him, and, more important, we knew our marriage would never end. We were in this for forever, and a deal's a deal.

My father was awful through the whole engagement. There's just no nice way to put it. He continually told me I was making a mistake and told Nick to his face that I was too young to get married. It was another thing for my parents to fight over, since my mom always took Nick's side when he would criticize me over some new thing. What you have to understand about my mom is that she is a tough crowd. My dad is a people pleaser, but people have to work to impress her. To this day, I think a lot of what I do is to win her approval. Her backing up whatever cutting thing Nick said to me gave it more weight and gave him license to do it more.

But trust me, I was no angel. I had upped my dosage of diet pills and was eating even less to be super-thin for the wedding. Speedy and hungry, I was easy to set off. Nick and I developed a reliable cycle: he would criticize me for something small, and I would blow it up to make it about something larger in our relationship or the pressure I was under in my career. He would feel attacked and raise his voice, then I would say, "Screw you," and pout like a child. Nick would then resolve the issue by being the grown-up in the room. Rinse, repeat. I know now that I have an addictive personality, so I am especially prone to falling into patterns. Thank you, therapy.

But gosh I loved him. I could not wait to marry him. I'd

always dreamed of getting married in a little white chapel in Texas, and I found it in the hill country on the west side of Austin. It was gorgeously simple, with white limestone walls and dark oak beams inside. When I walked in and I felt His grace, I knew this was where my wedding was supposed to happen.

We kept it small, inviting three hundred people to an afternoon ceremony on October 26. The week before, it rained like Noah was gonna show up, and each day I checked the forecast to see if we would get a reprieve so I could still have my reception outside. It didn't look like it was going to happen.

My father was a raincloud all on his own. At the rehearsal dinner the night before, my father acted as if the next day was his execution. It was so out of character for him, because my dad was all about appearances and acting like everything was, in his favorite phrase, "hunky dory." Through the dinner and all the toasts, he moped and kept shaking his head, right in front of Nick's family. My mother confronted him about being so horrible, so then they got into it in front of everyone. *Welcome to the Simpson Family Traveling Show, Lachey folk.*

I didn't want to see Nick the morning of the wedding, so I gave him his present that night. I'd torn a November 1997 page from my journal and had it framed for him with a picture of us. At seventeen, I wrote a letter "To My Future Husband," telling him that I was waiting for him. "I wish upon the heavens and all the stars for a light to guide me to where you are." Nick got choked up—he was sentimental, and I loved that about him. He didn't share my faith, but he understood that I really did dream of him.

"That's when our first album came out," he said.

"I'd probably seen a picture of you," I said, "and didn't even know you were my husband."

His gift to me was a music box of white and gold. When I opened the box, it played Shania Twain's "You're Still the One." I played it alone back in my room at the Barton Creek Resort & Club, where we would have the reception the next day. I sang the song, again trying on my Nanny's ring, my "something old" for the wedding. I stared in the bathroom mirror, certain I would look different the next night. I thought I was finally going to grow up to become someone's wife, and I needed to say goodbye to the child looking back at me. I went to bed and prayed, thanking Sarah for helping guide me to Nick. I also prayed for another miracle: that it would stop raining.

It didn't. I threw open the curtains as soon as I woke up, and all I could see was rain and gray. Throughout the morning, I think about ten different people burst into the "It's like raaaaaiiiinnn on your wedding day," from Alanis Morissette's "Ironic." But honestly, I stopped caring. I wore my "Soon-to-be Mrs. Lachey" sweatsuit and just let my wedding planner, Mindy Weiss, lead me around to get ready, a director and her leading lady. I was in love with my dress, a strapless ivory lace gown custom made by Vera Wang herself. The gown was encrusted with what seemed like a ton of baby pearls and crystals. We kept having to take it in as I went for my goal weight of, uh, weightless. I had borrowed an eleven-carat diamond headband from Harry Winston and pretty much anything my mother could get from Neil Lane. Hair clips, earrings, a pearl pendant, a bracelet . . . more was more. Throw in a six-foot train and you had yourself a princess bride.

Mom and Dad went with me and Ashlee—my maid of

honor—to the chapel in a 1937 Cadillac limousine we rented for the day. We all waited until the last possible second to get out in the rain, and they ferried me from the limo to the chapel under two umbrellas like I would melt. Inside, someone handed me my bouquet, a ball of five hundred tiny white stephanotis stems tied together that I later found out, when I got the bill, took twelve hours to build. Worth it.

My mother went in first, then Ashlee, and the doors closed, leaving just me and my dad in the vestibule, with an usher and photographer. I put my arm in his, fumbling with the bouquet. He cleared his throat, his usual signal he was about to say something important. I thought he was going to tell me he loved me or do something to make me feel less nervous.

"Are you sure you want to do this?" he asked.

I didn't answer, and he continued. "I'm right here. We can—"

"Dad, please."

"You don't have to."

I fixed a smile, knowing the doors would swing open at any second. "Dad, I'm walking down this aisle and getting married," I said through gritted teeth. "You're giving me away. You have to. I'll always be your little girl, but you have to do this for me."

The doors opened, and I saw Nick waiting for me. He gasped at the sight of me. I waited for my father to take the first step down the aisle, a white carpet lined with white rose petals. Instead, I took a step, dragging my father into movement. He briefly got it together but cried the whole way down the aisle. It was brutal. I took step after step down the rose-petal-strewn aisle, keeping my eyes on Nick.

He was standing on a slightly raised platform next to Brian Buchek, our officiant. Brian was a church friend from Richardson, all the way back to the fifth grade. He knew my dad well and seemed to sense what was happening. He started by keeping the tone light, talking about how I'd talked about this day since we were ten. "Is it everything you ever dreamed of?" he asked.

"Yes, it is," I said, truly meaning it.

I remembered when Brian found Christ when he was sixteen, and now here he was helping me marry Nick. I looked behind me on the bride's side and saw the faces of friends from all my worlds. My cousins, church family like Carol Vanderslice, and my music family like Teresa and CaCee. My dad sniffed and looked down. He had to stand next to me while Nick stood facing us.

Nick and his 98 Degrees groomsmen—his brother, Drew, was his best man—sang their song "My Everything" to me, and Nick could barely get through it. What I would always love about Nick is that he was sentimental, and as much as he tried so hard to appear tough, he couldn't help but show that he felt things deeply. I had both men in my life crying. I widened my eyes under my veil, determined not to cry and muss my makeup.

Then came the moment when Nick had to take my dad's place. It was almost too literal for my dad, who couldn't look at Nick but, as he turned to sit, let everyone see his face of doom. Nick lifted my veil for our vows. I know a lot of couples choose to write their own vows, but Nick and I used the traditional words, for the very reason that for hundreds of years many people had pledged their love using the very same promises.

When Brian pronounced us man and wife, I felt such a shock of happiness go through me that I almost laughed out loud. Nick kissed me, and we left to a gospel choir singing "Joyful, Joyful We Adore Thee." In for a penny, in for a pound, so why not have a twenty-piece choir show up? "Melt the clouds of sin and sadness; drive the dark of doubt away."

I had no doubts. I swear. At the reception, Nick spun me to our song, Van Morrison's "Crazy Love," with my friend from the USO tour, Neal McCoy, singing to us. I was twenty-two, and I had pledged my life and destiny to this man. And I don't regret it. Nick was meant to be my husband. No one else was supposed to have my virginity. I know that because I had talked so openly, with Nick by my side, about waiting to have sex until my wedding night, that people were curious. I get it. I'm the girl who spent three years doing interviews where everyone asked me about having sex, and I literally named the date it would happen. So, once that day came, all those interviewers found a way to ask me what I thought.

I didn't know what to tell them, but back then I felt obligated to give them an answer. I'd built up the anticipation in my mind that the first time I had sex with my husband had to be this transcendent experience where the heavens parted. What I didn't know then is that everyone's first time is awkward, and that is part of it. And that it's okay, but at the time, it's tough to understand. I had joined a long line of virgins in my family who said yes to forever for that one experience.

11

INTO THE FISHBOWL

"So, we thought it would be fun if Nick took you camping," the woman in my living room said. This was a production assistant whose name I can't remember. There were so many people in and out of our house that, in the beginning, we lost track of who was who.

"Nick wants to go camping?" I asked. My husband was not someone who randomly planned adventures. If we weren't working, we were on the couch. Or trying to figure out how exactly we were going to pay the mortgage on our million-dollar house in Calabasas.

"It would be funny," she said. "Fun."

"Where?" I asked. "Like, where do you even go camping in L.A.? Santa Barbara?"

"Yosemite."

I had no idea where Yosemite was, and I swear I had it confused with Jellystone. "Like with Yogi Bear?" I asked. "Are there bears there?"

"Oh, that's good," she said. "You should be worried about that. We can use that."

Welcome to the filming of season one of *Newlyweds: Nick & Jessica* and the first year of my marriage. Places, everyone.

When I packed for the trip, I stuffed as much as I could in my spring 2003 Louis Vuitton Murakami bag. Before I had children or my dogs, that bag was my child. It went everywhere with me.

"Is this okay?" I asked the crew.

They smiled. "You be you, Jessica,"

If I was me being me, I would have said no to going camping. But I guess they had enough footage of us sitting on the couch, so a-camping we will go. The plan was for us to drive up to Yosemite National Park with Nick's brother, Drew, and his wife, Lea, who were good wingmen on the show. They were family, and I could completely be myself around them. Which is to say that Lea and I could sit in the back of the car and commiserate about cramps.

My dad decided Nick and I were a twenty-first-century version of *I Love Lucy*, so early on, the producers were positioning Drew and Lea as our Fred and Ethel. They were there on behalf of the viewers, rolling their eyes at something I said. At least I had the physical comedy of Lucy: I wiped out twice on the hike through Yosemite, though I think that was because I wasn't used to wearing flats. If I were in my four-inch heels, that would never have happened.

We were just a few weeks into filming the show, and in the

beginning, there was this sense that you always had to be doing something so they could capture it. As Nick did stuff like load the car or cook the burgers, I asked aloud, "Am I supposed to be helping?" Not so much to fulfill my role as a new wife but to act out my role as a character.

It was one giant learning curve, figuring out how to be married and how to create content for a kind of show that had never been done before, something they were calling a "reality show." *The Osbournes* had premiered the previous year and had become the highest-rated show on MTV. As much as *The Osbournes* showed the "real" life of a celebrity family, they would have been the first to say it was kind of a circus. My dad pitched *Newlyweds* to MTV right after the wedding. This would be two celebrities, who viewers were used to seeing air-brushed to perfection, eating cereal and passing gas.

Dad's theory was that this would get me and my music on MTV—who never played my videos unless it was on *TRL*—while also undoing the damage of how I'd been marketed by the label. "If girls knew you, they'd like you," he said. "Columbia's been pushing them all away with this sexy-Barbie stuff. This show would be about your heart."

He paused a long time, then added, "And Nick."

He pitched it to us as a documentary, one that would chronicle our marriage and me working on my third album. If MTV was going to pay me to live my life and be on their channel, it didn't occur to me to say no.

Nick was slightly more hesitant, but only slightly. He wanted to start a solo career beyond 98 Degrees and needed to raise his profile. He knew it was tough to be in a boy band as a married man pushing thirty. He also knew that my dad was going to be a producer in the editing room and would have *my* back, so Nick's one request was that he wanted to be protected. His manager also got a producer credit so the show wouldn't be biased against him.

Tommy Mottola hated the idea, according to my dad. "He told me, 'You're going to destroy her career.'" But after the way my second album had been handled—a Frankenstein of whatever genres Sony thought would sell that day—I didn't put much stock in the label's road map to success. There was so little budget for my third album because Tommy, who left Sony in January, blew through a ton of money on my previous one. Now Don Ienner was in charge, and he was not a huge fan. Teresa came back into the picture and told me this was probably the last chance we had with Sony. We made a plan to get back to the natural person that I was, the one that people could relate to. Teresa put me in songwriting camps before writing camps were a thing that even existed in the industry. She and CaCee would get a studio with a bunch of empty office rooms and set them up with tables for writers to meet with me. She paired writers who had never worked together— maybe a country writer and a pop writer—and then put me right in the middle. Some of them thought it was odd to have me there. Teresa recently told me that one guy thought she was crazy. "Does she even write?" he asked her.

"I think she *can* write," she said. "She journals." I wanted to write my own songs, having realized that since the record company folks had no clue how to position me, I should cut out the middlemen and do what felt right to me. I met with Billy Mann, and together we wrote a song called "With You," which came from my heart. I wrote it about Nick and how he loved me and made me feel beautiful as I was, "with nothing but a T-shirt on." On my own, I started writing lyrics in my journal, including a line about Tommy that would be in the song "In This Skin":

> *I know that my talent is real,*
> *So, don't tell me, don't tell me,*
> *I have to be 102.*
> *I don't have nothing to prove.*

I was tired of trying to look perfect—for the church elders and for Columbia—and I brought that to the television show. For five months, they filmed us in our natural habitat of Calabasas, putting a camera in the TV and corners of the house to supplement the crew walking around with cameras. The crew had to get permission from us whenever we were filmed upstairs, the bedroom and bathrooms were off-limits. We could say "stop rolling" at any time, but in the beginning, we tried hard not to. They would get to our house at about eight thirty or nine o'clock and just try to push it so they could stay as late as possible. We would have burn marks on our backs from the mics being strapped to us for so many hours.

I was used to the feeling of being watched—having grown up as the pastor's daughter and then as Tommy's project at the label. But now we wanted to embrace "reality" and ourselves as much as possible, even if they would put us into situations just to get a story for the episode.

We shot that entire first season that spring and summer, and MTV had us set for an August premiere. They kept having to take breaks when I traveled for work, which was a lot.

Throughout that season, I did minimal makeup and let everyone know that, yes, I can burp at the same volume as my singing voice, which is very, very loud. And *you* try not to pass gas like crazy when you're on a strict protein diet. A girlfriend who was filming with me came completely done up in full makeup and was surprised when I farted in front of Nick.

"Have you heard *him*?" I said. "Besides, the only thing worth hiding from your man is receipts."

I was fine being me and finally finding out who exactly that "me" was in a very public way. But I did have one blind spot: I wanted my marriage to look perfect. I didn't mind if I looked dumb, but I wanted people to see the fairy tale in Nick. In us. I had the Instagram-girlfriend syndrome before it was a thing, and I wanted the world to see my husband in the best light because I was hopelessly in love with him.

But this was a reality show. The camera caught me hanging on his every word and him doting on me, but it also caught our struggles. How I would whine and how he would get mad at me over stuff that didn't matter. He didn't want me to have a housekeeper come weekly, he hated that we ate out so much, and he didn't want to hire anybody to do home projects. He was frugal, but it wasn't about money. He always wanted to do everything on his own to prove he could. And he held me to that same standard. Nick wanted me to be a housewife making all the meals, and I admit I went into that marriage hoping to be that way, too. I was the girl who registered for everything at Williams-Sonoma thinking I'd be like my mom. But I wasn't even *home* to unpack my house, let alone cook those meals. For most of my first year of marriage, I was very aware that I was a midlevel celebrity still paying off her wedding and not in a position to say no to any gigs. I would come home, go grocery shopping to try to be the normal wife Nick wanted, and then leave again. When I returned two weeks later, the crew would get us in the kitchen with Nick complaining about the bread that got moldy and the salad that went bad because I'd bought them two weeks before.

But if Nick acknowledged how much I was working, he would see that he wasn't, and he was too much of a hard worker to face that head on. The first real fight the cameras caught was about him decorating the house while I was away. It seemed so dumb, but it was about much larger issues in our marriage. I had been away for something like two months, and I didn't so much resent him decorating without me as I wanted to be able to focus on my career and have a nice home. But I had no time off. To have the home I wanted to give Nick, I needed to bring in professionals to help. Nick didn't want that. I'm sure a lot of women have been caught in that bind of having it all while trying to *be* all to somebody.

Throughout that fight, the closer we got to the real issue, the more frightened I became. I was very aware that the crew was dancing around us, silently getting all the angles. When I get scared, I freeze, so they had to hustle to create a feel of action.

When Nick accused me of being a spoiled brat, I knew how to handle that one. I knew I was spoiled, and I was working on that. But then, when he said, "Go away and leave me alone," I slipped.

"I *am* away," I said. "I'm always away."

He tipped his head back just slightly, and a realization moved across his face like a storm cloud.

"Oh, boo freaking hoo," he spat. "You know what, sob sob sob. Like I'm not doing the same shit you are."

Don't say it, Jessica, I thought. *Too real. Too real.* But it was out of my mouth before I could stop it. I said, "You're not do-ing *half* of what I'm doing, baby."

"Oh, now we're into this now," he said, reaching for his Miller Lite. "You think you're gettin' it all figured out."

"Baby, I'm not trying to act like I have it all figured out," I said, aborting the mission. I was too afraid of wounding his ego, so I said I would hire him to do stuff and pay him with sex. Talking about our sex life was a classic way to get the crew distracted from some issue. That was always something they seemed to react to and would use to lighten up a plot.

I got up and went to the couch to sad-watch TV while Nick finished his beer outside. When he came to pick me up and carry me to bed, I distinctly remember wondering if someone had told him to. If that was true, it was just too sad. Too real.

WHEN THE SHOW PREMIERED ON AUGUST 19, IT WAS LIKE SOMEONE slammed the accelerator on our lives and marriage, pushing it to the highest possible speed. It got huge ratings for MTV, and the stand-out moment that every late-night comic and news magazine talked about was when Nick and I ate our Atkins-approved Chicken of the Sea for dinner, watching a game in the living room.

"Is this chicken what I have, or is this fish?" I asked.

Nick turned his head to stare at me, dumbfounded.

"I know it's tuna, but it says chicken," I said. "By the sea. Is that stupid?"

The resounding answer across America was *yes*. My airhead moments—and there was a genuine doozy in each of the first ten episodes—became known as "pulling a Jessica." The show started titling episodes with my gaffes, "The Platypus" for when I thought it was pronounced "plata-ma-pus," and "Buffalo Wings" after that time I told Nick I didn't eat them because they were made from buffalo meat. Yes, these were all legitimate ditzy moments.

I didn't care if people made fun of me, because we were pulling in nearly three million viewers a week. My album, *In This Skin*, was released the same day as the show's premiere and did okay numbers, but sales rose as the show became more and more of a pop culture phenomenon. Two months later, my second single, "With You," was my first number one on the *Billboard* pop chart. I shot the video at our house, and it highlighted all my gaffes. "With You" became a *TRL* staple for months without me having to beg anybody to call in.

Hand it to my dad, because he was absolutely right. People who had dismissed me as a Britney-bot now heard me in a different way. Being the butt of the joke ironically gave my music credibility. I was the girl who burped, but, hey, did you hear her singing to herself right after? There was no autotune in my kitchen. It turned out I had an amazing voice.

My record sales got a huge bump from *Newlyweds*, so when Nick's *SoulO* album came out in November, everyone expected it to do as well as, if not better than, mine. Instead, it bombed. In his debut week, he sold a tenth of what he got his first week on the last 98 Degrees album. He had two singles—the second of which was even the theme to our show—and neither even charted on the *Billboard* Hot 100.

Still, we were both getting many offers for appearances and endorsements. We could pick up a hundred grand to sing three songs at a Bar Mitzvah or crazy money to surprise employees at a Chicken of the Sea staff meeting in San Diego. We had once been these also-rans in the music industry, rating vague "I think I know you" second glances in public, and now we couldn't walk a foot without five people coming up to us.

The fame was new, but it was also a new kind of fame. Reality television knocked famous people off the pedestal. Girls felt like I had hung out with them in their living rooms, and so when they saw me, they ran up to hug me like we were girlfriends. Couples identified so strongly with us. A man came up to Nick and me early on, pointing to a shy woman at his side who looked nothing like me. "I'm married to a Jessica," he said. "She can say the dumbest things, too."

I looked at her and took her hand. "Like 'I do,' right?" We smiled at each other and laughed. "Yes!" she said. It was little moments like that, where I was in on the joke and invited others in, too, that made me feel powerful.

MTV signed us for a second season to air in January, with filming set to start on our October 26 anniversary. In the weeks before we went back to work, the media coverage escalated. When Justin Timberlake hosted *Saturday Night Live* for the first time in October, he put on a blonde wig and shawl to play me trying to defend my intelligence on *Saturday Night Live*, with Jimmy Fallon doing his best Nick. We watched a tape of it together.

"Hi, I'm Nick Lachey," said Jimmy, "formerly of the band 98 Degrees, and currently of . . . well . . . nothing."

"And I'm his wife, Jessica Simpson," said Justin, "formerly of the band . . . Jessica Simpson." He gave me a strange Long Island accent.

I turned to Nick. "I don't talk like that, do I?" I asked.

"Nah," Nick said.

Maybe if he did my actual voice it would be too close to his then girlfriend Britney. "I know my arms aren't that hairy," I said. "Bet he didn't think he'd be playing *me* someday."

A couple days later, we were set to shoot the cover of *Rolling Stone*. I know Nick saw that as the pinnacle of fame. And then my dad called me.

"They just want *you* on the cover, Jessica," he said. "Without Nick."

"Oh," I said. I hung up, and I remembered a story CaCee had told me when the *Newlyweds* deal was presented to Sony. Tommy might have hated the idea, but the marketing people loved it because they saw what it did for the Osbournes. Nick was at a different label, and one of the Sony guys pointed to the agreement.

"I just want everybody to know there's going to be a winner and a loser in this situation," he said. "And let's just hope our girl is the winner."

The problem was, if Nick lost, so did I.

WHEN WE STARTED FILMING SEASON TWO ON OUR FIRST ANNIVERSARY, we and the whole crew knew the stakes. Whatever we needed to do to keep that ATM spitting out money would be fine with us. The conceit was that my dad had booked me a gig that would put me in Atlantic City on our anniversary, so Nick would surprise me afterward with a weekend trip to New York City. I was supposed to believe that my husband arranged for rose petals to lead me from the hotel door to the bed and then a horse-and-carriage ride to Tavern on the Green. Oh, and he also had the top tier of our wedding cake re-created and sent to the restaurant so we could eat it, a tradition that neither of us had ever heard of.

Nowadays, we all know how much production goes into "reality," but back then, people believed. Of course, Nick had nothing to do with any of that, but I wanted people to believe he was everyone's vision of a leading man. The problem is, Nick could hit his marks, but he couldn't improv any lines. While eating the cake, I asked him what song we were dancing to a year before on our wedding day.

When he hemmed and hawed, I tried to help him. "Baby, you don't remember our first dance?"

He didn't. I put my head in my hands, not because I was mad at him, but because I was frustrated that he couldn't even act the part MTV handed to him.

"It was 'Crazy Love,'" I said quietly.

We had become actors in our own lives, playing ourselves. Worse, we slowly started acting out our parts even when cameras weren't rolling. When we did appearances, we didn't want to disappoint people by not doing the whole act. It didn't feel wrong, because it was just exaggerated, idealized versions of ourselves. Heck, I wanted to be that happy. Performing as Nick and Jessica became constant, because we had eighteen or so gigs booked for December alone. We didn't even bother to get a tree, even though MTV probably would have decorated one for us. We went to Ohio first to see Nick's family, then my Nana and Papaw's house in Waco. Of course, we took the *Newlyweds* crew along to film every minute.

I couldn't hide my sadness in Waco. Partly because the holidays always made me miss Sarah, especially when I was with her brother and parents. But I was also starting to feel detached from my real life, and seeing my extended family perform for the cameras made me realize how much *I* was playing a part. Nowadays, I see so many people performing their identities on social media, but I feel like I was a guinea pig for that. How was I supposed to live a real, healthy life filtered through the lens of a reality show? If my personal life was my work, and my work required me to play a certain role, who even was I anymore? I had no idea who I really was.

But fame and money are great distractions. When we hosted *SNL* together in January, timed to the premiere of the second season, my dad told us to think of it as an audition reel for other shows and film studios. We both wanted to do real acting and needed an exit strategy from reality TV, which we knew was about to lose the novelty. My dad came to me with more and more endorsement offers that requested me solo. Unless you're an athlete, it's a girl's world when it comes to selling products. When MTV produced the Super Bowl halftime show in Houston, they invited me to kick off the show. Without Nick. Just as he was trying to build a solo career, his success became tethered to me.

He was proud of my success, but Nick also wanted somebody who could make him feel like I did when I was nineteen years old, fawning all over him. I don't think he understood how to have the kind of relationship where I didn't need him to tell me what to do. It was not a happy time for us, and people were no longer satisfied with just seeing us on *Newlyweds*. The tabloid industry realized we sold covers, and paparazzi began to swarm both of us, but especially me. This was before everyone had a phone in their pocket, so the paparazzi industry was incredibly lucrative. You just needed a camera and a willingness to run red lights to chase someone down.

As the frenzy built, the camera crew tried to shoot us as they always had. But soon, that became impossible. If they arranged for us to sit outside somewhere, people would pull up chairs like they were watching the show. It became impossible to hide. The simplest errand would lead to eight to ten cars following me and getting in front of me to block me to get a shot of me with my new Fendi bag.

Still, the fame seemed manageable. And then it wasn't.

"YOU KNOW, THE ENERGY YOU PUT INTO HUFFIN' AND PUFFIN' AND TRYIN' to get out of things, you coulda done them four times by now."

I can't tell you how many times I heard CaCee Cobb say that. I built my reputation in the industry for showing up on time on the back of CaCee dragging me places. In early 2004, Sony allowed her to keep her A&R job while she became my full-time assistant while Columbia relaunched a deluxe edition of my *In This Skin* album to capitalize on my new fame. By then, Teresa's artistic leanings weren't valued at Columbia, and she was now over at Jive Records. To help promote the rerelease, I was set to do signings in four cities around the country. Thanks to file sharing, the bottom had dropped out of the music industry, so the budget was miniscule. Like someone went through the couches at Sony to collect change for me.

On March 3, Sony flew us to Boston on a red-eye in coach because they were too cheap to pay for a hotel. We even did our own hair and makeup in the airport bathroom at Logan until a group of girls realized who I was and started to gather.

"I'm a celebrity," I informed CaCee for the millionth time. I was joking, but she was there to check me as usual.

"Okay, crazy," she said, "Let's just get to the venue."

The "venue" was a Walmart. Our driver was a very brusque, older Boston guy who had no idea who I was and didn't care either. I whispered to CaCee in the backseat. "Doesn't he think it's kind of weird that he picked us up at the airport and we need to go right to Walmart?"

"Maybe he thinks we're from corporate," she said. "Career girls."

"We're here to discuss the numbers—"

A car behind us honked, and I realized we were crawling on the interstate. "I've never seen traffic like this," our driver said.

There were stretches where cars just weren't moving at all, and CaCee began to get anxious. "I'm calling them," said CaCee. "We are going to be *so* late." But there was no answer at the Walmart. She left a message, and I yelled so they could hear, "Don't blame me, I'm tryin'!"

Traffic creeped and creeped until we finally got to our exit. CaCee seriously wondered if we should just get out and walk. When we got to the parking lot, we saw thousands of people waiting outside. "Oh, Lord," I said. "What is going on?"

And then they saw us. We were just in a regular old car

with clear windows. News reports said I was in a limo, but trust me, Sony didn't spring for a limo. People rushed the car, literally climbing on top of each other to see in as our poor driver freaked out. CaCee and I screamed and dropped down to the floorboards, half in terror but also with a huge sense of amazement because it finally dawned on us that this wasn't a zombie apocalypse we had stumbled into. It was for me.

"You're like a *Beatle*," said CaCee, and then caught herself. "I mean, your version."

The Walmart had expected five hundred people. Five thousand showed up. Walmart called the police and cancelled the event because there was too much of a chance for danger. Jessica Simpson: Menace to Society. Afterward, we called basically everybody we knew to tell them. The funny thing was that nobody believed us.

"Well, y'all didn't get out and do it?" said my dad, thinking of the five thousand sales left on the table. "What the hell?"

"Dad, they would have had to call the National Guard."

Three people were arrested that day for disorderly conduct, and another was charged with assault and battery. For the signing in Philadelphia the next day, they had a SWAT team on standby. Walmart went ahead and just canceled the Dallas signing out of fear that the hometown girl would draw an even bigger turnout than Boston. I did one more signing at a Tower Records in Los Angeles, wearing jeans in case I had to run. CaCee wanted me to wear sneakers, but I refused. The compromise was Louis Vuitton sandals with a lower heel. There was such a huge crowd that in order to accommodate everyone, I had to start signing just my initials.

"I love you," strangers kept telling me.

"Aw, I love you, too," I'd answer, meaning it. In one week, *In This Skin* jumped from number sixteen on the *Billboard* chart to number two. (Darn you, Norah Jones!) That morning, Dad read an industry article to me about the success of the album, making sure to emphasize the part where they credited the well-oiled campaign to roll it out.

"The sales went up two hundred percent," he said.

"Do percents go that high?" I asked.

"They do now," he said. I felt like I had won the lottery, because as much work as I put into things, I usually didn't get that kind of return on the investment. There was always still more I needed to do, things I needed to change. "Okay, now, *next* time . . ." But this time, I let myself enjoy the moment.

Life was always ready to keep me humble, though. On March 14, I performed for President George Bush at Ford's Theatre, and afterward my dad I went to the White House for a reception. The room was just stunning, and I kept looking around because I had no idea who anybody was. Someone brought a blondish-gray-haired woman up to me.

"Hi, I'm Gale Norton," she said. "Welcome to the White House."

"I'm Jessica," I said, shaking her hand. I made a stab at small talk. "And what do you do?"

"I'm the secretary of the interior," she said.

"Oh my gosh," I said, waving my arm high to take in the room. "I *love* what you've done with the place. Everything is beautiful."

My dad pinched my arm, and she just walked away. I was trying to be nice and give a compliment, but that's her Jessica Simpson story. *Now* I know the secretary of the interior manages federal land and national parks. Believe me, I beat myself up so much over that one that I could ace a test on it. At least I'd made it to the White House again. I couldn't believe my good fortune.

I don't think Nick could either. In countless interviews, people asked him in front of me if he was jealous. "Her success is my success," he said again and again, so convincingly that even I almost believed him.

12

SUCCESS HAS MADE A FAILURE OF OUR HOME

AUGUST 2004

As we left the club, the flashes of paparazzi cameras blinded us, and Nick reached back for my hand. The photographers walked backward in front of us, knocking each other over and yelling to get us to look right at them.

We were in L.A., a rare night that we were together. The valet had already brought the car, and Nick got in the driver's seat. I pulled on the passenger-door handle, but it was locked. The paparazzi yelled to Nick to open the door, hoping I would smile at them for a shot. I didn't. He finally unlocked the door, and I got in.

I put sunglasses on, even though it was after midnight. The

paparazzi surrounded us to get a two-shot of us in the front seat, then about half scrambled to their cars to follow us. They would be right behind us to the gate of our neighborhood, just to make sure they didn't miss us doing something. Anything. A kiss, a scowl—either way, the photo would sell and fit whatever story line a magazine chose that week.

I waited until we were driving to ask him how he knew the girl.

"Who?" he said.

"That brunette by the door," I said. She worked at the club, one of many that let us right in to drink for free, knowing they'd get an item in the tabloids that advertised their place to customers who would pay more to get in if they knew celebrities would be there. Girls always smiled at Nick, right in front of me. Groupies will always be groupies, but there was something different about the way he had looked at her.

"You gave her that nod," I said. "Like you knew her."

"I nodded?" he said. "Jesus, Jess."

Cue the cycle. I would accuse him of having a wandering eye, and he would rip into me, making sure I knew I was the one causing the problems in our marriage. Everything was my fault. In a real way, I agreed. There was something Nick wanted from me that I no longer had, an emptiness I couldn't fill, and neither could he.

I would freeze in conflict, which I know now was something that started with my abuse. My anxiety kicks in, and I can't get words out. I would have the words, but I would weigh and measure each one in my mind. But they stayed there. Because I went silent, each argument would quickly become one-sided. His defense was an offense, and his words cut me deep. We were not one of those couples that screamed at each other, let whatever fly out of our mouths, and then make mad, passionate love. No, we would yell at each other, and then he would go out of town and not answer his phone. Vegas or Miami with his boys. Or he would just stay out late to teach me a lesson. He had a group of guy friends who used him to get into places and enjoy VIP treatment at strip clubs and bars. He liked that scene, and I thought it was gross. There were times I tried to be sexy like that for him, and I even jumped out of a cake for his thirtieth birthday party in an outfit that I thought was burlesque but was really just sad. *If I dress like those women,* I thought, *maybe you'll look at me.*

But he barely looked at me anymore, period, and I had *Newlyweds* to remind me how much had changed. They still ran our wedding in the opener, that moment when he sees his bride for the first time. He gasps, and all the ladies at home say, "I wish my man looked at me that way." It reminded people that there had been real love between us. Trust me, if he had still looked at me like that, all my resentment would have melted away.

We were in a place where we loved each other fine, but we just didn't like each other. I could feel him *trying* to like me, but everything I did seemed to annoy him. Divorce was not an option for me, if only out of an obligation to my vows. I'd made a promise in front of God and all our loved ones. I couldn't imagine telling people I wanted a divorce. For generations, my family passed down a marriage guide that only had one tip: "Hang in there." I was afraid of letting everyone down. We both were. So many couples had told us we were just like them. What would it mean for them if we couldn't make it?

We got to the gate of our neighborhood, and the paparazzi relented. Nick was still muttering at me, but I was somewhere else, withdrawing again, which I knew he hated, but I couldn't help it. He parked in the garage, and I closed the car door softly. I withheld even the satisfaction he'd feel if I slammed the door like a child. Instead, I was just a ghost returning to her haunted little mansion.

Without looking back at Nick behind me, I entered the house that I'd never thought of as mine. I'd moved in and immediately treated it like a hotel where I never quite unpacked. Without the camera crew buzzing around, people holding up boom mics and lighting, it was like an empty soundstage. I went upstairs to bed and took a sleeping pill. I didn't care if Nick went back out or if he came upstairs.

It was only when I went to take off my makeup that I realized I still had my sunglasses on. I took them off, and the harsh light blinded me once again. I washed my face and looked up to stare at the ghost in the mirror.

THE ONE THING THAT BROUGHT ME JOY WAS WORK. ON A SUNNY AUGUST afternoon, I drove onto the Warner Brothers lot, repeating my lines in my head. This was the make-or-break screen test for the Daisy Duke role in the *Dukes of Hazzard* reboot. The studio had wanted me for the film, but I knew the director, Jay Chandrasekhar, was resistant. He had a strong comedy background and had seen a couple episodes of *Newlyweds*. I think he thought I was too dumb to play a character as strong and smart as Daisy Duke. But I knew Daisy's heart, and I wanted to do her justice. Jay agreed to see my chemistry on film with the Duke brothers already cast, Seann William Scott and Johnny

Knoxville. I knew from the casting agent that Mandy Moore and Jessica Biel were going before me that day, and I tried not to let it shake me.

I walked in to do the scene and saw Johnny. I immediately felt something I didn't understand, something literally attracting him to me.

"Jessica Simpson," Johnny said, shaking my hand. I reflexively smiled at his voice and gentlemanly Southern manners. I didn't expect that from someone who had created the *Jackass* franchise. He was magnetic, and just so charming.

The screen test was a blur, and when it was over, Jay said, "You're it."

"Really?"

"It was your smile," he said.

"Welcome, Daisy," said Johnny.

We would start a three-month film shoot in early November, which I thought would help get me out of filming *Newlyweds* for MTV. Nick and I just didn't want to do it anymore. We didn't want to lie to fans and pretend everything between us was fine. We also knew that even if we tried, we would have a hard time hiding our problems. At the end of August, we had a fight at an afterparty for the MTV VMAs, and the tabloids had a new story line: the Newlyweds under pressure.

The truth was far worse. "I'm starting to feel we can't have cameras on us anymore," I told Nick. "Our marriage is scary." That was the thing: we were still enough of a team that we could talk about our marriage going downhill, as long as we didn't approach specifics. Then we would have to do something about it.

MTV held us to our contract and set filming to start on our anniversary. The production team arranged for Nick to take me to the Saddle Peak Lodge in the Malibu mountains, probably because it had wild game on the menu and they could have me mispronounce emu or something. By then, Nick and I knew exactly what they wanted the episode to be about, so we knew what to say to get them out of the house or leave us alone. We were living life for a line. It would sometimes be the one thing we agreed on. "Let's just say this and have off time."

Of course, it rained. It had rained on our wedding day and our anniversaries. And right before this big romantic dinner, a production assistant showed me a brand-new tabloid story.

"Did you see this?" she asked.

Two weeks before, Nick had been at a bachelor party for a sound engineer friend of ours. The bride was a stylist, and I was a bridesmaid. Whoever had organized the bachelor party had started it at a strip club and then moved to a private home. The tabloid said Nick did some vague thing with a porn star named Jessica. I stopped reading.

"Why are you showing me this?" I asked.

The production assistant looked embarrassed. I realized they wanted a reaction on camera. If we can't get them to interact romantically, let's have them fight. Happy anniversary. I then had to sit through this dinner, another weird, quiet meal where they shut down the whole restaurant to film so nobody could approach us. There were so many tabloid stories about Nick in strip clubs or talking to girls that I just didn't know what to believe. Did he feel caught in this marriage? He kept putting himself into situations where he could be so easily accused of cheating. It was self-sabotage. And I was supposed to stay home and be Betty Crocker?

Nope, I was going to go be Daisy Duke.

I WAS SCARED TO DEATH FOR MY FIRST SCENE ON THE *DUKES* **SET IN BATON** Rouge, but at least Johnny and Seann were there. It was freezing, even for early November, though you would never know it by the amount of clothes I wear in my scenes. For this first scene, we all had to gather around a car, and I had to lament that the Duke brothers were going to get up to some foolishness, and I was going to have to shake my butt to distract the authorities to save the day. I was so prepared, because I wanted to prove to the whole cast and crew that I'd gotten this on my own. Not because I was Nick Lachey's wife or because my dad had squeaked me in with some deal.

I did the scene in one take, and everybody cheered. "Yeah, you got your first line," Seann said.

"Great job, lady," Johnny said, giving me a hug that we let go right to the edge of going on too long. Lady would always be his nickname for me.

I smiled at him and started to worry. I felt a force drawing us together. I wondered why I was open to this. I was already living in a distrustful situation with Nick, and now I was afraid I couldn't trust myself. *Oh my God, I didn't know my heart could do this,* I thought. And then, *Shoot.*

At the end of the first day of shooting, I went back to the house the production company had rented for me, a simple two-story home near the Louisiana State University campus. I had brought along four friends from L.A. to the movie shoot, CaCee, two girlfriends named Jessie and Mary, and my trainer, Mike Alexander, who was a friend from high school. And my little Maltipoo, who I had named Daisy as a sort of wish that I would get the part. I went upstairs to call Nick to share how great my first day went. He seemed distracted when all I wanted was for him to be proud of me. Or to at least listen to me. Everyone else on the set was happy and proud, why not my husband? When I asked him how his album was going, he seemed relieved.

When I hung up, I heard laughter downstairs. CaCee and Jessie were whoopin' over something. I realized that I had created a sort of dorm room of friends. My parents hadn't tagged along for once—they were both focused on my younger sister, Ashlee, and her new pop career. My father and the label positioned her as the antithesis of me—she even dyed her blonde hair brown—and it was working because she had the talent to back it up. Her deserved success brought their focus to my sister, so my parents went from being around me constantly to barely. So, down in Louisiana on that set, I'd decided to give myself the college experience I'd never gotten to have because I was always working, moving from living under my dad's eye to Nick's.

And for the first time, work was 100 percent fun. Let's be honest, I wasn't carrying the movie, and it's not like I had a lot of lines. I could just be Daisy, and I felt my cousin Sarah close to me. She was that Southern cool girl, too. In the film, I even wore red boots like the ones Sarah wore. Once I became Daisy, I wanted to be her for the rest of my life. *Oh, people underestimate me because of the way I look? How can I use that to my advantage?* I felt powerful.

But I also had to look the part. I was living on protein, dreaming of chips. I knew I was hired for my body and treated it like an athlete would. Poor Mike had to listen to me whine every day at the little gym we went to. When I did the scenes in short shorts or the bikini—and, really, those were my scenes—

I had a heavy robe to cover me the second the camera stopped rolling. "Run it over," I'd yell. "I'm nekkid out here." Lynda Carter was in the movie, and she understood the pressure and body scrutiny. Daisy Duke got to meet Wonder Woman and bond with her in hair and makeup.

"Get ready," she warned me. "People are gonna want you to be in those Daisy Duke shorts the rest of your life." Putting on the shorts on the set and having a group of people lean back to see if my butt looked good enough. Lynda had been there—fighting for our rights in her satin tights—but she also told me to embrace playing such a strong, forthright character as Daisy or, in her case, Wonder Woman.

"There were times," she said slowly, "I think she saved me."

I waved my hands at my eyes, afraid to ruin my makeup because I was so touched by her kindness. She hugged me. "It's nice to be someone else for a while," I admitted. "To not have to play me."

If Lynda was my mentor on the set, Willie Nelson was my guardian angel. He played Uncle Jesse in the film and insisted on calling me Daisy even when the cameras were off. He invited me to hang out on his tour bus, the Honeysuckle Rose, and soon he and his beautiful wife, Annie, took me under their wings. The Honeysuckle Rose is famous, and Willie always stays in his beloved bus when he's on the road or shooting a movie. He was just so satisfied with his life, this country Buddha who's happy to connect with his fans. I'd hang out on the big old couch inside, and he'd play me music by country greats like his friends Waylon Jennings and Patsy Cline.

"You know I wrote Patsy's 'Crazy,' right?"

"Oh, wow," I said. I knew it by heart and began to sing it.

"Yeah, but I wanted to call it 'Stupid.'" He started singing, "Stupid, stupid, for feeling so blue . . ."

When he realized I believed him, hook, line, and sinker, he let out a big laugh. "Oh, Daisy," he said, "I'm just pullin' your pretty little leg."

As soon as I was settled in, I had to leave again to throw Nick his birthday party. I spent something like a hundred and fifty thousand dollars for him to have a birthday weekend in Las Vegas. Note: wasting that kind of money trying to make someone like you is never really a good idea, but I wanted him to be happy because obviously I wasn't enough. I wanted to tell him all my stories from my movie adventure, but he didn't seem interested, so I shut down. He seemed insecure, and I thought, *How do you make all these women swoon while you are the one threatened by me growing up to be the person I want to be? An adult.*

I missed my friends. I missed Johnny.

Sigh, Johnny. The boy from Tennessee, as I coded him in my diary. First off, we were both married, so this wasn't going to get physical. But to me, an emotional affair was worse than a physical one. It's funny, I know, because I had placed such an emphasis on sex by not having it before marriage. After I actually had sex, I understood that the emotional part was what mattered. And Johnny and I had that, which seemed far more of a betrayal to my marriage than sex.

Our friends would all hang out together in the bars by LSU, which added to the college vibe. Eventually it would get down to me and Johnny talking over Macallan, the scotch whisky he introduced me to. I could talk to him for hours, and his stories brought things to life, surging with a mix of adrenaline and intelligence. Ten years older than me, he spoke of writers who inspired him, like Jack Kerouac and Hunter S. Thompson, and how they brought a spirit of adventure to everything they did. It was something he emulated. Nothing was ever average with him. It had to be the best night of your life, or it wasn't worth doing.

This wasn't a performance. He made me feel that spirit of adventure as he asked me about my life. Not just my present, but about who I wanted to be. I could share the deepest authentic thoughts with him, and he didn't roll his eyes at me. He actually liked that I was smart and embraced my vulnerabilities. He didn't make fun of me, he laughed with me. He believed in me and made me feel like I could do anything. And the only person who had ever made me feel that way was my dad. Certainly not my husband.

We were open about the challenges of our marriages and why we felt we had to honor those vows by sticking with the marriage. He had a daughter, and he spoke of her like his life began and ended with her. I had never seen someone's eyes shine like his did when he talked about his child.

"I just feel like I'm going through so many changes," I said to Johnny one night over scotch. "It's hard."

"Nah, change is easy," he said. "Staying the same is a lot harder on you."

I lifted the Macallan to toast that, and held it in the air, lifting it higher to see him through the amber of the drink.

"Don't be looking at me through whisky-colored glasses, lady," he said.

"Too late," I said.

"Let's just promise to be there for one another in our imminent and enduring times of trouble and thunder."

"Deal," I said. He always talked like that. I would moon over him to CaCee, using that same lofty language.

"He's saving me," I told CaCee.

"Jessica Simpson, you don't need him to save you," she said. "You can save yourself." She paused and continued in the big-sister tone I usually listened to. "What you are doing is not right, and it's not respectful to Nick. Either get in there and fix your marriage, really work on it, or you need to separate. If you want to leave Nick, talk to him. Johnny's not a bad guy, but there is nothing healthy about this thing."

"I want my marriage to work," I said.

"Well, then, act like it," she said.

I think CaCee felt guilty because I saw a freedom in her life that I wanted. She knew that I needed that and was going to go find it. But she didn't want to feel that it was her fault if I left Nick. Not just because they were close, but because CaCee never wants to hurt anyone's feelings. To this day, she still remembers the name of every person we've ever met together on set. She'll tell me about being excited that some random person had a baby, and she knows because she follows them on Instagram!

We had to break for Christmas, so I went back home to Nick. We could both feel it was ending, and that reality made him angry. He kept accusing me of changing.

"Of course I have," I yelled. "Nick, you married a *baby*. I'm not that person anymore."

His anger always made things worse, but in a way, I craved it. I wanted him to be angrier with me. *Yeah, give me more reason to leave,* I thought. *I don't want this to be all my fault.* Now

I know it wasn't my fault, but at the time, I still thought I had failed him.

When I returned to Baton Rouge, I became more brazen in flirting with Johnny. While I used to purposefully not call Nick at night so he would wonder, I now realized that I just wasn't thinking of him at all. I was inconsiderate, hoping he would make the decision for us, because I was too afraid. The *Newlyweds* crew came to Baton Rouge, but I didn't give them much. They were desperate, so they set up a camera on my computer just so they could get us in the same frame. It hardly seemed worth it: Nick would talk about working on his album, and I would say I was tired from work.

Nick showed up in Louisiana in late January, the day after the premiere of our third season of *Newlyweds*. He was suspicious about what I was up to, hanging out with Johnny and his friends, so he announced he was moving his album writing and demo sessions to Sockit Studios in Baton Rouge. It was probably the worst time in our marriage. He was seething with anger, which I matched with an increasing coldness.

The *Newlyweds* crews came to the scene, hoping to get footage of us. I didn't want to be around him, and I think Nick was surprised that I wouldn't even do the bare minimum of playing along for the cameras, sitting in the studio and watching him work. The crew was there, so I felt obligated to shoot. But I was sick of lying, and I resented that it was disruptive to the film. Not that I had to do much to get into the role of being Daisy Duke, but I was still trying to work, and they were coming onto the set of this fifty-million-dollar-budget movie like it was my living room.

I also knew that the cameras would reveal that I was over the marriage. I was right. What little they got of us together would quickly devolve. We were about to have another fight, when Nick said, loudly, "Stop rolling." That was our safe phrase—the signal that we didn't want to be filmed—but the crew continued.

"Will you just get out of here so we can have a conversation?" he asked.

A producer stepped forward. "If we keep having to stop rolling," he said, "there's no show."

We looked at each other, and said together, "Stop rolling."

From then on, we filmed as little as possible, save for a Valentine's Day episode where we did nothing to hide that there were problems. They had to do a clip show for the last one, where we pretended we wanted to move out of the house but changed our minds. It was bizarre, and I never watched it. We finished out the run and fulfilled the contract. Now there was a sense that we at least had to see what it was like to have a marriage without cameras. I think we both knew we couldn't blame all our problems on the cameras, but we felt obligated to at least try. Like I said, finish out the run.

Near my last day of shooting *Dukes of Hazzard*, I started to worry about what was going to come next. The movie was a great excuse for not being with Nick, and for being with Johnny in this fantasy land. I got the courage one day to ask Willie Nelson for marriage advice while we were alone on his bus. I felt I could talk to him about anything. I told him about Nick, and how I just wasn't sure what to do.

"I'm not the guy to give advice, Daisy," he said. I could tell he saw my disappointment.

"I had a father-in-law," he continued. "An *ex*-father-in-law, so, you see? But he said, 'Take my advice, and do what you want to do.' That may be the best advice I've ever heard."

He picked up his guitar, which was always nearby. "Uncle Jesse, can we sing together?" I asked.

He answered by strumming his guitar. I started singing "Will the Circle Be Unbroken," and he fell right into the rhythm. It's a beautiful funeral hymn of losing someone and hoping for a reunion in heaven. When that chorus first kicks in, there really is that question: "Will the circle be unbroken, by and by, Lord, by and by?" Is love really eternal? I'd married forever, to spend eternity with Nick in heaven. The place where I would see my grandparents, who'd hung in there like I was supposed to, and where I would see Sarah again. I'd married forever, and now I was certain that dream was over.

When you sing that lonely, scared song with someone, by the end, there's a connection. Doesn't matter if it's two voices in a bus or two hundred in a church, you feel a little less scared. As we sang, I started to cry, and I think Willie knew to just let me.

13

THE GILDED CAGE

SPRING 2005

We sat in the living room on a rare afternoon home together. By then, it wasn't often that we were even in the same city. I traveled so much that I no longer had jetlag, just a permanent back and forth of restlessness and fatigue. We were on the couch, and Nick made some crack about me, I don't know what. Probably one that I used to think was funny, and I said something mean. As usual, we launched into our long list of grievances with each other . . .

And we stopped. At the same time, we looked over to the TV and nodded to each other. Silently, we got up from the couch, left the house, and walked to an empty lot nearby. Only then, safe from anybody hearing, did we quietly scream at each other.

Production had stopped on our show, and the last sad episode ran in late March, but we were paranoid that we were still being taped. Looking back, I know we sound crazy, but when you live in a house with hidden cameras for years—in the TV and in the corners—it's hard to believe that they're all really gone. We had reason to be paranoid. Details of our conversations and troubles would show up on the news. Tabloids made up the dumbest things about us, but sometimes they would get something so right it was scary.

So we started leaving the house whenever we had to discuss something delicate. I kept thinking of *The Firm*, when Tom Cruise's character finds out his evil law firm has secretly wired his entire house with listening devices. When he tells his wife, she bolts from the house, terrified, and they go to a park where they can talk without anybody listening in. "Everything, every single thing we've said or done since we've been in that house," she says, "nothing has been between us."

He suspected my friends were selling stories, I suspected his. My protective mother had a guilty until proven innocent approach to everyone around us. The one friend we agreed would never do it was CaCee, but I was already becoming isolated from her. She was afraid to even go to restaurants with me because she was convinced someone would overhear *me* running my mouth and sell it, and I would blame her.

CaCee knew my biggest secret: That I was still in touch with Johnny Knoxville. We wrote these flowery love letters back and forth, often at night with Nick passed out in the bed next to me. We talked about music, and I would listen to the Johnny Cash songs he suggested just to feel like we were still together. Whenever I wanted to read CaCee some gushy letter from him, she would refuse. It was like Johnny and I were prison pen pals, two people who wanted so much to be with each other but were kept apart—by bars, by our stars, by our respective spouses.

I would delete every email, convinced Nick would find out. I rewrote each text and email in my Mead journal, the sanctity of which my husband respected, even if neither of us were doing a good job of respecting the rest of our marriage.

As there were more and more tabloid stories about our marriage falling apart, we became strangely more determined to make it work. Paparazzi would ask me constantly, as if we were pals, "Jess, are you leaving Nick?" Worse, Nick was asked, "Is Jess leaving you, Nick?" Our natural response was to protect each other, so whenever the press asked, we would vehemently deny that there were any problems. We didn't want to give anybody the satisfaction of seeing us publicly humiliated with a divorce, so we continued to play our *Newlyweds* roles. Sometimes we did this so well that we convinced each other. I thought, *Well, maybe this isn't enough, but maybe it's enough for me.*

In one of those moments, I deleted Johnny's number from my phone. I did it quickly, before I—or Nick—changed my mind.

IN APRIL, NICK MADE GOOD ON HIS PROMISE TO JOIN ME IN ENTERTAINING the troops, this time in Iraq. ABC cameras followed us for a variety show, and beforehand I'd started reading a paperback of Rick Atkinson's *In the Company of Soldiers*, an account of the ground war in the country. I wanted a sense of what these men and women were living through so I could have real conversations with them.

Before Iraq, our first stop was Ramstein Air Base in Germany, the main hub for U.S. armed forces in Europe, Africa, and the Middle East. The base was in Kaiserslautern, and on the plane, someone told me a good icebreaker was to ask, "How long have you been in K-Town?" I was relieved, because there was no way I was saying Kaiserslautern right. We were there for the first three days of the trip, doing a free show for six thousand people in Hangar 1 on the base. I had invited Willie to come along for the Germany portion. "Sure, Daisy," was his answer. He traded in his usual bandana for a cute USO one, and we did a duet of "These Boots Are Made for Walkin'," which was going to be on the soundtrack to *Dukes of Hazzard*.

Nick was so great on the trip, and it meant so much for me to see him in action, doing something meaningful to him. Not only was he perfect onstage doing most of the emceeing, but also when we visited Landstuhl Regional Medical Center, a one-hundred bed hospital that they told us was nicknamed the "Emergency Room" for the wars in Iraq and Afghanistan. Just as in my first USO tour in 2001, I wasn't ready for how young these people would be. But now, nearly four years later, I was twenty-four, and looking at eighteen- and nineteen-year-olds whose lives had been changed forever by war. A few had just been in Iraq for a very short time before being maimed by a car bomb. Most of the patients had legs or arms that were severely injured by shrapnel.

"These guys are just kids," I whispered to Nick in the hallway, trying to keep it together. Nick took the lead when he went into rooms, not sure what we would see. He'd walk in first and say "Good to see you," and his grace carried me and prevented me from having any appearance of pity. "This one put on lip gloss just for you," he'd say, gesturing to me. "Darn right, I did," I would say. He was kind, and when he struggled, trying to keep up a poker face, I stepped in. We were a real team again, and while I had no illusions that we didn't have problems, I saw what I used to see in us for that trip.

From Germany, Nick and I flew with my father to Kuwait, and then took a C-130 military flight into Iraq, where we would tour three bases in one day, then fly home that night. We had newly deployed combat troops on our plane, and just like the people in the hospital, they seemed so young. Praying for their safety helped me let go of some of my own fears about being in Iraq. I was only going to be there for one day. Who knows how long these troops would be there?

As we flew in, the pilot came over the loudspeaker. "Just want to prepare you that the Iraqis shoot rockets at us all the time," he said. "They are shooting from the ground, and they're not accurate. Just hoping they'll hit something else."

I looked at my dad with a "Help" face and laughed at the thought that I was going to better understand this life by reading a book about the war.

"When we land, we're not going to come in regular like a plane," the pilot continued. "We're gonna dump it and go straight in to avoid enemy fire, so prepare yourself for the sudden drop." He wasn't kidding, it felt like we were going to crash land on our first stop, Camp Anaconda, just north of Baghdad. Before we got out, they made us all put on bulletproof vests and helmets.

"We take a lot of incoming mortar fire," said the man as he casually adjusted my helmet. He said it the way my mom would say, "Bring an umbrella 'cause the skies are threatening."

I suddenly felt silly in my tight jeans, carrying my cowgirl hat. After a welcoming ceremony, our escorts took us to a mess hall to eat with service members. There was probably a thousand people inside, and we waited in line like everyone else, greeting anybody who came up to say hello.

After we sat to eat, I felt the entire ground start to shake. I panicked. There were explosions somewhere nearby. I looked around and noticed none of the soldiers were even registering that we were in a war zone. This was all so normal to them.

"I think the guns are a long way away," my father said when it happened again. He and Nick were in a contest to be cooler under fire, but I was a wreck.

"How do you know?" I asked.

"Take a look at these guys sitting at the table," Dad said. "When they move, you move."

"This is Mortaritaville," one soldier told me. "You get used to it."

"Well, when you're back home, I hope you get to Margaritaville," I said. "You can *really* get used to that."

After the meal, Nick and I sat at tables and signed autographs and shook hands for a long time, then they loaded us into a UH-60 Black-Hawk to go to the next base. They canceled our plan to go to the next base on the schedule because of the fighting that made the ground—and me—shake. We took a five-hour Black-Hawk ride straight to Camp Speicher in Tikrit to do another meet and greet, and when we were done, we got back on the Black-Hawk to take us to Kuwait. I confess I was relieved to be leaving. I was very aware of my privilege in my ability to go home. Just as we were about to fly out, we were told we couldn't leave because of an incoming sandstorm.

There was too much danger of a crash, and we would have to stay the night.

They put us in a bunker, and I freaked out. Not gonna lie. It was a small room with two sets of bunkbeds. My Sidekick worked—yes, in a bunker in Iraq—so I called my mother and started reciting my last will and testament. She then freaked out and called my dad while I was saying my goodbyes to CaCee. "Tina, we are under attack by a sandstorm," he said. "It's fine."

I started sending long letters to my friends, telling them how much I loved them. It occurred to me that God had placed me in this bunker with my two protectors, Nick and my dad, and I still didn't feel safe. There was a soldier guarding the bunker, and she took me aside before lights out.

"Here," she said, handing me a little angel figurine. "My daughter gave me this to keep me safe. You can borrow it."

I looked her in the eye and thanked her. It felt precious in my hand, full of power. I slept with it in my hand all night, and that angel got me through all my anxiety. In the morning, I tried to give it back to her, but she told me I could keep it.

"No," I said, "It's too much." But she insisted.

"My daughter will love that we all have something in common," she said. "Just think of us, okay?"

"I promise," I said. I have since lent it out once, to my friend Koko, when her husband was facing a long deployment. She was scared. "Here," I said, just like I'd heard in that bunker. "Take this angel and then give it back to me when he comes home."

I'm very happy to tell you she was able to. I still sleep with that little angel next to my bed. I'm grateful for that protection, and I still pray for the safety of service members all over the world. When I am rushing through an airport, my assistant hopes the doors of the plane are still open and that I won't see any service members. I always stop to find out if they're coming or going so I can give them a friendly word.

WE SAT IN THE OFFICE, MY NOTEBOOK ON MY LAP. NICK GLANCED AT ME and shook his head just slightly, knowing I had pens and pencils in my purse. The good student trying to impress the marriage counselor. Nick was against the idea that we needed therapy, alternating between two excuses: the therapist would probably sell us out to a tabloid, and we could get through this ourselves.

"I don't feel like anything needs to be fixed," he had said.

"Everything needs to be fixed," I answered. "There's not one thing that's okay."

If this therapist could give me the solution to making my marriage work, I would take it. He was a psychologist and life coach from Dallas who flew back and forth from L.A. and New York, meeting with celebrities and CEOs. We met in a nondescript office building to throw off the paparazzi.

On that sunny California day in May, the therapist, a forty-something guy with rimless glasses and thinning blond hair, patiently listened to us as we laid out our problems and received our marriage operating instructions. Nick said I was just too young and didn't know how to communicate. I would either go quiet or say things like "All bets are off" and "This marriage ain't gonna last." I felt I had to say things like that to get him to understand how miserable I was in the marriage.

"I know you hate me," I said.

He shook his head in disgust.

"I feel it," I said. "Whenever we are in the same room, it just comes off you. I feel it when you lie down next to me. I feel it when you can't even look at me."

The main diagnosis: he was withholding love while I was withholding intimacy and affection. "Even a hug," said the therapist. "Touching, of course, making love."

And him? I was supposed to take him at his word that he didn't hate me. He would stop saying or doing things in anger, and I, in turn, would stop bringing things up from the past. His actions needed to be consistent with valuing our relationship.

"You're doing the right thing getting help," the therapist said. "If you break your arm, you don't sit there yelling at it for being broken. You get it fixed." I left relieved that we had a list of things we could do to help each other. And for a few days, it was better. I tried to be more present and not be such a ghost. We stayed at home and cooked dinner.

The next counseling session, I sat there in the office, awkwardly stalling in the hopes that Nick was just late. He wasn't answering his phone, and I looked down at the blank page of my notebook.

Nick never showed. He stopped coming altogether.

Like some signal had gone up, Johnny then emailed me. I took out all my anger and drama on him, acting like he had abandoned me. I had deleted his number, and I guess he didn't notice that I hadn't contacted him, which only made me more upset. We had a ridiculous back and forth about who was at fault, and he accused me of attacking him for no reason. That triggered my need to please, so I smoothed it over, and convinced myself that this was just passion. I poured it into my songwriting, writing about Johnny and sending him the songs to get his take. I don't know what I thought that would do. Get him to show up at my door and say, "Get your stuff, we're running away together"? I began to realize contact with him was an addiction, and I would make these grand pronouncements that each time was the last time. I was grateful that he had expanded my worldview and made me appreciate so many things about culture, but I needed to walk away. This wasn't a game.

One of the songwriters I was working with told me he noticed that all the songs I was creating with him were about regret and a romance that was either lost or doomed from the start.

"You really need a love song," he said.

I smiled. "I know."

AFTER MONTHS OF HYPE, *THE DUKES OF HAZZARD* PREMIERED IN LATE July with a huge red-carpet event in Los Angeles. Johnny brought his wife and daughter, so the whole thing felt dangerous and foolish. I avoided him and kept Nick with me as I walked the rope line of interviewers. Every question was about how I got in shape to play Daisy Duke, and Nick got increasingly annoyed as we made it down the line.

Once inside, the movie started, and the audience cheered when my name came up on the title card. I shook with a chill going through my body. *Thank you, Lord,* I thought. Nick took my hand and smiled at me. He was proud of me, even if he had a hard time saying the words just to me and not the media.

Seeing myself so big up there, I found myself critiquing my body. My body was a machine, and I had given it over to the service of the character. I saw Daisy Duke on the screen, and then just the teeny tiniest stomach shadow of Jessica. While watching, my tell was that I'd pull a face with my lower lip. I was in the best shape of my life, and I didn't appreciate it, but also, it just shows the absurdity of how we always find something to criticize about ourselves.

Two days before the movie came out, Johnny went on the *Howard Stern Show* and took a lie detector test. They asked, "Have you had sex with Jessica Simpson?" and he said no. Of course he passed, but I just felt gross that he even submitted to doing that. My friends told me this was proof that he was toxic, but I still saw the good in him. How could I not, when I had made him into this fantasy man at the other end of a text or email?

Dukes came out in theaters August 5 and did huge numbers. In one week, I had the number-one movie and the number-one video on MTV with "These Boots Are Made for Walkin.'" Johnny emailed me that I was a bona fide movie star.

My success galvanized Nick to put more effort into his solo album, and he had part of the *Newlyweds* crew follow him around as he worked in the studio. I didn't want any part of that, and I was surprised that he did. He chose the crew members he could go out for beers with after they wrapped for the day. He'd built a recording studio in the house, and I tried not to be home when I knew the crew would be there. That said, I tried not to be home in general. I spent more and more time with my friends, especially my hairdresser Ken Pavés.

I drank too much on my nights out, and so did Nick. He didn't have a problem with alcohol, he had an issue with what it allowed him to say. One day I taped a Proactiv skin product commercial all day, and afterward a bunch of us went to dinner. Nick was at a bar, and said he'd come to dinner but never showed. Late that night he came home drunk. He was swaying back and forth, angry at me for a laundry list of reasons. I knew I deserved it. I was a terrible wife, and he was a terrible husband. But I knew deep down he was a good man. I wanted that man back.

I started to speak. "My friends say—"

"Your friends don't *exist*," he spat. "You just pay them to be around you."

It was a knife, cutting me down to the rawest marrow. My mouth dropped open. The one thing I always had was my friendships. I'd been so cold, so unresponsive to him for so long that he must have seen a flicker of something. So he twisted the knife.

"And your parents are only around because they are on the payroll."

I closed my eyes, willed myself away. I turned to go upstairs.

"All bets are off," I quietly said to myself. The next day, I would tell him what he said. He wouldn't remember. But I would.

14

I'LL FLY AWAY

I arrived in Nairobi a little after six in the morning. I was in Kenya for Operation Smile, a decades-old medical charity providing reconstructive surgeries for children worldwide with cleft lips, palates, and other facial deformities that were either life-threatening or socially ostracizing. They were doing a two-week mission providing surgeries at three sites in Kenya: Nairobi, Mombasa, and Nakura. I'd brought my hairdresser friend Ken, who had been the one to introduce me to the charity. When I heard Operation Smile had scheduled the mission, I wanted to go along because I had made the charity a priority for me.

It was October 26, my third wedding anniversary, and Nick and I had arranged to be nearly four thousand miles apart. He was in Sweden, working with producers on his album. I was in Africa. It didn't matter, really. We were barely speaking.

We got there in the morning, and I had the day to myself before we took a bus west to Nakura that night. I thought I would sleep, but I wanted to see if I could be anonymous so far away from America. I washed my face and threw on jeans and an oversize army-green jacket. I stood in the mirror, wondering if another tourist would notice I was Jessica Simpson. I decided to pull my hair back with a black bandana, the same way I had on mission trips as a kid. As I did so, I saw the shine of my wedding ring in the mirror. I looked at it, and it felt suffocating and heavy on my hand. I watched myself as I slipped it off to place it in the tiny pocket of my jeans and exhaled. The ring left a line of white on my finger, and I rubbed at it, trying to make it disappear.

I went to Nairobi National Park, a forty-five-square-mile nature preserve just outside the main part of the city. I walked in through the main entrance, and I had the feeling of being on a space walk as I got farther and farther from the safety of the car. I felt untethered, afraid that if someone spotted me, a crowd would form, and then I would have to run. I opened my backpack to get out a bottle of water and sipped nervously as I moved into the park.

"Excuse me," said a woman behind me. The voice was British.

Please, I thought.

"Excuse me," she said again. I turned to see an older woman with a husband who matched her to a tee.

She smiled. "Your bag," she said. "It's open."

A wave of relief washed over me. "Thank you," I said. They kept walking, and so did I, blissfully invisible. Near the entrance, the David Sheldrick Wildlife Trust runs a sanctuary for orphaned baby elephants and rhinoceroses. As I blended in with a small crowd of people standing behind a light rope line, keepers led a dozen or so baby elephants to a mud bath. The parents of these animals are usually killed by ivory and rhino horn poachers, and the orphans are found close to death themselves. They grow up there, bottle-fed until they are old enough to be released.

"In the beginning, they follow us around," the keeper told us. "But then they start to make their own decisions about where they want to go, and so we follow them." Usually, around two years old, the elephants have the confidence to go back into the wild.

I watched them frolic, dropping themselves on the ground and rubbing up against each other, their huge ears flapping. I took my sunglasses off so I could look them in the eyes. People slowly left the viewing area, but I stayed, transfixed. It had been so long since I had spent that amount of time alone among people. This was my sanctuary, too.

I heard the click of a camera's shutter like a gun cocking. It was to my left, but I didn't want to turn my face to see it. I shoved my left hand in my pocket and tried to fiddle my wedding ring onto my finger, like Houdini with a hidden key.

Come on, Jess, I said to myself. I scrunched my finger up to catch the ring with my nail.

Another click. *Got it.* I pulled out my hand and put my sunglasses back on with my left hand to be sure my ring was in the shots. I turned just slightly to see a heavyset white man training a Canon camera on me. I was the game, and I was caught.

I deadened my face, put my sunglasses on, and left the park.

That night, on the bus to Nakura, I wrote in my journal and asked God to replenish my heart so I could be of use to the children coming in for screenings and surgeries the next day. I was so tired of focusing on my own sadness and anxiety.

"I release this pain to You, so You will free me," I wrote. "Lord, use me as I deny myself anything having to do with 'me.' That 'me' is denied, passed on, set aside."

I meant every word, and I thought the same when I walked into the hospital the next morning. "Use me," I said again to God. There were so many children, and the surgeons would perform over 150 procedures on this mission trip. I stood around and posed for photographs, knowing my job was to bring attention to the charity. The real work was done by people like Dr. Bill Magee, the pediatric plastic surgeon who cofounded the organization.

And then I met Boke. She was eighteen months old, gorgeously chubby, and had come in to have surgery on her cleft lip and palate. Her mother had terrible anxiety about the procedure and had gone outside to calm down. I later learned they had traveled twelve hours to get to the hospital. She must have been overwhelmed to work so hard to get somewhere, only to then face the fear of her baby being operated on by strangers.

Boke began to cry, and I lifted my arms to a nurse out of some instinct I didn't know I had. The nurse sat her in my lap, and I smiled at her, making soothing *shh* sounds as I rocked my body to be one big cradle for her. She looked up, and we regarded each other for a moment, two strangers brought together in a place unfamiliar to both of us.

"Look at you," I said. "You're so pretty." She had the tiniest bit of short, tight curls, and as she relaxed, I couldn't help but kiss her pretty head. Her cleft lip was on the right side of her face, and the wide split went up to her nose, exposing her front teeth.

We relaxed together, and people moved on from watching us. Everyone was so busy that day that Boke and I just blended in until it was her turn. I went to give her over, and she started crying again. Dr. Magee was doing the operation himself and asked if I wanted to scrub in so I could stay with her. I nodded yes, and after I was scrubbed up and capped and gowned, I carried Boke in myself.

"You're already so beautiful," I whispered to her. "This will just make things easier for you." I held Boke when they gave her anesthesia and stroked her head as she slipped off to sleep. I thought I'd leave, but Dr. Magee invited me to stay. I watched, wanting to be a witness to this miracle. It took what, forty-five minutes? And it would change Boke's life forever. And mine, too. I had come to Kenya thinking I would be blessing these kids with good works, and I was the one being blessed. When it was over, Dr. Magee said he was impressed I didn't flinch once. It was one of the best reviews I've ever received.

I went with Boke to recovery so that I would be the first person she saw when she woke up. I sat cradling her and marveling that you could already see the transformation of her mouth being made whole. I held her in the crook of my right arm, and in her postoperation sleep, she wrapped her little hand around my left index finger.

When she was fully awake, someone went to get her mom to tell her that the surgery was a success. She came in, and we smiled at each other. She had no idea who I was and wanted nothing from me but to step in when she was in need. I hugged her, thinking how scared she must have been.

The doctors worked all day, so I stayed late and did the same the next day. When it was over, Ken and I were exhausted, and I could not stop thanking him for getting me involved in Operation Smile. It gave me perspective on what mattered. I hadn't planned on doing so much soul searching, but being so far away gave me an opportunity to look inward in stillness.

As part of the trip, we arranged to take a Jeep out to the Masai Mara National Reserve to camp. As we drove farther and farther into the flat grassland, I looked out at the trees dotting the landscape here and there and felt a growing freedom. I could have been anybody to Boke's mom. Could I be anybody to me? And who did I want to be?

That night I slept in a tent. Don't worry, it was luxury glamping. I don't want to make you think I was suddenly roughing it. I was changing, but I was still me. Still, under that blanket of stars woven by God, I didn't have my usual fear of the dark and what could happen. I went to bed early, not putting it off like I usually did, and slept soundly. I dreamed something about my life in Hollywood and being chased by paparazzi. I was so grateful when the Kenyan sun woke me, safe, a world away from all that.

I went outside and saw I was the first up. There had been just the lightest rain. Now the early-morning sun was shining. It was so beautiful that I bowed my head to pray, thanking God for giving me clarity. I knew now what I had to do.

When I opened my eyes, I looked up to the sky and saw it: a double rainbow. I know how that sounds, but it's true, and it was the confirmation I needed. I stared at it, my hands on my hips, and began to sing softly up to the sky.

"If happy little bluebirds fly beyond the rainbow," I sang, "why, oh why, can't I?"

When I got back to America, I would make steps to start my new life. I had to escape, and I wouldn't be leaving Nick to be with anybody. I was escaping to be with myself.

THERE'S A LINE IN MY JOURNAL FROM THAT TIME THAT I KEPT RETURNING to: "We must be willing to get rid of the life we've planned, so as to have the life that is waiting for us." It's a quote from Joseph Campbell, who studied mythology to describe what it takes to be a hero. I probably got it from one of the many, *many* self-help books I devoured back then, underlining points and dog-earing the pages that seemed to tell me a way out. I repeated that quote to myself for weeks, in the shower, on a red carpet, driving in my car. *There was a life waiting for me,* I told myself. I owed it to the people in it to be brave.

On the night of November 22, two days before Thanksgiving, I couldn't make that life wait any longer for me.

"I think I want a divorce," I told Nick.

I later heard that he told the press he was blindsided. I don't know how. At that point we were not even speaking to each other. Maybe he was just shocked that I stood up for myself. I don't think he ever thought I would take the leap. He immediately tried to talk me out of leaving him, saying we should sleep on it.

When I told him the next day that we should announce a separation, that seemed to make it real to him. I knew I would be disappointing so many people. He went to the studio to record a song he said he wrote the week before, called "What's Left of Me." I later found out he had his camera crew record him singing the demo.

That evening I rushed through LAX to make a flight to Dallas so I could be with my family in Waco. I was dressed like I was trying to disappear: black jeans and a black button-down, with a black-and-white-plaid newsboy cap and the darkest, biggest sunglasses I had to hide behind.

I made it to the gate as they were boarding and got out my phone. There was one more person I had to tell: my father.

"Dad, I have to do it," I said. "I have to leave him."

I waited to see who was going to respond, my father or my manager.

"Absolutely, baby," he said. "I love you, and I'll do whatever you need me to do."

That was my dad.

"We should do a statement," I said. "That way I'll stick to it."

"Jess, don't talk about it out loud," he said. "This is gonna break and break hard. We need to control it."

That was my manager speaking. *There was no controlling this,* I thought. My life was about to turn upside. "Okay," I said. "But do it right away."

"I'm so proud of you." And then he paused. "I wish I had the courage that you have to do that with your mom."

"What?" I asked. "What are you even saying?"

He didn't speak. I couldn't handle what he'd just said, so I immediately shelved it. "Dad, the plane's about to take off," I said, and hung up on him. I was confused by what he'd said, but I put it aside because I was so overwhelmed.

I settled in my seat, and it was only when we took off that I started to cry. This was before Wi-Fi on planes, so this was my last three hours before the storm hit. The statement went out while I was in the air, but nobody on the plane knew a thing, except that Jessica Simpson was loudly sobbing in first class.

Then they announced that the movie we all had to watch was *The Notebook. Oh God,* I thought. The most romantic movie in the world, and I was leaving Nick. I knew exactly what the movie was about because I had read the script but turned it down because they wouldn't budge on taking out the sex scene. And it would have been with Ryan Gosling, of all people. The movie was on every screen, and I was swept up into it, wishing I had that great love that would be forever.

The flight attendants all felt sorry for me, and I was trying so hard to be polite every time they came over with more Kleenex. I was a total wreck.

When I landed, the announcement had made the news in the airport. With my head down, I ran to a car to take me to my Nana and Papaw's house before anybody could find me. It was a new house my family had bought them, one that they got to build themselves to make it perfect. I got in late, and they greeted me at the door. I collapsed into their arms. Safe.

My parents were coming the next day on an early Thanksgiving-morning flight, so it was just me and my grandparents for the night. Papaw seemed uncomfortable, not sure what to say. He went to bed while Nana and I talked late in the living room. I looked up at all the framed magazines covers and articles she had hanging up of Nick and me, like the *InStyle* wedding photos and *Teen Vogue* cover. She loved our love story and adored Nick for waiting for me. I know she prayed for him every night, and she probably still does. She was in denial that it was ending, and as much as she adored me, she was unable to hide her disappointment.

"You'll sort this out," she said.

"Nana, no. It's time."

"Pray on it. It's God's will that you be married."

My heart broke just a little more. "He's not really a Christian," I told her. "And I'm not being the wife he deserves. What about this marriage is godly?"

"Well, *divorce* isn't godly," she said.

I paused, realizing my grandmother, my prayer warrior, thought I was doing wrong in God's eyes. I closed my eyes for a second and took her hand. "Nana, this is the decision God wants me to make. It's not godly to stay together and be completely unhappy."

She looked off. I knew she had stayed through Papaw's struggles with drinking, but clearly, she loved him and saw the man he truly was. The Papaw I got to grow up with. My mother had stayed in a marriage with my father, who also apparently wanted out. Everybody just stayed, stuck it out, thinking God would close His eyes to them if we dared to ask, "What about *me*?"

Sure enough, when my mother arrived, she hung on to her natural inclination that if you just worked at something enough, you will get the results you want. She waited until a quiet moment to give in to that Southern impulse to smile and get through it.

"Just give it another shot," she said.

"Mom, you sound like your mom," I said. I knew that

would sting, but I couldn't help myself. Like all mothers and daughters, especially strong-willed, dynamic ones, they, too, had a complicated relationship. "I know I'm breaking Nick's heart, my family's heart, hell, the world's heart."

"You *are* America's couple," she said. My mom said it like she was seeing everything in a different way than me. This wasn't just some feel-good celebrity ranking. It was that in many ways we belonged to the public. She is a smart businesswoman, and she knew more than I did how many people might turn on me.

"What is the point in being a power couple if we're faking it?" I said. "There's no real power in this anymore. Real power is in authenticity."

She nodded and took my hand. She loved Nick, but she supported me. At the Thanksgiving table, we all talked about what we were thankful for. When it was my turn I didn't immediately speak, and my mother started to talk to smooth it over. Silently, I thanked God for the strength He gave me to leave the life I'd planned to find the life waiting for me. *Thank you,* I thought, and still do. *Thank you, thank you, thank you.*

I HID IN WACO FOR SEVERAL DAYS, BUT PAPARAZZI AND REPORTERS FOUND me. My mom and I were on a walk, and they took pictures and asked questions like we were friends.

"Jessica, why did you leave Nick?" they asked as I turned to walk back to the house. I refused to answer.

I told my dad I didn't want to talk to the press at all. "I will not allow for anything to come from my mouth that is disparaging to Nick or my marriage," I said. "They will not get me on tape talking about it. That's it." I wasn't naive. I knew that I had opened my marriage up to the world as a fishbowl. People were going to be angry about me putting up a sign saying the exhibit was closed.

I returned to L.A. and stayed at my parents' house in Encino. I was a prisoner there, with helicopters circling. My sister, Ashlee, lived behind my parents at the time, and one morning I called her. I had this idea to army crawl up and over to her house to escape without being seen.

"Is that crazy?" I asked.

"Yes," she said, laughing. "You must."

"I wish we had walkie talkies," I said. "Okay, meet me out back."

Halfway across the yard, I heard a helicopter and stopped. I wondered if all this was worth it. I could have just stayed in the marriage, and at least I wouldn't be crawling through the dirt to my little sister's house.

"No, I've got this," I said aloud. I cleared the hill and saw the glass and concrete of her home. Ashlee was waiting for me at the back door, and she hugged me when I jumped up and ran in. She laughed when I realized I got the dust of the California valley all over myself.

"Can I borrow some clothes?" I asked.

We went upstairs, and we spent the day lying on the floor, our heads touching as we listened to music and talked. She would make amazing playlists, almost like medicine. "I think this song applies to your life right now," she'd say, my emotional deejay. It had been so long since we had hung out. I needed her strength as I mourned, and we became so much closer through my divorce. It took me losing a part of my life to appreciate a part of my life that always will be, my sister.

"You're going to be okay," she would say. "Just give it time."

But I had to work. On December 5, I was scheduled to perform at a Christmas gala at Cincinnati Music Hall, right in Nick's adopted hometown. A local billionaire named Carl Lindner was famous for his lavish holiday parties and had done a deal with my dad to pay me nearly a million dollars to sing for one night in the city where everyone loved Nick.

CaCee went with me, and I dressed all in black because I thought I needed to be somber for the crowd, who I was certain would hate me. Just before going on, I froze.

"I can't go out there," I said.

"Jessica—" said CaCee, starting with the big-sister tone. "Don't you be doing this here."

"I don't have anything to sing about," I said, hearing my introduction. "I can't sing love songs."

"Then sing about Christmas," she said, handing me the mic.

I walked on, hit my spotlight, and waited for the boos. They didn't come. It was just a quiet uncertainty. "I'm sorry," I said into the mic. I started to cry, and then walked off. CaCee stepped forward and grabbed my face with that U-shape of her hand.

"You get back out there."

"No one wants me without Nick."

"You were singing before you met Nick, Jessica," she said, physically turning me around to push me back onstage. "Remember that."

I think CaCee was afraid if I didn't get back out there and walk through the fear, I would never get on a stage again. I sang some of my songs, but then hit my stride with the Christmas songs. I wiped away tears during "What Child Is This?" thinking about all the times I sang that song in churches in Texas. When I got to "O Holy Night," I turned a corner in the concert and in my life. It was during that line I love, when Christ appears and the weary soul feels its worth. That thrill of hope.

I felt it. I looked out and saw that people were crying with me. I could do this life without Nick, because I would never be alone.

TWO WEEKS INTO DECEMBER, NICK STILL THOUGHT WE COULD HAVE OUR whole life back. I was afraid to see him, knowing his fear of change would make me relent. I thought that if I officially moved out, just took my journals and the clothes I wanted to keep, he would understand this was real.

It was my mother's idea that we would go to our house and move me out while he was away. Some boys' trip or event, I can't remember. The Simpsons were not good with conflict at that time. I admit it was rude, and CaCee told me as much. She was still close to Nick and saw him as a sort of sibling.

"I just think this is the wrong way to go about it," she said, over and over.

My mom had an empty party rental truck brought to the house because a U-Haul would be too obvious. I got about eight of my girlfriends together, and I went over with the intention of getting only the things that were sentimental to me.

I entered my own house, and it was more like a haunted mansion than ever. I didn't even want to turn too many lights on—I just wanted to get in and get out. Daisy came and greeted me, jumping up and down as I bent to kiss her.

"Daisy Mae," I said, scooping her up in my arms. Once we were inside, and my mom saw how little I wanted to take, she was shocked. She knew how hard I had worked in my life to afford some of these things, and she didn't want her baby taken advantage of.

She said, "Are you sure you don't want—"

"Mom, we are not shopping my house."

I didn't want any of it. I never wanted to see that couch again or the china we picked for our wedding. But there were some things she felt I had paid for, and I saw them carrying them out the door. I shook my head, but I was too mentally exhausted to fight. Even now, I sometimes think about some object and think, *Now, where did that go?* And I have to remind myself it was just another thing I let go of.

But there was something—someone—who was coming with me. At the door, I just couldn't put Daisy down. "Let's go," I whispered in her ear. I turned off the light, shut the door, and didn't look back.

Divorce is messy. I know he came home and was furious. Nick felt like he'd been robbed, and I know he told someone, "She even took my damn dog." I wish we were the kind of people who could divorce and stay friends. We weren't, and I regret that my actions hurt him.

Despite his anger, and maybe because of it, he was still intent on not letting me go. On December 15, I called Nick to tell him I was about to file for divorce and that he needed to sign the papers. The next afternoon, he drove over to my parents' house, where I was living. He came in, and we sat on the couch. He tried talking to my parents, getting them to rethink things, but I asked them to leave. This was my decision.

"It's not over," he said.

"It is over," I said. "You have the papers in front of you."

"I'm not signing them," he said. He promised that he would go to counseling now and sputtered about how he had the number of the best counselor in Los Angeles.

"You didn't go when we needed it."

"I'll go," he said. "I'll go now. I'll change."

"No, you won't," I said softly. I didn't want to hurt him more. He didn't like me, so I didn't understand what it was he was trying to save. "And I don't even want you to. Nick, I'm continuing to change, so *I* don't even know who you're gonna get. But it's not gonna be the girl I used to be."

He started to cry, and in that moment, I left my body for a second and just saw the scene. Nick in tears, and this girl keeping a poker face like a hostage eyeing the door. *Jessica, you should cry,* I told myself. I thought it would make him feel better. I couldn't. I'd been living with sadness so long that I was used to the feeling.

"Please don't leave me," he said, and I was back in my body, looking into his eyes. "I love you so much."

"Love is not enough," I said. "If love was enough, I would stay forever. But it isn't enough. We have to like each other. We have to be friends."

He walked out, and I slammed my fist against the couch. I had expected to be sad, and instead I was seized by anger. At Nick and at myself for not thinking I was worth doing this sooner. I'd thought my soul was held captive, and I had the key the whole time.

I filed that day, citing irreconcilable differences. Soon after, I moved from my parents' house to the first place I ever thought of as mine and home. The first time I saw it, I walked into a courtyard with flagstone terracing, and the house had ivy climbing the walls. "I feel like I'm in *Hansel and Gretel*," I said.

I was told by the realtor it was a "starter mansion," which made me laugh. To me, it was a storybook house, an enchanted cottage with a secret garden and a pond with lily pads. When I walked inside, it felt like a hug, and I let the house embrace me. I bought it on the spot. I finally had my own home, not anybody else's. I didn't have to share it with the world or camera crews, my parents or a man. It was mine.

It was in Beverly Hills, on Coldwater in a gated community. It felt safe, and it made sense that I was surrounded by high-profile single women who were also in transition and finding themselves. Nicole Kidman, Penelope Cruz, and Cameron Diaz. It made the gate a paparazzi resting place, but inside, we ladies of the canyon were free.

I had virtually no furniture, and in the beginning, I slept on a mattress on the floor. I was alone and wanted to keep it that way for a while. My first night there, I sat on the floor by one of the glass doors to the balcony overlooking the backyard. I looked out at the full moon while I sipped on white wine. Daisy was sleeping on the mattress, tired out from exploring our new place. Near me were a pile of my journals, and I pulled out the one I'd used to plan my wedding. I leafed through it, smiling at the hopeful twenty-one-year-old girl who was so excited to be engaged, already making notes about bridesmaid gifts.

The last pages from the journal, the beginning of my marriage, were blank. I'd stopped writing in that particular one because as soon as I got married, I was already different than the naive girl who took copious notes about cake testings and flower arrangements. I'd thought she was silly, and had blamed her for rushing to get married. Now my heart went out to her.

I grabbed a pen, and in words made swirly and flowery by wine and tears, I wrote on the very last page of that girl's journal:

"Old journal, new life," I wrote. "Married, divorced. Love, love lost. I'm lost, yes, but believe in this moment that I will be found. Found by me. I need to outgrow passing time pretending womanhood and actually find the woman waiting. Acknowledge that she resides deep in me, but I haven't met her. I move only by faith, and the strength You give me to introduce us. It's a full moon, and I forgive myself and the girl I was with this moonlight. I'm sad, but happy with the new day and the wonderful sun that will come."

It did.

Whatever you are going through, the sun will come.

part three

15

GOING OFF-SCRIPT

There was a time when I went out. A lot.

I was twenty-five, and I wanted to have fun. My girls and I would go to restaurants and clubs with my Ken, and I would insist on driving. I always loved having that feeling of control. At the bottom of my street, the paparazzi would be waiting, twelve cars deep, and the chase would begin. We had a new girl in the car with us once, and I wanted to get away from the pack. I knew a turn where I could gun it, then cut down another street that had a fork in the road. As I swerved, my new friend began screaming and didn't stop until I'd made the turn and lost them.

"Don't worry," I said calmly, as I slowed down and checked the rearview. "I had to take a stunt driving class for *Dukes*."

Photographers were not going to stop me from being free.

Their mission was to catch me on a date, and I was frankly on a mission to get one. I needed to see what kind of guys I actually liked. I never gave myself much of an opportunity before, and neither Nick nor I were waiting until the divorce was final to start our new lives. He and my father were haggling over money, and I couldn't wait forever.

I also had to give up on Johnny. I hadn't left Nick for anybody but me, so I didn't have the illusion that I could turn to Johnny and say, "Okay, now your turn." He needed time, and I didn't have time. I wanted to go have fun. But I was the same diehard romantic, reading his love letters through the whisky amber of the glass.

In one of his texts, he asked me how I did it.

"Did what?" I asked.

"Leave," he said back.

"You just have to do it," I said. He didn't, at least not for another year. But by then, it was too late for us. I finally let the idea of him go.

So I was free to date and explore, like some Jane Goodall studying the mating habits of Hollywood's celebrity bachelors. I would meet guys in clubs, or their people would call my people. Our shared fame would mean we couldn't be seen together, or we'd fall into the sausage grinder of the tabloid fame machine. We rented cars or met on private planes, probably loaned or rented to impress me, who knows. It was intensely glamorous and all completely secret.

And easy. There was a shorthand to dating while famous. If he was a star, he was not a stranger, because we already knew everything about each other. What landmines to avoid in conversation. You knew who had a rep for never settling down, who was on a rebound like me, and who was not getting anywhere near me because I just saw them with their wife in a magazine. I had a list of guys, and I checked every box. And all my girlfriends were jealous. They still are.

I may have approached my research like a dude, but I was still that girl from Texas who thought every kiss was the start of a love story. I realized this when CaCee and I were out for drinks with two girlfriends at Chateau Marmont. One of them had been on three dates with a guy and wondered if she was accidentally dating him.

"*Three?*" I said. "He's your boyfriend."

"Whoa, whoa," said CaCee. "Jess, no. Listen." She asked me if I remembered when I dated someone in January, naming a high-profile actor. She said "dated" like it was a joke.

"Yeah, of course," I said.

"Did you ever leave his house?"

"Well, no," I said. The girls all looked at each other and smirked. "What?"

"Dating is when someone takes you on a proper date," said one of my girls. "To, like, dinner. Or, like, outside. Where they can be seen with you."

"Jess," CaCee said. "You fall in love too easily."

"I fall in love too fast," I sang back to her, one of my favorite Chet Baker songs.

Guilty. I had no concept of what it was to date and get to know someone, no matter how casually I approached it. These cloak-and-dagger meetups were fun, but I wanted real. I dreamed of going to readings or museum trips to learn about each other through describing what you saw in the paintings. Or, you know, meeting at a bookstore, reaching for the same self-help book on codependency.

I said this to my girlfriends, and they rolled their eyes, knowing how much fun I was having with Hollywood's most eligible. Still, I prayed that God would send me someone who longed for love like I did.

I began spending more and more time with Ken, and in some ways, I had that fantasy relationship with him. I have a hard time being alone, and he was always willing to be around. We'd sit around my house and read poetry to each other. It was to inspire me as I wrote my next album, but also because it made us feel fancy. One day, I'd successfully avoided having paparazzi follow me, so I took advantage of the peace to drive to an out-of-the-way bookstore in Los Feliz, an arty neighborhood in Los Angeles. When I went to the front with my arms loaded with Lord Byron and Elizabeth Barrett Browning, the woman at the register kept looking at me. I had my glasses on, my hair pulled back with no makeup.

"Please don't take this personally," she said. "But you look like the smart version of Jessica Simpson."

I laughed out loud, and I think the poor girl realized who I was. "Thank you," I said, and went to the car. I smiled in the rearview.

"You're not so dumb," I said.

I AVOIDED ALL THE PRESS ABOUT NICK AND ME AND DID AS FEW INTER-views of my own as possible. I was still writing songs for my next album but was blocked every time I tried to write about my ex. I thought that maybe that was the answer: just write a fun album. It was around this time that I followed Charlie Walk, one of my early champions at Columbia, to Epic, where he was the new president.

CaCee, Ken, and I rented a house in Santa Fe while I filmed my next movie, *Employee of the Month*. I loved it there, and I felt like I had the space to get to know my new self. I realized that I'd wasted a lot of time avoiding acting on decisions because I feared regret. I was good enough to be my own friend, and a friend wouldn't let me do that anymore.

Reporters followed me to New Mexico, trying to get me to say something about Nick. *Take the high road,* I would tell myself over and over. And then the steamroller came behind me. On April 19, he released a tell-all interview with *Rolling Stone,* where he pretty much talked about me the whole time and apparently cried a bunch of times, too. I don't know, because by then I was back in L.A. and the article was kept from me. By then, we had also cut off all communication. I knew he was creating an ad campaign for his next album, *What's Left of Me,* around the divorce. As much as that hurt me, I still felt responsible for him in many ways. If this would help him heal—and make a living—give it to him.

As part of the divorce album rollout, three days later, MTV did a much-hyped prime-time airing of his documentary about the making of the album. The one he had the *Newlyweds* crew following him around for. It was a Saturday night, and, yes, I stayed home alone to watch it in bed. I didn't have my popcorn, but I did have my wine. I just wanted to know what he was going to reveal, and I also wanted to know what he thought of me now, because at that point I had no idea.

Well, I soon learned that he hated me. They showed him

playing a song for his dad called "I Can't Hate You Anymore," and he said, "Kind of sums it all up for me." *He didn't write that yesterday,* I thought. He wrote that while I was married to him. I had been right all along.

I watched him portray himself as a victim, casting me as this selfish person. He then mentioned that the door was still open for us to get back together. I kept pulling the blanket up over my face to hide because I felt so exposed. It was so disrespectful and dragged me back into his orbit when I was just starting to leave it. Look, I respect artists, and you can't stop them from drawing on their lives and saying what they want to say. But this was different. This was PR and spin. It felt like I was pulled back onto *Newlyweds*, only it was just him talking about me with faraway looks and dramatic pauses. He blamed opening our lives to cameras for ruining our marriage *to the same camera crew he'd then hired.* I even watched the *Making the Video* special that aired after and saw that he'd re-created our life for the video, casting his future wife Vanessa Minnillo to play me as this cold, unfeeling person. I knew he did this to hurt me.

It didn't make me cry, it made me mad. But he was breaking down in front of the world, and, again, I felt responsible. How many times are women made to feel responsible for the actions of men? I know now that I wasn't, but back then, it felt like I needed to fix him.

So I called him. And I asked to meet him at my house. I don't know what kind of rental-car or secret-driver agent tricks he pulled to fool the paparazzi and get through my gate, but he managed. He rang the bell, and out of reflex I hugged him. I meant it, too. Despite my anger, I missed him.

Nick brought his album to play for me, and I had to sit in my living room listening to his songs about me. He even sang along and would look at me for praise. Or glance at me when there was a particularly cruel line about me. I was numb, just blank. How do you react when you find out you have apparently hurt someone so deeply that they feel entitled to such actions? I felt manipulated into some revenge fantasy, but I had put myself in this situation.

I didn't know any other way to make it better, so I slept with him.

I know. I wish you were there to stop me, too. It was emotional, yet there was no connection. There is nothing more to say than this was the confirmation that this man was not my husband anymore.

He didn't stay the night. I was relieved because I could feel his hate. The whole situation was very dark. I didn't want the energy in my home. When he walked out the door, I knew I would never see him again.

I didn't call anybody afterward to tell them that I had let that happen. I was too ashamed. I had so much to step forward to in life, and I'd put myself back in the same old boots. Nick would always be one of the loves of my life, and he taught me how to love in that way, so I appreciated that. But I had to leave him in the past.

But to do that, I had to finalize the divorce. Nick and my dad continued to fight over how much money I had to give him. I finally asked my dad and my business manager what the sum was. They said Nick wanted a certain number, and honestly I don't remember what it was. If it sounds crazy that I can't remember, it was crazy to me that we had that kind of money to fight over after just three seasons of a show. We were both blessed by God, but Nick had a better lawyer.

"Just give it to him," I said. "You all gotta stop. Just give him the money. He deserves the money."

"No way, no how," said my father.

"Dad," I said. "This is for my freedom, and you can't put a price on that. Do it."

He relented and agreed to pay him the money just to be done.

"I'll make it back," I said. "I promise, I'll make it back."

And then I did. Give or take a billion.

16

PLAYING DRESS-UP

The fit models walked into the showroom one by one to line up in front of us. I looked over at my mom, and she was beaming. Next to her was Beth Pliler, my old dance teacher, whose smile widened with each model's step. Mom was the president and creative director of the Jessica Simpson Collection, while Beth was brand manager.

"The stitching on that one," I said, pointing at one shoe. "Let's make it—"

"Tonal," my mom and I said at the same time. We laughed. The Collection was a godsend for us. Starting a fashion line was my mother's dream, one she'd held on to since she was a little girl. My great-grandmother, who had a sixth sense, used to watch my mom cut paper dolls to dress them up in scraps of fabric. She gave my mom a Dearfoams slipper box to keep them in. "This is your dream box," she told her. "One day, you're gonna be a fashion designer."

"What's that?" she remembers asking.

She always styled me when I started out, and during *Newlyweds*, people would contact her to give me clothes to wear. Mom noticed that what I wore on the show would then sell out in stores. Since everyone was always asking my mom what I was wearing, she wanted to cut out the middleman. She told my dad to find someone willing to do a licensing deal so we could just make the clothes ourselves.

One thing that was important to us was that whatever we did had to be affordable. I had a shawl, a simple cream one, and girls constantly asked me where I got it. It was from Barney's, and I felt bad telling them that because the price tag was out of reach for a lot of my fans. I wanted to give them the feeling of luxury without having to spend a lot of money.

Dad put out feelers and approached Vince Camuto, who became our fairy godfather. He was a footwear legend who had created Nine West, then sold it for about $900 million. Vince was a suave but kind mastermind who first learned what women really wanted to wear when he was a poor Lower East Side kid who started out as a cobbler and then charmed his way to the floor of a store on Fifth Avenue, selling to rich New York City ladies. When my dad approached him, Vince was nearly seventy, and I think he was too busy working to know me from MTV. He asked his son John, who had seen me on *Newlyweds*, what he thought of me.

"I'd bank on her," John said. And my life changed.

It only took one dinner with Vince and his beautiful wife, Louise, for us all to click. I talked about my own passion for dressing girls going back to childhood, when I styled everyone for prom, and I would sometimes pick out clothes to buy myself because I knew it would also look cute on one of the girls in youth group. I'd lend them out, and it made me love the piece even more. With Vince, I was adamant that I make clothes that could appeal to all women. "Not everybody has the body of someone who lives in New York or Los Angeles," I said, and Vince smiled. "I want to sell to the average girl because I love that girl."

Vince had built an empire on footwear, but he didn't just want a shoe license with me. He saw the potential for a lifestyle empire. Vince paid me fifteen million for the master license, and people thought he was crazy. "Jessica really is America's sweetheart, and I think her fans will grow with her," he told *Women's Wear Daily* when we announced. "If this is not a one-billion-dollar or two-billion-dollar brand, I'll be shocked."

He built a seven-thousand-square-foot showroom for me in the Macy's flagship store in Herald Square in New York, and then went to Italy to find these gorgeous chandeliers and white marble fixtures to put in the showrooms in both Macy's and the Southern chain Dillard's. It was a sign to the customer, and to me, that this was a serious venture. My mom created an office for her and Beth right over the garage of her house. She was at it almost every day, creating the color palette and picking out materials and fabrics. Beth helped with logistics, and we gradually involved more family friends, still keeping the operation tight.

We started the line with shoes, specifically a high-heeled red cowboy boot that cost $69. With Vince, everything was for the love of shoes. We all wanted to make money, too—and we did right away, but Vince showed me how important it was to put your heart and soul in the sole of the shoe your customers are walking on. The cowboy boot sold out immediately, and we brought in $50 million in wholesale goods the first year alone.

As we expanded to denim and sportswear, then handbags, home, and accessories, my mom and I hired designers in every category. We would collaborate with them in an initial design meeting, suggest a color palette and styles that we thought should be part of the brand. The design team would then go do their magic and come back for a second "mid-design" meeting where we would see mock samples so we could make tweaks and changes. From there, we would have a "final design" meeting, where we see the finished samples that would be making their debut on the market. That's where we would pull the pieces that just didn't work and add finishing touches to the collection.

My mother could execute ideas like none other. She brought all the efficiency and penny-saving of a preacher's wife to her new calling. Then I would do eight- or ten-hour days at the showroom, either approving or tweaking the designs. I have an attention to detail that sometimes drives me crazy, but while being a perfectionist is hard, when it comes to design, it is so rewarding. If I asked for a change, I would remember it the next time I saw the piece. I think people were surprised by how involved I wanted to be. I trusted my mom with the keys completely, but I still liked to get in and drive every now and again.

Which is what I was doing that day in the showroom. One of the fit models was new, a cute girl with long brown hair, pulled back. She was willowy and graceful, and kept turning her heel to better show the shoe.

"Would you buy it?" I asked her.

She paused, her eyes widened. This happened with the new models every time. They were so used to being treated like mannequins by designers, so they didn't expect that I was genuinely interested in how they felt wearing the shoe or the accessory. The fit models make the rounds of all the showrooms, and they know the quality of other people's stuff. I want to know if they will wear the shoes. And can they actually walk in them?

"You're not hurting anybody's feelings," I said. "We're in these meetings to fix things. You'll still get paid if you hate the shoe."

"I like it," she said.

"But?"

"But I'm tall," she said.

Mom and I looked at each other and did a quick nod. I'm on the shorter side, so the higher the heel, the more confident I am. I tell people I live on stilts. But I needed to translate my preferences to make something for everyone.

"Maybe we should take the heel down an inch," my mom said.

"Half-inch?" I begged.

"Three-quarters," she said and laughed.

"That work?" I asked the model.

She smiled. "Yeah," she said. "Then I'd totally wear them."

I put my fists up in triumph. "Sold!" I said.

It was interesting to see my mom in action. This was her calling, something she could work on with me that didn't involve my dad. Until recently, my mom was very shy and always turned down magazine profiles and generally refused to walk red carpets with me. This was all hers. This was what they lived and breathed.

Fashion wasn't my dream, though of course it's been fun. My payoff was always making people feel beautiful and confident. That moment the model smiled. The bigger girls I'd meet who thanked me for not making plus-size looks that were only about covering up. Curves should be glorified. People think they need to hide a mom bod, but that body literally built life for someone else. I want all girls to put on my looks and have five people telling them they love their outfit.

It's why our fit models have a range of body types and why I never diet for my ad campaigns. If I am ten pounds heavier, then I am ten pounds heavier. Sure, it helps that I have control over the shot, and I get to choose the photographer, so there's trust. But once I was handed the reins of the Jessica Simpson Collection, I could just steer the business where my mom and I wanted us to go.

A lot of celebrities crash and burn with clothing lines, mainly because they let their pride get in the way. They either try to sell something that isn't like anything in their Dior-stuffed closet, so it is out of touch with what is truly wearable, or they try to do super high-end sample sizes at four hundred dollars each. I don't need the price tag on something with my name on it to be high just so I feel fancy. I might buy that stuff—like, a lot of that stuff—and I respect it. But I don't need to sell it. You have to let go of your ego in this business. I always say, "People can walk all over me as long as it's my logo on the bottom on the shoe."

Another reason I have succeeded when other celebrities

haven't is one small but very important decision I made when I signed: a noncompete clause. I didn't want Vince to be able to sign any other celebrities without asking me. I am not giving up my floor space in department stores so some pop star or reality TV person can launch a line.

The point is that you must take care of yourself, even when you are given an amazing opportunity. My mom could ace the bar exam if she took it tomorrow because she has read so many contracts. "I just google the words I don't know," she tells me. You need to nurture your dream the way you would a best friend or child, and you need someone you can trust on board with you. I am beyond grateful to my mom for all she put into this brand.

You've been listening to me talk, so I want to hear from you. Press pause for a second on your life and ask yourself, *What is my calling?* What makes you feel passionate? If you don't immediately have an answer, try broadening beyond something specific. My mom's was specific—fashion—but mine was more broad. I like making people feel good. Whether I am doing that through music, which came naturally to me, or through writing, which is harder on me but brings a different reward, I'm driven by the same impulse.

I think sometimes we get so caught up in the vessel of the work rather than what matters: the spirit that fills it.

WHILE I WAS IN THAT SHOWROOM, I HAD A SECRET. I AM SURE AS SOON AS I left, I texted him.

I first met John Mayer a year before at a February 2005 party Clive Davis threw during Grammy weekend. He ran up to me to tell me how much he loved the song I wrote, "With

You." We were on the same label then, Columbia, so he would randomly show up at events, like my album release party.

"What the eff is John Mayer doing here?" Nick asked me then.

"I didn't invite him," I said.

Nick didn't trust him, and he probably shouldn't have. John began to write me immediately, and I was flattered, but only interested in him as an artist. He was about two albums into his career, but everyone could tell he was a singular talent as a guitar player and songwriter. His notes quickly became more intimate, and he told me he saw something in me that no one else did. He asked why I would want to just be famous as a wife. He said I was so much more than what the world perceived me to be.

As soon as I was single, he made his move, and this time I was interested. In the summer of 2006, I was still dating, and using those "relationships" to figure out who I was. There were a few guys with big hearts and strong personalities, and I found myself changing to suit them. John wasn't having it and told me he wanted to have all of me or nothing. He assured me he didn't want to make me into anybody else. Early on, he wrote a song about me, and he made it so plain that I thought, *Oh, he does want me to be myself.* So I chose him.

CaCee felt uncomfortable with my decision to date John. I always saw CaCee as my friend first, but she was always very professional as well. John was a Columbia artist, and she knew John from even before he signed. She had already been put in the middle of the situation with Nick and she didn't want to go through that again. But CaCee was also uncomfortable with a lot of my decisions back then. She was worried in my rush to start my new life, I was losing the girl she had first met. She quit being my assistant, telling my father first and then offering to help train a replacement. I'd grown so dependent on her that it felt like she was leaving me. I felt abandoned. Our friendship was strained for quite some time.

John and I dated in secret for months, with dinners at my house and meetups in hotels. My security team would lead me through a back entrance of a SoHo hotel, then up a shabby service elevator. When he visited me, he would have his hood up, but he wasn't on the radar of any paparazzi. John was a night owl like me, both of us unable to turn our brains off. He said that I had kept him company in the middle of the night with my Proactiv informercials. In the beginning, there was a give and take. I saw him combing his hair and told him not to bother, that it looked better wild. Like a dark romantic hero. He would ask me for advice on outfits, and just seeing him wearing something I picked out made me feel proud. He saw me writing in my journal and left a note in there for me. "If I wrote you a note, would you read it?" it began, the sureness of his jagged handwriting so different than my whirls. I was in love.

It seemed mutual. Again and again he told me he was obsessed with me, sexually and emotionally. The connection was so strong that he made me feel seductive, and he spoke about sex and my body in a way that made me feel powerful, at least physically. His focus on me was the opposite of my marriage. I would get up to go to the bathroom, and John would ask, "Where are you going?" While I was married, my ex-husband couldn't be bothered to figure out what city I was in. It felt safe to be so desired. I knew John would never cheat on me, and that confidence was a new feeling for me.

Where I felt insecure in the beginning was that I always felt that I was falling short of the potential he saw in me. I constantly worried that I wasn't smart enough for him. He was so clever and treated conversation like a friendly competition that he had to win. He would get going, riffing from one subject to another so quickly that I would get lost. One minute he was explaining the start of his Rolex collection, and then another he was going on about a collector who he was jealous of, then the nature of jealousy, then the construct of time and the heft of it on your wrist . . . When I tried to leap back in and say something to add to the dialogue he was having with himself, he would challenge what I said, because that's how he saw the give and take of conversation. Sometimes he wouldn't let go of questioning why I thought a certain way until it had me second-guessing myself.

I'd get quiet, take another sip of alcohol, then another, and wonder why I couldn't just sit on a couch with him without getting so anxious. I even asked one of my girlfriends who knew him for advice just based on her *speaking* to him. It was the start of a bad habit: asking people who were not dating John how to date John.

"You have to be a strong person to make a contribution in the conversation," she said. "You can talk to him about anything because he just wants to learn about stuff. You don't have to just talk about what you think he wants to talk about."

So I spoke about what mattered most to me, and what I was most confident in: my faith. He found it fascinating but of course would challenge me on what I believed. I think he envied that steadfastness, because it was one of the few things in life he couldn't quite figure out.

But I could only do that so much. My anxiety would soon take over, and because I am such a sensual person, my solution was just to give him love. The mix of sex and love was the easy part, because I had plenty of both to give.

We were able to see each other in secret throughout the summer and the start of my campaign to promote my album *A Public Affair.* As opposed to Nick, I wrote a fun album, an eighties radio throwback that was an ode to freedom. Not one single song was about him, even though people assumed the cover I did of Patty Griffin's "Let Him Fly" was directed at him. It was my way of assuring myself that I needed to let go of Johnny Knoxville. I was proud that I had writing credits on ten out of the thirteen songs. The first single was "A Public Affair," and when it came out June 29, *Billboard* called the first single "a perfect record." It did fine numbers, but it was clear when I tried to promote the record that people weren't ready to see me so happy after my divorce.

The album came out August 26, a month before John's release of his album, *Continuum.* I got the highest first week sales of my career, but the numbers fell a lot immediately. That album was never going to do as well as *In This Skin.* Still, I was excited that John and I had albums coming out around the same time. We loved that we had this amazing secret we had kept.

And then we didn't have it. The week of my release someone from my team broke the story to the tabloids. Coming just a week after my album came out, it looked like a full-on, amateur stunt orchestrated to sell both our albums. I fired the person. John was worried he seemed in on it and felt that his artistic integrity was in jeopardy.

I was in New York, and he exploded on me, breaking up with me over email. On August 31, he posted the cover of Public Enemy's "Don't Believe the Hype" on his blog as his response to the media. I was humiliated and thought he was out of my life for good. He wasn't.

Still, I was trapped in the middle of promoting an album. I had hired a new PR agency and clicked with Lauren Auslander, who would later become one of my best friends. She was my age and understood what I was going through. I was lucky to have her with me in that tough time. The initial conversations with reporters were already a pretense to get to their "What about Nick?" questions, and now I had to play dumb when asked about John out of respect for him, too. I didn't lie, I just said he was a musician I truly respected and that I had known a few years. I left out that he had put me on a pedestal and kicked it over on his way out the door.

There was one bright spot: the breakup was right before the MTV Video Music Awards, and one day I was in a VMA swag suite at New York's Bryant Park Hotel. A swag suite is where they give celebrities things they didn't need so they will become walking advertisements for products. I won a silver 2007 Chrysler Crossfire luxury sports car, a two-seater paparazzi magnet. I wasn't really surprised, since of all the celebrities there, I was the one most likely to have a photo with a car featured in the tabloids.

Maybe because I was so depressed, I wanted to make something good happen. I had stayed in touch with the Casa Holgar Elim orphanage, which I'd first visited nine years before. With the money I'd made, I was able to help Mama Lupita make the place a comfortable home for the kids. Not just running water and electricity, but basketball courts and vans to take the kids to school. Doing my part helped me realize that I was blessed and reminded me that God had given me this grace. I didn't take it for granted.

It seemed ludicrous that I was getting a free car now. I also knew that the week before, Mama Lupita's van had broken down, and now she was using a beat-up old truck. I dutifully took photos with the car outside, giving the camera a look of shock as I held the key fob. When it was done, I motioned to the Chrysler rep as I took off my sunglasses.

"Um, is it okay if I swap this for a minivan instead?" I whispered.

She looked at my stomach. "Why would you need a minivan?"

"I'm not pregnant," I said, rolling my eyes. "It would just work better for me."

They gave me a white seven-passenger Chrysler Town & Country, which I later drove through the gates of the orphanage to hand the keys to Mama Lupita. The kids knew I was coming and had saved up money selling bracelets and necklaces so they could have a mariachi band greet me. Everyone was in clean red T-shirts, except for a few of the tinier girls, who had brightly colored dresses on. I lifted one girl when she hugged me, and we danced around to the music.

I was truly happy, and at least for that moment, no man could take that from me.

17

DESIRE AND POSSESSION

I had planned everything. The "I Belong to Me" video was going to be my way of introducing my fans to me as a grown, single woman. It's a ballad by Diane Warren, and there was a lot of pressure to make the video about Nick, but I resisted. Instead, I chose to show people my new life. I wanted the video to open with me on a mattress on the floor, just like I had had at my new house. Then I went to the mirror and cut my own hair, taking a cuticle scissors to give myself a jagged bob. When I washed the makeup off my face, so I could look myself, and my fans, in the eye, I cried real tears on that set, surprising everyone. I said good-bye to the old me, to the hopes I had for Nick, Johnny, and John, and just embraced Jessica.

I was very proud of it, but people weren't ready to hear "I

Belong to Me." They thought it should have been, "I Belong to *Nick*." I didn't anticipate so many people being mad at me, but my real fans stayed true, and could see my heart. I broke a blood vessel in my throat before a round of live morning shows, so I couldn't even count on my voice, but they got me through. "I'm sorry," I told them over and over again. I was apologizing about my voice, but so much more. I was so sorry that I had let them down.

It was bad timing for *A Public Affair*, an album I genuinely loved, so I relied on my girlfriends. At the end of September, my new assistant Adrienne and I planned a girls' trip to London to see my sister Ashlee in her West End debut in *Chicago*. Adrienne is good company, direct and funny, and basically took the job as a lark. She grew up with family money, so she wasn't impressed by any of the trappings of my life. We'd go shopping and she'd leave with more bags than me. Which takes doing, I'll tell you.

We had a few days to hang out in London before seeing Ashlee's debut, and we had the best time. When I was in L.A., even when I wasn't photographed, I was watched. There were still lots of paparazzi in London, but less people cared about taking note of what I was eating in a restaurant. The British public just let me be. Ashlee had only been in town about two weeks, but she already had this cute apartment and whole new life in London. She seemed so grown up, and I was again struck by how she always had the life that she wanted, and on her terms.

I know I irritated Adrienne because I kept finding ways to bring the conversation back to John. I kept seeing signs and spooky-spiritual things that would make me think of him. I would see a white feather and ask Adrienne what it meant. Oh, Lord.

We were at our hotel one day and I went out on the balcony to look down at the London streets. I saw someone staring up at me, but I was too high up to make out his face. His hair was wild and curly, like I pictured Romeo.

"Adrienne," I yelled. "Is John in London?"

"What?" she said. I didn't have to say Mayer. He was always John.

I turned inside to get her to look. "I swear I just saw him," I said.

"No way. You are crazy. Bonkers."

I looked down again and he was gone. I did feel crazy. I still hear myself now, too, and wonder if I imagined it. But John had a gift for showing up out of nowhere.

Sure enough, the next night we went to a small party with Ashlee, and John was there. I didn't have the nerve to ask him if he was outside my hotel, because I knew how it would sound. He came over and started riffing with me, and that's all it took. I was hooked again. That he even talked to me was a relief, and that he wanted to be with me that night felt like I was released from solitary.

It was on that trip that I felt the full intensity of his obsession with me. And it was a drug to me. He studied every inch of my body, every detail of my face. He photographed me constantly, to the point that I worried he was keeping souvenirs before dumping me again. He was only in London briefly, and when he flew out we stayed in touch. Our secret was safe again.

I was on a high from being with him when I went to see Ashlee onstage, and she was amazing. As soon as she made her entrance, I started crying with pride. Ashlee had become a pop star, but this felt like it was in her heart. I loved that little girl who sang her heart out to *Phantom of the Opera* and *Les Miz*, but now she was a woman playing London's West End. Someone I didn't know but wanted to get to know. I thought about all the times she had been my backup dancer, when I was too busy performing to look back and admire what a star she already was.

"You were shining even brighter than the lights on the stage," I told her backstage. She smiled and started to look away, but I wouldn't let her. "I always knew you were so talented, but to own that stage is such a gift. It was your stage tonight, Ash."

We looked at each other for a long beat, and so much that was unspoken was released. She started to tear up, this girl who was always so tough. Who'd protected me all those years even though she didn't realize she needed to. I started crying again, and then laughed at myself for being so sentimental. There's something wonderful about rediscovering each other as sisters, when you're in your twenties. You have more perspective. That night, I was able to let go of a lot of the guilt I had about her missing high school to join me on the road. She was living the artistic life she was destined to have.

Ashlee had to leave to do an on-camera interview with a U.K. show backstage, and they wanted me to join in. I looked at her, not wanting to steal her spotlight, but she nodded. My face was swollen from crying so much, but I didn't care. I wanted to make sure people knew how proud I was of her.

We started waving our fingers at our faces to dry the tears. We Simpson girls, always ready to be on.

IT WAS TWO MONTHS LATER, LATE NOVEMBER, AND JOHN HAD ALREADY broken up with me again at least once. Honestly, he did it so many times I lost track. Always in an email.

Sometimes it was out of the blue, other times I knew it was coming, because my light would start to go dim. John loved me when I was shining, and he drew strength and inspiration to write from that light. He would grill me about my life, asking me questions about the men I had been with and the choices I had made. When he tapped me dry, he looked at me like I was withholding something from him. He would tell me that my true self was so much greater than the person I was settling on being. Like there was some great woman inside of me waiting to come out, and I had to hurry up and find her because he wanted to love *that* woman, not me.

He'd dump me, then come back saying he had discovered he loved me after all. I always saw it as him mercifully taking me in from the cold. Every time John returned, I thought it was a continuation of a love story, while my friends saw a guy coming back for sex with some foolish girl.

One of those times, I wrote him a gushing letter thanking him for realizing I was worthy of love, and it breaks my heart to see how I practiced the wording in my journal: "I promise to be myself as I search to become the woman you already see."

I can't even believe the acrobatics of promising to remain true to your own self while becoming the person someone wants you to be. I had gone from trying to find that woman for me, and now I had to be that woman for John. Only he could deem when I had made it. He had that kind of hold on me.

He said a lot of our breakups were about me drinking and not being present for him, which was not, I would only find out much later, the full truth. But I took him at his word about his motivations, and that's why I always went back. It was my fault, and if he forgave me, that was all that mattered. Or at least he made me feel like everything was my fault. He has since admitted that he has abused the ability to express himself. I had always prided myself on being smarter than everyone thought I was. For a long time, he took that from me. He made me feel dumb. I stopped understanding what was real and what was in my head.

I was so afraid of disappointing him that I couldn't even text him without having someone check my grammar and spelling. This drove my mother nuts. "That is a terrible relationship," she said, "if you have to be scared you misspelled something."

Because we were so often long-distance, our relationship was often over text. I treated even the most basic texts from John as make-or-break riddles to solve. If he was annoyed with me, I would invest *hours* decoding a basic fact, trying to find the poetry so I could respond accordingly. Did it mean we were over? Was I supposed to stand up for myself? My anxiety would spike, and I would pour another drink. It was the start of me relying on alcohol to mask my nerves. After overanalyzing his text, I would write back paragraphs of tortured words, and hand it to Adrienne to proofread.

"Jess, you don't need to send all this," she said to me once when we were in a car heading to an appearance. "Don't."

"Then what should I say?"

She deleted the paragraphs I'd written, wrote one word in two seconds and handed it back to me.

I looked down. "Just say 'Sorry' "?

She nodded, and I sent it. Minutes later, I heard a ping and braced myself.

"Thank you," he wrote.

That was all he needed to hear. So, I took responsibility for my actions. But I also got to a point where I overintellectualized everything he said, because I felt I was not intellectual enough for him. All he really wanted was me to be myself. But I didn't know who that was for him, or for me at that point. Some of my friends say I can't blame him because I handed him this power.

I don't know. Did he repeatedly stab me in the heart, or did I just keep running into the knife he aimed at me?

18

THEY LET YOU DREAM JUST TO WATCH 'EM SHATTER

DECEMBER 2006

I was in my suite at the Mandarin Oriental hotel in Washington, DC, out of my gown after a State Department dinner hosted by Condoleezza Rice the night before the Kennedy Center Honors. Steven Spielberg, Andrew Lloyd Webber, and Smokey Robinson were among the honorees, and of course Dolly Parton. The next night, I would be onstage at the Kennedy Center, one of the lucky performers chosen to sing in tribute to Dolly.

She's my idol. The queen of one-liners, she's the deepest of people, but can find the light in anything to make that depth hilarious. *Steel Magnolias* is everything to me, and I knew her version of "I Will Always Love You" before I knew Whitney's. But I felt closest to her as a fan during my divorce, listening to her song "Little Sparrow" over and over. It's a song about the fragility of hope, and how it can be crushed by men. Her vocal on that is astonishing, and I bet she did it in one take.

The concert would be taped to air on CBS later in the month, and I got to sing "9 to 5." I thought I was ready, having rehearsed many times on-set in Shreveport, Louisiana, where I was shooting *Blonde Ambition*, a *Working Girl* redo with Luke Wilson. Between scenes, I wasted time in my trailer fighting with John on the phone or over email. He would accuse me of making a fight out of everything, but there were times he would bring up someone from my past just to have something to be jealous about. I stopped journaling, because my self-esteem was so low that I thought anything I wrote was stupid.

I lost focus on my work, which was obvious, at least to me if not everyone else, when the director's aunt, Penny Marshall, came to the set to do a cameo. It was a huge opportunity to impress a film legend. Penny Marshall had directed *Big* and *A League of Their Own*. Plus, her brother Garry had directed *Pretty Woman* and a million other romantic comedies. This was the family to impress, a chance to prove myself to someone with unbelievable connections in the industry. The old Jessica would have been right there, ready to be their Goldie Hawn or Bridget Bardot, whatever their scripts called for. Penny and I had one scene together, and I needed more than a few takes. I should have nailed it. I told everyone, including myself, that I was just intimidated, but really, I hadn't fully prepared. Still, I got by. No one ever said a word.

And now I was in DC, out of my gown and ready to check my email. My plan that night was to get to bed early, and instead I was soon on the floor, crying.

John had broken up with me via email, again. He'd followed it up by sending me a song. Aerosmith's "Angel," a twenty-year-old message in a bottle that I wasted near about the entire night trying to decode. It's about begging someone to save them with their love, which is exactly what I always wanted to do for John. It was so high school, I know, this notion that the secretly deep cheerleader was going to save the hot band geek from the path of destruction he had put himself on, but that was the kind of roles we played over and over in our relationship. It was the usual complicated word problems of dating John: If a tortured artist hurls a nasty email at 10 p.m. and then a love song at 11:20, are you up or down?

I called him, but he didn't answer. I was left to listen to that darn song over and over, when I should have been listening to "9 to 5."

I was a mess all the next day, and it's a blur now when I started drinking. I know I started backstage at the Kennedy Center. My mom had helped me into this *Breakfast at Tiffany's*–style black strapless cocktail dress with a diamond necklace. I looked the part of Jessica Simpson, but I just had to trust that she was gonna show up.

Shania Twain was there, warming up in the staircase behind the stage to get the reverb. She seemed nervous, which scared me because I admired her so much. There were so many greats walking around: Reba McEntire, Reese Witherspoon, Allison Krauss, and Vince Gill. And I kept going back to my dressing room, where the Macallan was.

"You need to not be drinking," my mom said.

"This doesn't make me drunk at all," I replied.

"Um, okay, whatever," she said. "But yes, it does."

Ken was trying to lift my spirits as I ran through the song, making up fake lines to be funny. I started repeating them, confused. My mom saw me take another drink.

"You need to put that down," she said. I had never gone onstage drunk before. My dad was anxious, but he didn't say anything. I think we all trusted that I would show up when I actually got onstage. The same way I'd always done my whole life.

Just before it was time to go on, John called me back. It was ugly.

"How could you do this to me?" I asked. "Why do I have to be thinking about you all of the time? If you are gonna let me go, *let me go!*"

I tilted my head back to keep my makeup dry. I think he hung up. He wouldn't talk to me if I was drunk. And I finally realized I was.

Reba kicked off the tribute, introducing a video she had narrated about Dolly's life. It opened with the first, haunting line of "Little Sparrow," and my entire body tensed. The video then showed her as a kid, singing her way onto radio shows and leaving for Nashville the morning after she graduated high school. I thought about my life, and what Dolly had done with the gifts God had given her. She'd written so many songs, and I was afraid now to even write in my journal. When they played a snippet of "I Will Always Love You," I lost it, heaving big hyperventilating sobs in a dress I wanted to burst out of, a necklace that seemed to choke me.

I began to pace around, and who knows how many people were staring at me. It came time for my part. Reese Witherspoon went out to introduce me, and of course she was perfect. The band started "9 to 5" and I waited for God to save me like He usually did. I'd get by.

I got through the first verse and chorus, and I was gone. I got lost and had no confidence to turn these lyrics into a song. I couldn't understand the melody, the phrasing, or the tempo. And I didn't know how to get back in.

I looked out at this bright room. I saw the President, all these dignitaries, and then Dolly. She looked so concerned. The band stopped, probably expecting me to start again, at least for the cameras.

"I'm so sorry," I said, to her and to everyone. "It's an honor to be here, but this song is too good for me. I'm so nervous."

I turned, and as I stepped, I started to hop to the wing, a childish move to pretend none of this had happened. I ran to my parents, who were in full panic mode. They kept repeating, "What are we gonna do?" They were still so used to thinking we would lose everything if I messed up.

George Stevens, the producer, sent someone to ask if I wanted a redo when the show was over. My parents said yes for me. In the dressing room, it was like someone had died. I kept staring at a printout of the lyrics, and they all blurred together.

The show over, there was a knock on the door. I assumed it was my cue, and stood up, ready to walk the plank.

It was Dolly. She was wearing a white gown that sparkled, her blonde hair falling around the rainbow medal on her chest. She looked like an angel.

"Now, I hear you're gonna sing that song again," she said.

"Before you do, I want you to know I wrote that damn song and I don't even remember the words."

It was a lifeline, her kindness and grace, in that moment. There are people whose cups run over—and yes, I worry I am risking a boob joke here when both Dolly and I are in the frame—but whose cups run over with love and grace. She is one of them. That she took the time to make me feel better on her special night will always mean the world to me.

I went back out to the stage, and the band was set. The audience had gone home, and it would just be us in the empty opera house. A producer told me they would dub in the applause later. I went out to the mic stand, and I looked out at the theater. With no audience, you could appreciate its beauty, like the red velvet lining of a jewel box. But there was no feeling. No warmth.

I had to sing to no one. Alone. I tried, but it was too sad. "I'm sorry," I said. "I can't."

I looked at the band, whose time I had wasted, and I wanted to disappear. I walked off the stage and looked back at the empty seats, and then into my dad's eyes. "I will never sing again," I said.

There was an afterparty, and I didn't want to go. I didn't think I deserved to. My parents made me. "This is disrespectful," my mom said. "You have to go."

I recently asked my mom why she was so intent on making me go to the party. "That was the thing that I had to do a lot that I hated," she said. "Making you do stuff. But it's business."

I'm glad I went. I avoided everyone, but I wanted to thank Dolly again. Reese stood by her, when she saw me, she said in a full southern drawl, "Oh, *honey.*"

Dolly asked how it went, and I shook my head.

"Don't you even worry," she said. She probably knew I'd pull a Cinderella and flee the ball right quick. She gave me her number. "If you need anything," she said. "*Anything.* You call me."

A photographer wanted a picture, and Dolly called a bunch of the girls together. She put her arm around me, and Shania put her hand on my shoulder as Reba hugged me from behind. Reese and Allison bookended all of us.

"Smile!" Dolly said. And I did. Because you do what Dolly Parton tells you to, even if it's hard.

That picture ran in a lot of places and for a long time I hated it. I hated that girl trying to smile in the center of these incredibly talented people. But now that I have learned to forgive myself, I see the bigger picture. I see four women and one fairy godmother supporting me solely because they knew I needed it. To Reba, Shania, Allison, Reese, and especially you, Dolly: Thank you.

I TOLD MY THERAPIST THIS STORY A FEW MONTHS BACK, ABOUT JOHN breaking up with me right before I went onstage.

"That's not love," she said. "You know that, right? I mean, he never loved you."

She said it so casually, like this was something I should have figured out a long time ago. I felt a dagger, right in my heart again. I was still protective of him.

"What do you mean, he never loved me?"

"He was obsessed with you," she said. "Love and obsession are so different. One is healthy, one is not."

I didn't know the difference then. Thank God I do now.

It wasn't long before he was back in my life. I flew out to New York City to be with him for a New Year's Eve party. We were in a good place, at least for us, and John seemed to welcome the press attention this time. Our rule was that we would never acknowledge in interviews that we were dating. We'd hide in plain sight.

He asked if I wanted to join him when his winter concert tour kicked off in Florida later in January and I dropped everything. From then on, I abandoned my life to be the girlfriend on the tour bus. It reminded me of when I was touring with 98 Degrees, and sometimes that felt right, and other times it brought back memories that made me uncomfortable. You create a family on the road, and there's a feeling of intimacy as you arrive at a new city at four in the morning. Though this time around our bed was at a Four Seasons. John was a superstar in music, respected by veteran performers as much as he was loved by his fans. People just loved to watch him play, and he brought an improvisational spark to all those years of preparation, playing guitar until his fingers bled.

I remember sitting alone at a soundcheck at Veterans Memorial Arena in Jacksonville, my feet up on the seats as he played guitar onstage. I'd worshipped Nick in concert halls, but Nick wasn't always happy when it was me on the stage. How would John react to me performing again? I was so intimidated by John professionally. John was this guitar god, truly one of the greatest in history. He would look at me during certain songs, always reworking the playlist depending on his mood. If I was in the crowd up front, security would take me back to his dressing room during the last song of the encore so I could be there waiting for John. I'd think of *Almost Famous* and sing "Tiny Dancer" to myself, the L.A. lady in love with a music man. The groupie with her own platinum album and the clothing business raking in hundreds of millions.

I would periodically take breaks to go back to do work in L.A. The paparazzi started taking pictures of John even when I wasn't around. In the beginning, he made a joke of it, putting an arm up to where my shoulders would be. Embracing my ghost as he walked. That's what they wanted, right? Me. He already had fame, but I was a paparazzi target. And he welcomed becoming collateral damage.

In early February, Ken and I dyed my hair brown. I did it because I was trying to be someone new. I was going through a more "artistic" phase, carrying around my Leica camera and becoming really passionate about photography. I was obsessed, spending at least thirty minutes on each picture, color-correcting and making certain aspects pop. When I mentioned my hobby in magazine interviews, it became a cue for the writer to sneer at me to the reader.

But John encouraged it. First, he bought me vintage books on photography and technical manuals, then he decided to get his own Leica and he became better at it than me. *Aw, damn,* I thought, *that was my thing.*

With my camera in hand, I realized the tour was an amazing opportunity for the Collection. I would be in the middle of the crowd, taking note of what everyone was wearing. I photographed what women looked and felt good in before it got filtered through some fashion magazine. I wanted to know what jeans women really wore on a date, and how high a crop top people really wanted. John loved clothes, so when we went shopping together, I would pull luxury items, like something from some Japanese designer he was suddenly crazy about and think how I could make that spirit translate to something more accessible to our buyers. I sent tons of photos back home to the Collection, and on a tour bus, I had nothing but time to create mood boards and tear inspiration from magazines. I still wasn't ready to go back to music. My acting career wasn't satisfying me either. I knew *Blonde Ambition* could have been a lot better and wasn't surprised when it later bombed.

Besides the Collection, my creative outlet was simply John, the two of us working at each other like puzzles, not sure if we were putting each other together or breaking us apart. We went to Sony's Grammy afterparty together, and I was so happy he posed for pictures with me, because Grammy night is like the prom in our industry. He was nominated for five awards and won two that night. He broke up with me that night at the Four Seasons in Beverly Hills. I can't even recall why. I just remember knocking on his hotel room door and begging until he finally took me back in the middle of the night.

From there I joined him on the road, Minneapolis and then Madison. That Wisconsin stop was Valentine's Day, but he told me he didn't believe in that stuff. Not for cool people. I watched him sing "I Don't Trust Myself (With Loving You)," a song about winning a lover's trust just so you can break her heart, and then do it all over again. It was his MO set to a gorgeous rhythm, as irresistible as him. I sighed, but I told myself being with him was enough.

The next day we were back on the bus, heading south to a February 16 show in Kentucky. Somewhere in Illinois John had an idea, and started calling around on his phone, talking quietly. He told the driver he needed to make a pit stop. He jumped out, yelling for me to come along. He took me to a Tiffany & Co. store. We went inside and he picked out a diamond necklace.

"I've always wanted the first diamond I gave a girl to be from Tiffany," he said, putting it around my neck.

I told myself this was our Valentine's Day. The following month he took me to Rome. We had a private tour of the Sistine Chapel, and as I looked up at God and Adam reaching for each other, I thought of how much Sarah would have loved this.

Afterward, we visited another church. Fendi. Oh, I'm just kidding, but we did go, and it did feel like a miracle, because when we walked in he said, "Pick anything you want." The extravagant gestures continued, and made my anxiety kick in. The higher he lifted me, the longer the fall would be when I disappointed him, and I knew I would. I was still self-medicating with drinking but doing it less so now that we were spending more time together.

I went along on his tour of Australia the following month. When he saw me start to drink, he stopped me.

"Don't drink," he said. "Try this pill. Just take this and it will take the edge off." It was a Xanax, and he was right. It softened the edges of my fear and anxiety enough that I could be normal and present. But it frightened me into the realization that I clearly had a problem. Not with drinking, but with whatever I was covering with the drinking. This Xanax was a quick fix, but for what? I didn't know, and I wasn't ready to face it.

In Adelaide, a girl working the concert leaned over to me and asked if I wanted a water. She was sweet, my height and age, with brown hair.

"When are we going to hear you sing again?" she said with that Australian accent.

I smiled. "Oh, soon," I lied, turning my face back to watch John onstage.

JOHN COLLECTED GUITARS AND HAD SO MANY THAT THERE WAS ALWAYS one in reach, the way an average person would be with a cell phone. Each had a story, like it was Eric Clapton's and, by the way, it was the one he used for "Layla." He would idly pick one up, play some gorgeous melody, and then look at me to join in. I would give a closemouthed smile. We did not have that spark to make music together, or maybe I resisted it. I know I had moved on from my ex-husband, but I still grieved singing with him. We were great together, where we were at our best. I wasn't ready to share that with another man, even one I was in love with.

And John knew. He hated that I couldn't let that part of Nick go. So, he presented me with an idea. He was obsessed with a song I wrote for *A Public Affair* called "Walkin' 'Round in a Circle." I'd used a sample of Fleetwood Mac's "Dreams," and that familiar tight rhythm allowed me to be a little looser with how I structured the song. I wrote it about the patterns I fall into, and how fear often keeps me stuck walking in a circle, where I can't tell the beginning from the end. Jimmy Jam and Terry Lewis produced the song, and John's idea was to redo it, make it less breathy and more direct, like my "With You" or his own music. As an artist, I knew he was right. It would be better that way.

"The song's a hit," he said. "I'll produce it. I'll release it."

"No," I told him. "I don't want people to be like, 'Oh, she's using John Mayer to better her career.'"

He told me I needed to stop caring so much about what people thought. I don't remember if he mentioned the idea to my father or if I did, but dad was cheering it on. "Yes, oh my God, he would be the best thing ever for your career."

But I didn't want my career to be about my relationship anymore. I had already broken my own heart with that approach.

John didn't listen to me, or maybe he mistook my growing resignation as a yes. He went ahead and booked a recording studio for the next time we were in New York City. Chad Franscoviak, his sound engineer and roommate, was there, always calm around the storm of John's energy and talking. Anybody would have taken advantage of this moment, and I didn't. So, I sabotaged myself. There was Pinot Grigio, and I began downing it.

"You don't need a drink," he said. "Just be yourself."

"You make me nervous," I said. "I have to get comfortable."

"Why do you need to drink to be comfortable?"

I busied myself with stalling tactics—lengthening my vocal exercises, "centering" myself, pouring another—until I had to get in front of the mic. The windowless studio seemed tighter, more like a prison cell than a place to create. John was on guitar. I don't know if the plan was for him to do backing vocals later or if it would be a duet. I just knew he had a vision for how I should sound, and I worried I wouldn't live up to that.

We started in. "Life is a curve ball, thrown with the wild arm, and if I'm gonna swing in, I must get motivated—"

I stopped, and said, "Sorry."

He said something encouraging, but all I heard was the critique, which is what a producer is supposed to do. He wasn't being out of line. But it brought back Nick producing for me in the studio. We started again, and we went on like that for a long time. If you told me it was thirty minutes or three hours, I would believe you either way.

"Just stuck in a dream, where the answer's clear," I sang. I'd written that song as a promise to myself to change my habits. Now it felt like I was narrating my current life with John. Caught in this cycle of make up-to-breakup and back again, no longer growing into myself. I got too in my head, wondering if this was God putting me in a position to sing the truth of my life. Or John. It occurred to me that I had always done well when I worked to be worthy of God's gifts, and I had spent a year trying to be worthy of John's love. Finally, it was as if my vocal cords became frozen. I couldn't sing.

"Why are you doing this to me?" I asked John. "I hate it."

"I'm trying to share this with you," he said.

"I can't share this with you," I said. "Singing together was what I did with Nick."

He looked down and sighed. I tried to continue. "I don't know what to do, I—"

I started to cry, feeling like a failure. Maybe I was. I ran. Literally ran out of the studio, taking huge gulps of night air when I got to the sidewalk. After the quiet of the sealed recording studio, New York felt loud. The sound of traffic moving and trucks turning was like the steady crash of waves, sirens here and there. A couple walked toward me and I coughed to put my head down and my hair in my face. I didn't want to be Jessica Simpson right then. I went to my hotel to hide.

I sat on the bed. I hadn't shown up in the studio—not for John, but for me. I didn't know why. I was starting to realize John was someone I could focus my anxiety upon. My pain walking around in skinny pants and a cool scarf. No, I'd let myself and my song down. It could have had a new life, and I let drinking get in the way. I let my fears get in the way. I used my drinking to cover my fears. I realized it in that moment, and I let it pass. Owning my faults is an easy thing for me. Learning from those realizations and breaking the cycle of making the same choices, that's the work.

John never discussed it. Not once. He broke up with me again soon after. I was twenty-six, the world at my fingertips, and I let the cycle continue through the summer. I took him as my date to the Met Gala, and then he broke up with me. At the Cannes film festival in May, I promoted my upcoming military comedy, then called *Major Movie Star*, but eventually released as *Private Valentine*. It was a princess moment, and maybe he saw the pictures of me at Cannes, because suddenly he was in love with me again. In Miami, I got to sit next to my mom as we showed at our first Mercedes Benz fashion week. I lost track of if we were back on or not then. Of even if we were ever really on at that point. I was having these incredible experiences, and I allowed him to steal my joy.

At the beginning of the fall, I was alone again. This time I was off the John merry-go-round long enough to catch my breath and stop being the ideal woman he had in his mind. I had room again to have a conversation with myself. *You're the only one who has the power to be the best you,* I thought. *Nobody else can do that for you.*

You may have had that lonely conversation with yourself by

now, but if you haven't, let me tell you. You can have people encourage you and talk to you all day long about your potential, but if you're not there, ready and willing to be that for yourself, you'll never be fulfilled. For me, I wouldn't know myself until I faced my fear of singing again. I had to walk through that fear. I needed to write again, get back in the studio, do what I loved. My first call was to my manager—my dad—and the next was to the friend I knew I couldn't do without.

CaCee picked up on the third ring, sounding concerned. I didn't blame her. She was now doing A&R at Sony, fulfilling the dream she started with in Teresa's office. I told her my plan before I lost my nerve. "So, will you do A&R on the record?" That was the Artists and Repertoire creative work of helping choose songs, just as her old boss Teresa had done for me in the beginning.

She was quiet on the other end, and finally said, "I don't know, Jess."

"What don't you know?"

"If it doesn't go well, you'll blame me," CaCee said.

"Well, I'm pretty sure it's not gonna go well," I joked, "so let's just do it. At least I'll have my best friend."

"Okay," she said.

"I love you," I said. I hung up, thrilled.

Now I had to do it.

19

RETURN OF THE SOUTHERN GIRL

We drove through a nondescript neighborhood of Nashville, convinced we had our directions wrong. But we kept going, making one turn, then another until we got to the address. Finally, we arrived at a corner lot surrounded by politely low stucco walls.

CaCee pressed the button at a low-key gate. A pleasant voice answered.

"Good morning," CaCee said. "We have an appointment with Dolly."

The doors opened, and once we saw the building it all made sense. There was a beautiful stucco-and-timber compound with red tiles, and at its center, there was a mission-style chapel right out of an Old West movie. It even had a little dome with a bell inside and a cross on top. This, of course, was Dolly Parton's office and rehearsal studio.

Dolly and her kindness were the inspiration for me to come to Nashville to do a country album. As soon as CaCee, my assistant Adrienne, and I got settled in our rental house, one of CaCee's first suggestions was that I call Dolly about the possibility of working together. I was afraid to call the number Dolly gave me after the Kennedy Center, so I made CaCee call Dolly's manager, Danny Nozell, who was so lovely to her. Dolly called me right away and told me to come on in. She did her business work between four a.m. and ten a.m. At seven o'clock, we were her second meeting of the day.

"Jess, are you shaking?" CaCee asked me.

"I'm just nervous is all," I said.

As soon as we walked in, there she was yelling, "Hey!" She hugged me like we were reuniting after a long absence. There are people who embrace themselves so fully and live so authentically that you feel like you grew up with them. That's Dolly.

She immediately started showing us around, and the first stop was the chapel, a tiny little candlelit place that reminds you of those rooms tucked away in hospitals for prayer or quiet reflection. A place where anybody can come and feel at home, no matter what you believe in. She lit a candle for us, and we all prayed together. Dolly put me at such ease.

From there she took my hand to lead me to her office. She sat behind a desk and CaCee and I sat on pretty chairs. She put her hands together and looked at us. This was Dolly the businesswoman. My heart swelled, and I thought, *This is how you build a career like hers.*

I talked about my goals for the album, and she nodded.

How I wanted to get back to singing from the heart, not to sing to sell records but to make people feel. I was aware that I was a pop star coming to the country world, and I wanted to be respectful of that. I said that it would be an honor to write with her.

"Yeah, I'd love to," she said, "but I'd like to send you some songs, too, that I think you might like."

"Please!" I said. "That would be amazing." I couldn't imagine being so talented that you had good songs that you hadn't gotten around to recording yet. But this was the woman who wrote "Jolene" and "I Will Always Love You" on the very same day, so it made sense. We went into her rehearsal space, and she played us songs to get a feel for what I could do. CaCee and I sat on a beat-up leather couch, luxuriating in her voice as she worked to get the songs right. When it was over, she gave me a bunch of demos to bring home. And a big hug to keep with me.

"I'm glad you're doing this," she said. "You are just so sweet and precious."

I put my hand on my heart and teared up. When the door closed behind us, CaCee and I looked at each other like we'd seen heaven. We were still shaking our heads when we got in the car.

"It is so powerful for your idols to actually be who you thought they were," I said. "I can't believe she even met with me."

"Of course she did, Jess," CaCee said. "She loves you. People like Dolly Parton or Willie Nelson, they don't need a single thing from you. They're nice to you because they want to be."

"I don't know why, though," I said.

CaCee looked at me a long time. "You're just a beat-up little bird, aren't you?"

I nodded, and we drove back to our home away from home. That night I was still flying from my time with Dolly. I didn't know what awaited me in Nashville. The tabloids were already sneering about me going country like it was a gimmick, but so far everyone I'd met in town had been kind to the new kid.

The new kid. I had been that so many times when my family moved around, and that's why I always sat with the lonely kids at lunch. I knew what it was like. CaCee was right: Dolly and Willie were so kind because they didn't need anything material from anybody. They had it to give, and they'd sit with me.

I WAS IN NASHVILLE AT A TIME THAT IT FELT LIKE IF I RAISED MY HEAD TO DO anything in the public eye, someone had a peashooter pointed at me. I had started dating a nice, normal guy, Tony Romo, the quarterback for the Dallas Cowboys, around Thanksgiving, and even that was something for people to pick apart.

Tony had seen my dad out a lot for about a year and had asked to be introduced. I always told my dad no, that I wasn't interested in athletes. "I'm a musician girl," I said. I believed that I could only date people who could relate to me because they were in the business. Which I guess was my code for, "I like emotional torture and fixing dark people." But I was watching ESPN one day at my parents' house, vegging on the couch, and they did a little interview with Tony. They asked him something like, "Who's your dream girl?"

He answered, without a beat, "Jessica Simpson."

My dad laughed. "Told ya," he said.

I thought about it for a minute. I liked his smile, and he

seemed nice. What if I went off script and took a break from the dark and twisted?

"Dad, call him," I said. "Tell him I'll see him."

We met in secret and hit it off. A few days later, our families both watched him win a Thanksgiving Day home game, then all had dinner together at our hotel restaurant. He sat next to me, and near the end of dinner, he started giving me puppy dog eyes, kind of leaning in like he was willing his lips to mine.

"Are you seriously trying to have our first kiss in front of all these people?" I asked.

"Maybe," he said.

Is this what real dating was? You simply went for it? "Well, try it," I said, to him *and* to me.

We had a very chaste kiss and it felt right. We went public quickly, which was also new for me. It was easy. He had no interest in drama. He said the Lord's Prayer every night before bed. A solid person who was the kind of guy that, as a kid, I imagined marrying.

Because we were so public from the beginning, I was very proud when he invited me to the December 16 home game against the Philadelphia Eagles. It was a Sunday, and close to a hundred thousand of football's true believers all filed into the sacred church of Texas Stadium for the 4:15 game. The biggest thrill for me was that I got to bring my grandparents to sit with me. Nana and Papaw kept looking around, amazed at it all.

The Cowboys had a 12-2 record but had just had a lousy game the week prior. This was a chance for redemption. I proudly wore a pink version of Tony's jersey with his number nine on the front, and there I was, cheering on my guy. *Annnd* he proceeded to play the worst game of his career. It was bad from the start, and when the camera showed me huge up there on the screen, people found the reason. Why was this guy, who just signed a six-year, 67.5-million-dollar deal, playing so poorly? It must be the blonde in the bleachers.

"Send Jessica home!" the chant began. "Send Jessica home!" I couldn't quite make it out at first, because it didn't occur to me that anybody would be giving me a role in how the Cowboys were playing. If I didn't hit a note at a concert, the audience wouldn't start screaming at Tony to get the heck out of the arena. My Nana and Papaw understood what was happening, some protective instinct kicking in as their beloved Cowboys booed their granddaughter.

"Don't you listen to them," Nana said. I became mortified that this was happening in front of them.

Can I just tell you how much I knew about football? What it's like to be a coach's granddaughter growing up in Texas? When there were four minutes and nineteen seconds left in the game, Eagles running back Brian Westbrook got the ball and gained twenty-four yards before suddenly taking a knee just inside the one-yard line; everyone around me thought he was hurt. Did I? Nope, I knew what he was up to. Dallas had no more time-outs. If he actually scored the touchdown, we might get the ball back, and if we got the ball back, we might at least go out fighting. No, he wanted us to suffer. He took a knee three more times, letting the clock bleed out. It was insult added to injury, a humiliating 10–6 loss.

And, somehow, it was my fault.

"Jinx" was the word everyone used. The media was cruel, and even Tony's teammate Terrell Owens talked about me to the press. "Right now, Jessica Simpson is not a fan favorite," he said, "in this locker room or in Texas Stadium." He also helpfully added that the last time Tony played close to this bad was the year before, when he had dated Carrie Underwood. T.O. later apologized and I held no grudge, but people had a new villain. They printed huge photos of me and made giant popsicle sticks of my head to taunt Tony with at every single game. People dressed like me and acted stupid in the crowd. I didn't want that kind of power. I found myself having to assure people that I wanted the Cowboys to win.

Perhaps sensing I was vulnerable, John inserted himself into the national conversation about me, because why not? He posted an open letter to Cowboy fans on his blog, telling them "That girl loves Texas more than you know. It's one of her most defining traits as a person. So please don't try and take that away from her." When Lauren, my publicist, called to tell me what he did, I threw the phone on the couch like it was the boogeyman.

I figured Tony would get sick of people calling me a jinx and tell them to knock it off. He was constantly interviewed on the sidelines or at postgame press conferences. He could just look the camera in the eye and tell people that he was responsible for his performance, and to leave his girlfriend alone.

I waited.

UNWELCOME AT MY BOYFRIEND'S GAMES, I WAS FREE TO FOCUS ON MY work in Nashville and see him when we both were off. It was what I needed. I got to work with the best people, including my producers Brett James, who wrote Carrie Underwood's "Jesus, Take the Wheel," and John Shanks, who'd worked with Stevie Nicks, Bonnie Raitt, Kelly Clarkson, and a cool girl named Ashlee Simpson. At my writing sessions, I would bring my notes from journals and even old emails from snuffed-out flames. Like Dolly had, musicians and songwriters in Nashville accepted me, making me feel like I belonged. I loved hearing about their journeys, how they would just write a song and then bring it to the famous Bluebird Cafe to test it out for an audience.

Artistically, that winter was a magical time for me, but it was extremely taxing emotionally. It helped that I was in a good relationship with Tony, despite the apparent football jinx, which allowed me to write happy songs like "Come on Over" and "You're My Sunday." But there was also a reckoning with my weaknesses and the pain I'd experienced. The daily writing sessions were like therapy, tearful and raw. Doing songwriting, I felt nekkid in front of fluorescent lights. Adrienne and CaCee would come and get me, and I'd get in the car all talked out. At the house, I wouldn't even take off my heavy ski jacket. I marched into the kitchen, pulled down a bottle, usually Ketel One, and sat at a little desk. Night after night, I sat at my laptop, going down Google rabbit holes or Skyping with Tony. I kept the bottle next to me, drinking until I'd take the edge off all those bubbling emotions and kept going until I couldn't even feel the smoothness of simple thought. I was just a body, needing to rest until my brain kicked in again for the next writing session.

CaCee had never seen me like this, and Adrienne didn't want to play nursemaid. It was scary. They started marking the liquor bottles to keep track of my drinking. This went on for some time, until Adrienne confronted me. I closed the door on her, and later I let her think I was too drunk to remember that she said I needed to stop drinking so much. But I remembered. It was only recently, when we talked about that time in Nashville, that I told her I could recall everything she had said. A lot of people, even when they're out of control, have an ability to control others. Your anxiety and your addiction team up like viruses that need to grow in the host body. You train other people to work around them, to keep their peace.

I told myself that this was an extreme time, and sure enough, once I was done songwriting, I didn't need that crutch of alcohol so much. There was something about getting close to all that truth that my mind couldn't handle. It was another early warning sign of what would come, but again I ignored it.

By the time I got to the recording sessions, I had worked through so much that it was the most comfortable I'd ever felt singing in a studio. I did three songs the very first day, and when we did that last cut, I thanked myself for walking through the fear. I cowrote all but three of the songs on the album and decided on Dolly's song late in the game. It was called "Do You Know" and I loved it so much I wanted it to be the title of the whole album. It was one of the last I recorded and I sent the finished version over to get her blessing. I wasn't about to mess up a Dolly song.

She loved it so much she asked if I would be interested in doing it as a duet. "I think our voices would sound good together."

"*Yes*," was my answer. If I did nothing else with my career, Dolly Parton wanted to sing with me. One of the many benefits of the Jessica Simpson Collection taking off was that I could make the music I wanted. I no longer needed a label to dictate my every move. I could offer it to people, and if it provided a soundtrack to one of their decisions or put words to something they couldn't quite get ahold of, that's why I did it. I did it for me, and I did it for them.

When *Do You Know* came out in September, it hit number one on *Billboard*'s country chart. I went just about everywhere to promote the album, and it was nice to be able to be less guarded with the press. I had a simple life with a nice guy, and if people asked about my marriage or John, I could easily side-step the questions.

I didn't have to do much to promote *Major Movie Star*, which went almost straight to DVD as *Private Valentine*. Before it came out, I held a special screening of the film and a concert for troops stationed at Camp Buehring, an Army base in the northwestern desert of Kuwait. It was about twenty-five miles from the Iraqi border, a stopping point for many troops on the way to their deployment. A threshold between their life at home and a life at war in the desert.

I embraced my fear this time and made it less about my experience, and more about understanding what these men and women were facing. That night I slept in the barracks with my little angel figurine to watch me.

"See, Jess?" I said aloud to myself. "You're growing up."

IN NOVEMBER, TONY BOUGHT A HOUSE NEAR TEXAS STADIUM, SO I BEGAN to spend more time there when I wasn't working. I would stay with him for a few days, and then go back out on the road for an event or to work on the Jessica Simpson Collection. When I started talking about Dallas as my home base, my friends didn't understand it, but I was trying out normal life with a truly committed relationship. If John texted or emailed, I would hold up my phone and tell Tony immediately. He knew the hold John had over me, and it was like telling your sponsor when you're triggered. He'd seen how I reacted when John randomly showed up at my parents' Halloween party in Encino. I had no idea he was coming and was shocked. I had gone full-out, dressed as Chewbacca from *Star Wars*, fur all over my face. I was having a good time, safe with my family, and then there he was. My heart was in my chest, and I turned around— trying to blend into the crowd, a five-foot-three girl *dressed as Chewbacca*. Not how you want to run into your ex with your current boyfriend standing right there. John routinely used his friendship with Ashlee's then husband, Pete Wentz from Fall Out Boy, as an excuse to stay in the Simpson family orbit. My parents knew what he had done to me, but John was always so charming. They also knew that I still loved John, and before I got married to Tony, I needed to either have closure or go back at it again.

Tony wouldn't come out and admit it, but I know he worried I would leave him. One of the few parameters he put on the relationship was actually a big one: He didn't want me to do any movies that required an on-camera kiss, which basically ruled out any romantic comedy, the type of movie for which I was most likely to be cast. I get it, some people can't handle another person making out with their girlfriend—even for work—but there were only so many plucky fish-out-of-water stories with no male romantic leads. I think it was more about how he would be perceived, than the love scene actually happening. What would people think of *him* for allowing that to happen?

He was less vocal about his real fear that, given my past

and my proven ability to fall in love on a film set, I would do it again. I didn't have a good defense for that, I'll admit. "Your honor, the prosecution would like to invite the following actors to the stand . . ." But I would never have done that to Tony.

When my friends came to Dallas to visit, I would get them rooms at the Four Seasons or Hotel ZaZa. They wondered why they couldn't stay at Tony's, since his home had six bedrooms. But I was basically living in a frat house. He had his high school buddies there, always on the couch eating pizza. I remember the moment I realized they were all playing the Madden NFL video game and Tony was playing himself. It was just so bizarre.

Decorating was also not his thing, and I wasn't interested in overstepping and didn't have time to anyway. For a long time, he had garbage bags up on the windows instead of blinds. It wasn't that he was cheap, it never occurred to him to bother. He would have $350,000 checks as bookmarks next to the toilet, leaving them uncashed.

But I liked the easiness of Dallas, where I rarely saw paparazzi. I spent a lot of time with my old Sunday school teacher, Carol Vanderslice. She was as nonjudgmental as she was back before all the fame, and we fell back into the rhythm of me being able to confide concerns and hear back solid advice founded in a practical faith. She was one of the only people who knew how hurt I was that Tony refused to stick up for me. I'd taken to wearing a blue jersey on game days and told everyone it was that pink jersey that was cursed, not me. Things started to get better, but still when I went to the games, I would be so tense and twisted up watching from the box that the next day I would be sore.

In so many ways, we were supportive of each other, and

it turned out that it was easier when you didn't do the same thing. He loved my music, and when we'd go out on the boat I bought him, he would play my album so loud you could hear it across the lake. Then he'd sing along at the top of his lungs. If he had the guys from the team over, he would put on my music and I would jokingly hide as he rewound to certain parts. He'd say to them, "Did you hear how long she held that note?"

This was the kind of encouragement I was getting from the country community. I was really touched when Rascal Flatts asked me to take over for Taylor Swift as the opening act on the twenty-city leg of their "Bob that Head" tour starting in mid-January 2009. Joining them would be such a big deal for me. It was set to start just before I had a gig at a country radio festival on January 25 in South Florida. Alan Jackson would be there, along with Jason Aldean and Little Big Town—great exposure for me with the country audience.

It was an annual event, I was told. Something about a chili cookoff . . .

20

DEATH BY
MOM JEANS

I swear, I thought I looked beautiful. Maybe that's what hurts—
and still hurts—the most. That I had no idea I was about to
become a global joke. I was still flying from how well the tour
with Rascal Flatts had started the night before. I had forgotten
how much I loved to tour, to get up and sing in front of fifteen to twenty thousand people. We had sellout crowds, with
our grosses competing with the only other acts that were drawing those numbers, established bands like Fleetwood Mac, Van
Morrison, and Billy Joel touring with Elton John. I was so ap-
preciative of the Flatts for the opportunity, but I was also, for
the first time in, well, my life, content to be in that "now." I
had a cherry-red journal for the tour, and the first pages are

filled with joy and a sense of relief that I had regained my self-confidence.

"I just feel as if I am right where I am supposed to be," I wrote in South Carolina on my fifth night of the tour. "The best part about the certainty of this happiness is taking a bit of pride in knowing that I am starting to own my authentic self and trusting my faith to guide my travels. We beat ourselves up too much. We have nothing to prove to anyone, not even ourselves."

Oh, sweet girl. What I would give to hug you.

It seems ridiculous now, and over the years I've spun the story of the incident as I retell it for maximum laughs. "Of course it was a chili cookoff," I joke, anything to hide the humiliation I truly felt. "You can't get a better headline." My kids' generation will read that once upon a time Jessica Simpson wore a sleeveless black bodysuit top, high-waisted blue jeans, and a Fendi leopard-print belt onstage at an outdoor afternoon concert in Pembroke Pines, Florida, and they will have no clue how that could have started a decade-long international discussion about my body. Or why the media ran stills and slow-mos of me smiling onstage and twirling, images examined like film footage of the Kennedy assassination. On TV and in magazines, pundits would be asked to guess my weight and size, then in the same exact segment or article talk about what a shame it was that I was being so bullied. "Can't"—*kick!*—"this girl"—*punch!*—"catch a break?"

But let's go back to the before and just be with that happy girl for a minute.

"Should we tack down the pocket?" This was my childhood friend Stephanie, who was helping style me for the tour.

We were backstage at the concert, and I was about to go on in front of thirty thousand people. Stitching it down quickly would make sure there was no bunching.

"Nah," I said, looking in the mirror. "I might want to work the pocket." I was having such a good time touring that I liked the spontaneity of digging my hand in my pocket to brace myself for a high note. The choreography was looser than the second-by-second scripted movements of a pop concert. "Kick, ball change, look serious as the firework effect hits stage right, now smile for a JumboTron close-up . . ." It was so freeing to move how the music wanted me to. Stephanie had a plaid button-down ready if I wanted to do an open-shirt thing, but I said no. My hair was big and southern with dangly double-hoop gold earrings. I did one last look in the mirror and loved what I saw.

I bounded out to the crowd, who received me with so much love that it just made me even happier. I did an hourlong set and got conversational as I introduced the songs, playing some old hits and the new country songs. Before "You're My Sunday," I talked about Tony, who I was getting on a plane to Dallas to see that night. "I'm so happy!" I told the audience, meaning it.

I got offstage and did a meet and greet in a tent in the back of the park. Twenty-five fans won the 99.9 Kiss Country radio contest to meet me, and I made my way over grass in my Alexander McQueen platform pumps. I posed for tons of photos, and almost every person got around to saying that they were glad I was so happy. They knew I hadn't been, and we shared that moment of grace, being together in a good place.

The first photos were up on the internet late that afternoon and were everywhere by the time I was back in Dallas. They were mostly taken from below, and there just were so many of them. As if whoever was choosing couldn't pick a favorite and just said to the American public: "Here! Enjoy!" The equivalent of your frenemy tagging unflattering photos of you on Facebook, only times a million. Bloggers and commenters started in with "Jess got fat!" jokes right away, then mainstream sites picked up the story with headlines about my "new body" and "showing off my curves."

It was awful, but the worst part was this: my very first thought was not my pain at becoming a joke and everyone laughing at me. No, it was, "Oh no, I feel so bad that Tony has to be with the fat girl." What was he going to do when he saw this? Was he going to break up with me? Did he feel that way about my body and just didn't know how to tell me?

He didn't. He loved me for me, and he also thought the whole thing was ludicrous. But I was devastated and confused. I had been really feeling it that day onstage, comfortable after such great gigs on the road with the Flatts, finally back in my element. I think that's part of why people made so much of those photos. I looked like the girl invited to the dance as a joke, fooled into thinking everyone wanted her there. "Doesn't she know? How is she the last to know?" I was Carrie at prom, right before the pig blood fell.

Magazines and websites ran side-by-sides of me in a bikini as Daisy Duke and in the jeans. It was funny—whenever I saw those bikini pictures, I saw Daisy. I didn't see Jessica. And then there were these new pictures that didn't have much to do with me either. Wonder Woman herself, Lynda Carter, had tried to warn me of this very thing all those years ago. I remembered her words. "People are gonna want you to be in those Daisy

Duke shorts the rest of your life," she'd said. She knew what it was like to be frozen in the amber of pop culture minds. I didn't realize how right she would be. I had created a gold-standard Jessica, the "before" for every "Is she fat or is she thin?" story for the rest of my career.

I had always been in on the joke, and that gave me power. Now that it was everybody else making it, I didn't think it was funny. I was insulted for myself and all women. Here's the thing: women are beautiful at any size. I believed that, and still I had dieted for years, taken who knows how many diet pills. I did that because I thought that's what it took to be a success in the music industry and in Hollywood, but I didn't want anyone else to hold themselves to that impossible standard. I wish I hadn't.

So I wouldn't tell anyone that the jeans were a size 25 waist, which is an American 4. I wouldn't go on to talk shows to say I was about 120 pounds when those photos were taken. The media guesstimated much higher numbers. The fact that I was that skinny and that I was deemed overweight still frightens me. No way was I going to go out there and turn on my sisters by saying, "Oh, no, you're mistaken. It was the angle and the fit. I'm actually a size four." What would that do to my young fans, who may have been a size bigger or twenty sizes bigger? My publicist Lauren got so many requests for photo shoots and sit-down interviews to "set the record straight." It seemed like negotiating with a hostage taker. If I disavowed having a regular body, nobody would get hurt. Except everybody would get hurt. We refused the requests, unwilling to play into the game of shaming women.

The story just kept going. The *New York Post* gave me a

new nickname, "Jumbo Jessica," and the media declared that I was a cautionary tale about "mom jeans." There were fashion pages about how to avoid looking like me. Page Six, the gossip column everybody in media read, ran a cartoon of me with my features ballooned to represent every cruel stereotype of a person of size. It showed me dumping Tony to be with my true love, Ronald McDonald.

That caricature became how I saw myself. Even as I tried to remain body positive about everybody else, a dysmorphia set in. I no longer trusted the mirror. With every reflection, every single pane of glass I passed, I took myself in quickly to try to catch myself, to see what the world apparently saw. The worst part was that I had to get up in front of thousands of people in Charlottesville four days later for another tour stop. My confidence was gone, and Stephanie and I rethought my entire wardrobe. What could invite people to make fun of me? I instinctively added a black vest, just like my days of performing at church camps as a kid, when my body was continually scrutinized for the potential incitement of sin. The rest of the tour, instead of enjoying the sold-out audiences, I was conscious of people taking pictures. Reporters eyeing me, taking notes. What were they seeing that I didn't? It made me shrink onstage.

My mother worried about me, knowing my self-confidence had been taken away. She saw me withdrawing, not fully present. I was the same girl who had refused to go to school because the cheerleaders were cruel to her. Now, instead of graffitiing our house, it was people commenting on every image of me.

"Ninety percent of women go through this, I promise you," she told me. "You just have it on a whole different level."

"Why are people so cruel?" I asked. I may as well have been in my old bedroom in Richardson, refusing to get dressed for school.

She didn't have an answer, so she went to the go-to every mom uses with her daughter at one time or another: "They're just jealous."

I couldn't do anything about the media focusing on me, but I hated that *I* was so focused on me and my body. I had grown so much since I was that girl who'd pinched herself black and blue in 1999 because I had the smallest jiggle. I no longer needed to draw on abs with eyeliner. And here I was, still looking for the flaws. Old enough to know better, but unable to stop myself. Still, I had enough sense not to go on some crash diet, or worse, stop eating in order to fit the media's view of what was beautiful.

In those months, I can probably count on one hand the public moments when I forgot how much everybody was looking at my body, judging me. I was in the line at TSA flying out to L.A. to do some work on the Collection. I set off something when I went through the metal detector, and I got flustered. A female agent did a pat-down of my body. When it was over, she smiled at me, so I smiled back.

"You're really not that big," she said.

"Thanks," I said. *Jess,* I thought as I walked on, *that's not a compliment.*

I turned back. "I'd be fine if I was, though."

It took me a while to not just say those words, but to believe them. Like a lot of life lessons, I was able to incorporate some aspects of what I learned right away. Some took longer. It certainly informed how I expanded my clothing line. The Collection needed to stay inclusive as we branched into jeanswear and dresses, and our showroom always had to have fit models who reflected the full range of the customers I loved. I always wanted to dress the everyday woman, because I *am* an everyday woman. I want to wear the same things that everybody else wants to wear, and I wanted to be able to provide those things for people. To be the friend you go shopping with who gives you a thumbs-up when you come out of the dressing room because she genuinely wants you to look and feel good. The silver lining of the mom jeans debacle was that I felt women trusted me more, because now they saw what I was going through.

When my time on the Rascal Flatts tour was over in March, I found that my feelings of insecurity stayed with me, even when I wasn't onstage. Mom and I scheduled an appearance to promote the Jessica Simpson Collection at a Dillard's in Scottsdale, Arizona. When I arrived at my hotel room, I had some quiet time while everybody got settled in their rooms. But I resisted, because downtime at that point usually meant picking myself apart. I grabbed a remote and flipped the channel, only to see a photo of me in those high-waisted mom jeans next to a more recent picture of me onstage. They said I'd gone on a crash diet and lost twenty pounds. I switched off the TV.

"Why won't people leave me alone?" I asked the empty room.

This little tiny whisper of intuition answered. A voice from within spoke up. "It's okay to not be left alone," it said. "The moment people leave you alone, it will be because you stopped standing up for yourself."

I got chillbumps. The truest voice is always that one inside you. I wouldn't give in.

There was a long line of people at that appearance, and I always watch my team fade ever so slightly from standing around at these types of events. I don't help things by taking too much time chatting with each person as I sign a photo or the heel of a shoe. But I love those moments of connection. A woman who'd waited at least an hour finally got to my table and started to rush-talk at me as if she'd rehearsed what she had to say the whole time and had to get it out.

"Ijusthavetotellyouthatyoureallysavedoneofmy-students . . ."

"Who?" I asked.

She slowed down and said her name. "She's a great girl, but she was really getting . . ." she paused. "Bullied." She said it like it was her failure as a teacher. "It was about her weight. It's eighth grade, so kids can be . . . you know. I could stop it in my classroom, but not outside. She was just so sad."

I could feel my whole team leaning forward, listening as she continued. "Her mom told her about you, and she feels something akin to you. I asked her about it, and she said that because of you she knows she can get through it."

Soon we were all tearing up. I stood up and said, "If I give you a hug, will you give it to her for me?"

This was why people wouldn't stop their judgments and leave me alone. It was so I could stand up to them, and *for* that girl. When the world was trying to knock me down, to challenge who I was as a woman and the ownership I had over myself and my body, I could choose to get back up and be right in their faces. To say what I would want that girl and my daughters and all women, to say: "No, actually, I am beautiful because I believe in myself and everything God has given me."

I'm not saying it's easy. It's sometimes a daily struggle. But you gotta get up. You can't leave me up here all on my lonesome.

I COULD TELL TONY WAS RELIEVED WHEN THE FLATTS TOUR WAS OVER. HE was a traditional guy who believed in old-fashioned gender roles. He wanted me to be a Dallas Cowboys housewife, even without the ring. I spent more time at the home, which he encouraged me to think of as my own, but it was still as much of a frat house as ever. In interviews, when people got through the required questions about my weight, they turned to asking about my next project. I said I was still deciding, not letting on that my boyfriend didn't want me on a movie set. I think he was fine with me doing the Jessica Simpson Collection—it certainly made me financially independent from him—but maybe he also saw that as women's work. A more official version of a girlfriend who has a hobby making dresses for her friends.

I was in a bind: Tony liked dating Jessica Simpson, the star, but he wanted a wife like the other football players had. I cooked meals at home and went to the grocery store, where I saw my face looking out at me on the covers of magazines at the checkout line. I never identified with those magazine covers anyway, but now they seemed even further from who I was. One time, after I saw myself on a magazine when I was leaving the store, I went to sit in the car and had an imaginary conversation with Tony. I asked him all the questions I didn't dare say aloud.

"Is there room in your ideals of what a relationship is supposed to be," I asked, "to meet me halfway so I don't give up my dreams?"

I watched a teenager round up shopping carts, leaning on one like a Jet Ski. "Can you support me and what I do as much as I support you and everything you do?" I was on a roll now. "Is my giving up all I want to do truly what you want of me?" I paused a long time. "And why?"

It didn't occur to me then that I needed to ask myself those questions, too. Did I love Tony enough to give up my work and dreams? I didn't dare ask, because I knew the answer was no.

I talked about it with my father, who wanted to do more film producing and would jump at the chance to do another movie with me. I was honest with him, telling him that I would marry Tony if he asked, but I wasn't sure that I wanted him to ask me. I wanted to be what Tony needed, but I felt God had called me to use my voice and be an example for women.

"Well, the same God that called you to sing is gonna want you to do that," he said. "Maybe you need to walk away."

It didn't help that my parents told me they'd been hanging out with John Mayer. It was so bizarre. In early 2009, John rented a place in Hidden Hills, near where I used to live in Calabasas. He turned the whole place into a home studio to record what would become *Battle Studies*. It was about fourteen miles from my parents' house in Encino, and they told me about having him over. They would even go pick him up to spend time with them. Gated community playdates. At first, I thought they were kidding, but he had stayed friends with Pete Wentz and Ashlee. Still.

He told them he had read my *Vanity Fair* cover story that came out in May. My parents told me he went on and on about it. He emailed me about it, too, telling me how amazing it was and that he loved me and wanted me back. Because I was on the cover of *Vanity Fair*? I actually hated the story, which was mean-spirited and full of references to me not actually being fat—a word the writer used over and over again—and had one brief mention of the fact that I had created what was at that point a $400 million business. But the photographs, by Mario Testino, were beautiful. It's telling that being in *Vanity Fair* made John think I was worthy of his interest again. I also said one thing in the interview that, reading it now, I know would have been irresistible to John: "I feel like I'm at such a place that I own myself, and it's authentic."

Challenge accepted, I imagine him saying.

My parents knew how much John had toyed with me, and even now, I marvel that he could extend that manipulation to my family. I recently asked my mom why she spent time with him. "What were you thinking?"

"We were all in love with him," she said with a laugh. "We'd bring him over here, and we'd sit around the firepit, and he'd play his guitar. What's not to love about a cute guy playing you love songs?"

Sigh. They were under his spell. I can't really blame them. I know how persuasive he can be and how kind my parents can be. But I refused to let him have that real estate in my mind again and focused on figuring out how to make my life work with Tony's. I was turning twenty-nine in July, and every magazine said he was going to propose any minute.

Maybe John read one of them and thought so, too. As we got closer and closer to July and my birthday, he ramped up his wooing of my family. He told them in no uncertain terms that he had changed, and he could tell I had changed, too. "I need her back," he said. "I'm in love with her."

If it were just my parents, I might have taken that with a grain of salt. But he got to Beth, my old dance teacher who became one of the heads of the Jessica Simpson Collection, and her husband, Randy, who is now my house manager. Randy is no-nonsense. If you can fool him, you are a master. And Randy believed him. His profession of love for me was so over-the-top that it made my relationship with Tony seem like I was missing out on someone who truly adored me.

"Jessica, you don't even know," went the chorus. "He is so sincere. You have to at least hear him out."

Can I sigh again? Is two too many on two pages? A week before my birthday, I was in L.A. at my parents' house. I had this idea to have a huge party, and my mom and I were going over the details. My dad drove to Hidden Hills to bring John over while I was there. By a fire in the backyard, he stood and told all of us that he loved me and that we could all trust him to be a good man. I told him I would always love him, but I was with Tony.

But I didn't *tell* Tony. I broke my own rule of full disclosure about any contact, even accidental, with John.

On July 9, the night before my birthday, Tony went through my phone. He saw an email from John to me, something about not being able to get a shower door to work at my parents' house. Tony confronted me with it immediately. I wasn't even there, and no, I still don't know why John showered at my parents' house. He accused me of seeing John behind his back. I hadn't cheated on Tony at all, but I could not lie and say I hadn't even seen him.

"Nothing happened," I said.

Tony didn't believe that for a second. And within that second, he broke up with me right there. Two years, gone with an email. It was just immature that he went through my phone. If he didn't trust me, why was he with me in the first place?

I could trust that Tony would never tell the press that John Mayer caused the breakup. It would imply that he wasn't enough for me. Even though I canceled the party, I managed to keep the breakup secret for a few days. I think maybe I would have been able to keep it quiet longer if Tony had just gone back to Dallas. Instead, he stayed to go golfing with his friends and took his guys out to a Hollywood Boulevard club on my birthday. Kind of a red flag.

Tony soon realized I was telling the truth. Of course I didn't cheat on him. But our breakup had been so ugly that it shocked me into realizing it had been necessary. When he said he wanted me back, I was honest with him.

"No, you did what I needed to do," I said. "Thank you."

"This is really over?"

"You broke up with me, so yes," I said. "It's over."

If I hadn't already been through that cycle so many times with John, I might have reflexively gone back once someone "forgave" me. Tony's a wonderful guy, and he was destined to have beautiful babies with someone else, a lovely woman. Not me.

John got what he wanted. I wouldn't be with him because of Tony, and now Tony was gone. I lost my feeling of agency in my life once again and felt I should just give in and be with John. He had promised forever in my parents' backyard. Who was I to argue?

I went to John's house quickly. Driving over, I felt like I was in the closing scenes of a sweeping, epic love story, and the dark romantic hero had beaten out the star quarterback. *Wuthering Heights* in Hidden Hills, only this time Cathy chose Heathcliff. But did I? It seemed like the choice had been made for me.

Ah, but when I got to him, I found out my Heathcliff had other ideas. "Forever" could wait.

"Oh, you don't get me yet," he said.

It was a punch in the gut. I thought I was the one getting gotten. He had said all these things, practically asking my parents for my hand in marriage while I was in a serious relationship. Swearing to me up and down that he was a changed man. Now here I was, ready to pledge my love back, and to kiss him as the curtain came down. And it fell on my head.

He insisted on playing me songs off *Battle Studies*. "This one's for you," he said, again and again. I recognized myself sometimes. Other times I just felt the hurt again. I named a person he had dated. Weren't these songs also about her, too? He paused, then told me he could never find material to write with her.

I almost puked. I was material. Slowly, insidiously, a realization creeped into me, a monster with claws clutching my brain with one hand, then making a fist around my heart with the other. All this time, all those years, he was breaking up with me to torture himself enough to get good material.

"Did . . . were you breaking up with me to hurt yourself?" I asked. "Just so you could get a *song*?"

I had thought I was crazy. There were times he left, and it was my fault, and I have taken responsibility for those moments. But other times a breakup was so out of the blue that it seemed to come just as we were finally getting somewhere.

Now I knew the truth. I was a pet bird. He would throw

me into the sky and watch me catch air and soar long enough that it meant something when he pulled a gun from his back pocket to shoot me down, expertly aiming to graze a wing, never a kill shot to end the misery. To think that every single time I lay on the ground, broken and bewildered, he took his time walking over. Observing me to jot down notes and hum a new song of heartbreak.

And every time he "found me," I looked up at him, grateful to be taken in, sorry for the trouble I must have caused him.

I wish I had walked out right then. I didn't. He had me so messed up that inside twenty minutes I was all in on his "wait and see" terms. It felt inevitable to be in love with John, so I continued talking to him for months. I told friends I was "back with" him, and they stocked up on emotional bandages. But I knew now not to let him get close enough to shoot me down again. This bird wasn't going back in the cage, no matter how bad he needed a song.

21

TRUE BEAUTY

SEPTEMBER 2009

In the summer I reflected on what a hard year it had been. I knew there had to be a reason that God was allowing me to go through this, and it was my job to find some sort of light in all of it. I knew He wouldn't want me to suffer and have nothing to show for it. I'd become a punchline for weight jokes, tried to have a normal relationship, and then gone running back into the arms of a man who tortured me.

I was offered a television show, *The Price of Beauty*, where I would travel the world to examine what different cultures find beautiful. I knew it could be a way to show how we women try so hard to contort ourselves into these boxes of what appears ideal to men and what will make us deserve love, even from family. I said yes immediately and decided to bring CaCee and my hairdresser friend Ken along to be on the show with me.

For me, it was a very spiritual journey, and it upended a lot of my own notions of what was beautiful. In Thailand, we explored the complicated subject of colorism and discussed the lengths many people go to keep their skin light for social status. I was shocked to meet Panya Bunjan, a singer who had disfigured herself using bleaching agents. Back home I felt I had to tan to be attractive. In Uganda, we visited a village where members of the Hima people explained to us that a woman is only beautiful if she is what our society deems "overweight." We visited a fattening hut, where a bride prepared for her wedding by adding as much weight as she could. In Brazil, we examined the notion that plastic surgery was so commonplace that you were a freak if you didn't have it. CaCee and I were on an emotional *Eat Pray Love* kind of trip, whereas Ken kept trying to keep everything light.

Most heartbreaking and eye-opening for me was meeting Isabelle Caro, a French model with anorexia who was eighty-six pounds when I met her. In 2007, she became the face of the disease when she posed nude at *fifty-eight* pounds for a Milan Fashion Week billboard campaign to fight the pressure on models to starve themselves.

When I met her, she had worked her way back up to eighty-six pounds and still seemed so fragile. Isabelle's disease had started near the end of high school, when she was trying to break into modeling, around the same time I signed with Sony. While I was told I needed to lose fifteen pounds to be a success, she told me a modeling scout advised her to lose twenty.

As Isabelle talked, it was hard not to cry, seeing the skeleton move beneath her tight sheath of pale skin. I kept looking away, but her beautiful eyes pulled me in. We were two women who had been told we needed to be skinny to be worthy. That shame was killing her, and I felt lucky to have escaped that. I asked her how she found the strength to be so open, showing what anorexia really looked like. She answered that she was doing it for young girls. I thought about that girl I heard about in Scottsdale. I decided I needed to do more. Not just withstand judgment but call it out.

I left her side feeling bulletproof from all the criticism I still faced about those photos from a chili cookoff, or even the praise when people thought I looked "good." Nobody's words—compliments or critiques—should define the value of our souls. What if, all this time, our "problem areas" were not our stomachs or thighs but our brains? I'm not saying people aren't cruel—believe me, I know—but we can't allow ourselves to do the work for bullies. Give a girl an insult, she'll feel bad for a day, but teach her to hate her body, she'll feel bad forever.

After *The Price of Beauty*, I knew I needed to separate what really mattered to me and what mattered to my ego. In subsequent interviews, I worked hard to say, "I like the way I look," whether I was up or down ten pounds. All kinds of women started coming up to me, not to give me a supportive word, but to say that I made *them* feel good. "*We* look good," I would hear. They thanked me for setting an example that we don't need to measure our self-worth with a scale.

In November of the following year, Isabelle died at age twenty-eight. I think about her so often, and I am grateful for the experience of meeting her. She made her life matter, and wherever you are and whatever you believe, please say her name aloud so she is remembered: Isabelle Caro.

IT WAS WHILE WE WERE IN BRAZIL SHOOTING *THE PRICE OF BEAUTY* **THAT** I got the call about Daisy. On September 14, my sweet, wonderful dog was staying at my parents' house while I traveled. She was in the backyard when she was snatched by a coyote. The coyote ran off with her, and we never saw her again.

CaCee was with me when my mom called, frantic. I lost it in a way she'd never seen before. Daisy Mae was like my child before I was a mother, and I adored her as a constant companion. She was also, in many ways, the last reminder of my marriage. I felt a crushing sense of deep loss and a feeling of being truly alone.

Twitter was new to me, and I went on to ask people to help find her. I paid dog trackers to look for her and robo-call the neighborhood. People made fun of me for caring so much about a dog, but if you have ever loved an animal, you cannot fathom that someone wouldn't understand my need to find her. People contacted my family with prank leads, and some of the news stories about Daisy were grotesque in their meanspiritedness. The journey I was on, traveling the world—and the women I met—gave me strength. I didn't know how much I was about to need it.

While promoting his album, *Battle Studies*, John gave two interviews, one with *Rolling Stone* that was released in January, then one a month later in *Playboy*. He talked like he'd tied a cinderblock to the gas pedal, a man intent on destroying his image as a thoughtful singer-songwriter. The first one was just gross, with him talking about the women in Hollywood he's slept with and essentializing women down to their private parts. "You need to have them be able to go toe-to-toe with you intellectually," he said. "But don't they also have to have a vagina you could pitch a tent on and just camp out on for, like, a weekend? Doesn't that have to be there, too? The Joshua Tree of vaginas?"

I've only skipped through the *Rolling Stone* interview, but a girlfriend who cared about me wanted to make sure I knew about one sentence that actually mattered. He said lately he could only sleep with "girls" he'd already slept with, because he couldn't fathom having to explain to a new woman that, yes, the famous John Mayer was interested in her.

Did you catch it, too? *Girls.* Plural.

I confronted him about it, naming another person he'd been with. "Are you sleeping with both of us?"

"I'm not 'back with you.'"

"Yeah, but you got my ex to break up with me!" I yelled. "I was living in Dallas! You took me away from something. What is wrong with me that I let you get me back into this situation *again* with you?"

The February interview in *Playboy* sealed it. He talked about me by name in the most degrading terms. You can look it up, because I had to be asked about those quotes in every interview I did for about two or three years. I scanned it more than read it, horrified at whatever paragraph my eyes landed on. He called me "sexual napalm" and said he wanted to snort me like a drug. If I had charged him $10,000 to sleep with me, he'd sell everything he had to keep doing it. He also used the n-word and said he wasn't attracted to black women. He wasn't even interviewing. He was "Johnning." He opened the spigot of his mouth, and that's what poured out.

This time John emailed me a letter apologizing. It was the kind of letter that might have worked on me before I'd met women around the world who were facing their own reckonings on what they were willing to do or become just to be loved.

Well, I sat myself down and wrote him a letter back. This one I didn't have anyone proofread to impress him, because I had no interest in impressing him. Or ever even seeing him again. It was a goodbye letter. He did this to me just as I was about to do a press tour to promote *The Price of Beauty*, a passion project about female empowerment. And almost every interview began with a reference to me being sexual napalm. I found if I made a joke about it—saying he "gave away my game, because everybody thinks I'm the nice girl"—the interviewer at least moved on quickly. But the quotes followed me everywhere. Never had I felt men undress me with their eyes like then, and I was a freaking pop star. I was used to that, but this was something on another level. The guy got on the school intercom and said I was crazy in bed.

I didn't accept his apology. I deleted all his contact information from my phone. I was done with this man in a way I never thought was possible. When he reached out to me, I changed my number and changed my email.

Delete.

Look, I hold on to everybody. If I think about it, I can really start to hurt about past relationships. I can go there so easily, because I gave so much of my time and my *self* to these guys. You feel like you need some return on that investment, but sometimes it's just personal growth.

You probably have that someone, too. I think it's okay every now and again to reflect on that time. Get down the box from the top shelf of the emotional closet and marvel at the things that used to mean so much. The keepsakes of our mistakes, the souvenirs of lost years. But know when to start making new memories with people who deserve the you that you are now.

I can't tell you how many of my girlfriends have warned me not to write about John. "He'll come for you," one told me, genuinely concerned. But I am grateful he removed himself from my life so spectacularly. It cleared the way for destiny to knock on my door.

part four

22

LOVE COMES
TO MY DOOR

As I've started writing this section, we've had two earthquakes here in California. I am the first to admit that I am not good at earthquakes. I always tell my husband, Eric, that I'm a tornado girl, because I did so many classroom drills growing up in Texas. I know to shelter in place, find my foundation, and wait things out. Earthquakes throw me, because I am someone who relies on the ground beneath my feet. When I write or pray, I like to be close to the ground, and I draw strength from its sureness. When it shakes, something so permanent also seems fragile.

I have that same need to hold on to something when I think about all the chance moments that brought Eric and me together. My hands move to touch him or one of my kids, just to feel that sureness that we five souls all really found one another. They are the foundation I have built my life on. I know God put us together, but it still seems incredible that love literally came to my doorstep on a beautiful May evening.

So many things had to happen for our paths to cross—not just that first night—but in the thirty years we spent preparing ourselves for each other. I see us in a split-screen montage of scenes, crafted from the memories he's shared with me, and I know his heart so well it's like the faithful, musical girl in Texas is somehow there with Eric Maxwell Johnson, a smart and thoughtful boy growing up in Needham, Massachusetts. While I went to record companies in New York to pursue my dreams, he went to Yale, an Academic All-American wide receiver who graduated with nearly every receiving record in the book. If people talked about my voice, they talked about Eric's hands. He remains legendary at Yale for being able to catch anything. While I was three days away from releasing my first album, he was at the Yale Bowl, diving to make the impossible game-winning touchdown against Harvard with twenty-nine seconds left in the game. It was a moment so famous in Ivy League football history, it's still just known as The Catch, and by the time he graduated, the Massachusetts guy who'd broken Harvard's heart also broke every receiving record in the Yale book.

Our separate lives began to accelerate. While I was landing in the papers for my first USO tour, the *New York Times* was profiling him for transforming his body to play tight end for the NFL. Hall of Fame coach Bill Walsh, then San Francisco 49ers' general manager, watched a videotape of Eric's workout that his agent had sent around to get interest going for the

2001 NFL draft. Bill believed in his potential, just like people believed in mine. Eric played first for the San Francisco 49ers for six years, then spent one year with the New Orleans Saints. We both married people for love, and we sat with our spouses watching each other on TV, catching glimpses of each other as channels flipped by. Me on *Newlyweds*, him on ESPN. How many times we must have seen each other and yet not known, "Oh, there you are." Then each of our marriages had ended, his just as injuries forced him into early retirement, mine as I was forced to reevaluate who I really was.

The first part of 2010 was a time of renewal for each of us. He was finalizing his divorce and studying ways to heal his body from the trauma of football. He studied meditation and researched nontraditional medicine with Master Ming Yi Wang, a teacher/healer based in California. Eric lived like a monk, first sleeping in a tent on a roof in San Francisco, and after a long trip to China with Master Wang, he moved to Venice, a beachy neighborhood in L.A. While he went for long walks with his dog, I had stepped back from the spotlight and was happy to be single and alone. I needed to clear my head and heart because everybody who I allowed in I gave everything to. For once, I gave all that to me.

Here the memories start to quicken. Eric was going to go the University of Pennsylvania's prestigious Wharton business school and visited for an orientation welcome weekend. While he was there, he met another guy from L.A. named Matt. When they were back home in L.A., Matt called Eric and asked if he wanted to go out with some friends of his, Dan and Bret, to the Village Idiot. Eric said yes, but then realized he had basically agreed to hang out with a bunch of people he had never met. He thought about canceling but decided against it. Life was an open door. He was up for walking through.

Bret didn't get the memo that the night was supposed to be a guys night, so he brought his girlfriend, Lolo, who is a childhood friend of my sister, Ashlee. Lolo was like a fairy that evening, flitting about with wide eyes and a great smile. She called Ash, who was at my house. I'd invited a bunch of people over to watch a basketball game, though I don't even watch basketball. But it was a time when I didn't want to go out much and liked my friends knowing they could drop by whenever they wanted. It was kind of a Grand Central Station of nice people coming and going, and I liked it that way. It reminded me of my youth group days in Dallas, only with booze and rock music.

Lolo got right to it. "I'm stuck at a boys' night at the Village Idiot," she said. Ashlee told me what she said, and we made faces at each other like Tinker Bell was trapped on the pirate ship.

"Tell her to get over here," I said. But Lolo thought she could hang in, hatching the beginnings of a plan for Eric. Lolo had found one of those rarest of birds, a man in L.A. who was single, cute, and cool. At about midnight, Eric got tired of all the small talk with strangers.

"I'm gonna go," he said. "It was nice meeting all of you."

"Wait," Lolo said, practically jumping up at him. "I have a friend for you. Should I call her?" she asked. "See if she can come out?"

"Maybe . . ." Eric said.

"You're going to love her," she said. "Her name's Turkey."

No, that's not my nickname. She was thinking of setting Eric up with our friend Stephenie, who we called Wild Turkey because she was legendary in her pursuit of a good time. I've known Turkey since I became her babysitter back in Dallas when I was fourteen. She's fantastic, and I remain grateful that Turkey was in a songwriting session that night and didn't want to leave.

Eric went to go, and just as destiny's door was about to quietly close shut, Lolo asked, "Do you want to go to Jessica Simpson's house?"

He turned. "Well, that was out of nowhere," Eric said. "Okay, sure." He caught a ride with one of the people he barely knew to go to the house of a woman he'd only seen on TV.

When Eric walked through the courtyard of my Hansel and Gretel home, people were scattered both inside and outside. Ashlee sat at the glass table on the porch outside my kitchen, singing show tunes. She was wearing a black circle-brimmed hat and didn't stop singing as Lolo kissed her cheek hello. Ashlee nodded at Eric, and Lolo spotted me in the kitchen. I was with my friend Jeannia, standing next to a dream interpretation book on the counter.

"Hi," I said.

"Hi, I'm Eric," he said, looking down at the book. It was dog-eared, with tons of Post-it notes marking pages. "You analyze your dreams," he said, smiling at me.

Did I say something poetic? Something about how, as an artist I try to harness what my subconscious tells me? No.

"Oh, yes," I said. "Because last night I dreamed I pooped out a pig."

His eyes got wide, and he started to laugh.

"Wait," I said. "Then *that* pig had a pig. And then all of us played together."

"*Okay*," he said. "That's cool. I like dreams."

I looked up at Eric, a foot taller than me at six foot three. I was in my Uggs, wearing a big gray sweatshirt and short shorts, my signature look then for gatherings at home.

"Your place is beautiful," he said.

I offered them a tour of the house, and I could see Eric taking it in. I was proud of my home, the first one that was all mine. It was girly but sophisticated. The Old Hollywood style of Marilyn Monroe and Jean Harlow. Justin Kredible, a comedian who also did magic, had stopped by, and a bunch of people watched him do card tricks. I joined in, and he correctly guessed the card I pulled, a three of spades. People kept asking how he did it, but I was content to just let the mystery be.

It's sweet now to me that my first conversations with Eric were about dreams and the magic happening around us. I know the pig thing was silly—and maybe a little gross—but I see Sarah's hand there with her love of pigs.

We migrated back to the kitchen, he and I, making small talk. We then moved to make room for people dancing by and sat down in the little stairwell in the nook of my kitchen. It was one of my favorite parts of the house, a narrow hallway that snuggles you in with steps just wide enough for two people to sit. We talked, shoulder to shoulder, and an hour went by, then another. It was like we were catching each other up on our lives. We got deep real fast, talking about our own spiritual journeys. With other men, I was afraid to talk, but with Eric, there was no fear of judgment. This was completely new.

As it got late, people started to leave. I saw Eric's new friend Dan saying his goodbyes.

"You're cute," I said to Eric, before I even knew what I was saying. "You should stay."

"Stay?" he said. "Um, okay, I can stay, but you have to mean that because my ride is leaving."

"No, I want you to stay."

"All right," he said, smiling. "I'll stay."

We talked another two hours, the house finally emptied of people hugging us goodbye. It was like the end of a wedding. We kissed on those steps, and I led him up to my room.

The next morning, which was not far away, he was going to an all-day Marianne Williamson seminar about learning to apply spiritual principles to your career. He'd committed to going with a friend, who was coming to pick him up. I was dead asleep in bed, so he left a note on a paper towel in the kitchen, next to the three of spades I got from the magician. The note read: "Jessica, I had to leave early. Thanks for having me over last night. Will call/text later. —Eric."

"This guy just left Jessica Simpson naked in bed to go see Marianne Williamson," I said aloud.

He waited a day to text me. He told me later he didn't want to "push it." I wanted to meet him sober and didn't want to risk paparazzi. Why ruin someone's life if things don't work out? I invited him to come over to watch the *American Idol* finale with me that Wednesday. He told me he had a yoga teacher training that night and could come over after. When I hung up, I said, "Who *is* this guy?"

That night he came over with a four-pack of Guinness. I'd already invited my friend Lauren to watch the show, and I was excited that they seemed to click instantly. They were both from out east and had a similar smart sense of humor. We watched the show, talking during breaks about the performances. I am good at critiques of technique and material from all my years working with my vocal coach Linda and then the A&R with Teresa. I felt confident as I talked this way and not afraid that I might be showing off. There was no need to dim my light around this man. As soon as it was over, I got out my laptop to take him down a YouTube rabbit hole of live performances. Things like Mariah Carey's first-ever appearance on TV singing "Vision of Love" and Queen completely mesmerizing 72,000 people at Wembley during Live Aid. Then I made him watch every episode of *The Price of Beauty*, which I was so proud of. I realize now that I was unconsciously saying, "Here, these are my heroes. *The Price of Beauty* is who I really am. Let's get to the heart of this." I wasn't naive. I knew that I had been in the public eye long enough that Eric would have preconceptions of me. I could tell he was seeing past all that.

When he said goodbye to us, I invited him to a photo shoot I was doing the next day. "Maybe you'd want to stop by?"

"No, not really," he answered quickly. "That is absolutely not my scene." I wasn't hurt because it made sense. He wasn't interested in being some guy hanging out waiting.

"If we go out after maybe I'll call you," I said, having every intention of doing so. Once the shoot was finished, we met at Nobu in Hollywood, and Eric got a crash course in most of my girlfriends, my mom, and some of the girls who work on the Collection. Turkey showed up, a slash of red lipstick on her gorgeous mouth, and Lolo explained that Eric was originally meant for her. They thought that was hilarious, each certain it would never have worked out. They turned out to be soulmates in a different way and have become best friends.

It was at Nobu that I found out Eric was vegan and almost did a spit take. *Well, I'm changing that,* I thought. I did for a time, but he went back to eating that way. I watched him eat what amounted to salad stuffed into rice rolls and asked, "How are you happy? Aren't you starving?" But I liked that athlete's focus on his health, and I thought about my Papaw, and how he was always in tune with his body.

Eric and I kissed at the restaurant and then at the bar we all went to after. It's a miracle no one saw us and told the press, but for the first time in years, I wasn't even thinking of that. We came home and made love. It was Memorial Day Weekend, and he just stayed. In the morning, I watched him sit outside, with his feet in my koi pond, meditating. *Who is this guy?* I thought. I started taking pictures to send to my friends.

They got to see the real thing, because my friends were in and out all weekend. Through Eric's eyes, I appreciated them even more. Other times, a boyfriend had meant I'd gone into exile, abandoning my girlfriends to focus on a relationship. But now it was like he was holding each one up like a gem, turning it to see the glorious uniqueness of each one. They saw something special in us, too, and the care we took with each other.

"Why are we acting like an old married couple?" Eric asked me that weekend.

This light walked into my life, and I remember the moment I realized I didn't have to give him my light. We could share it and make things brighter for everybody. *Welp,* I thought, *that's refreshing.* Yes, I was instantly infatuated with Eric. You know

I fall in love too easily, but with him, we were both ready for the real deal.

Eric told his parents that he was dating me early on. Stephen and Mary Jo are from Boston and are very New England in their demeanor. They are brilliant and not very engaged with pop culture. His mother, who was a big firm lawyer at the time, expressed shock when he said he was dating Jessica Simpson, "the pop singer."

"The one that shaved her head? She has two kids, right?"

"No, no," he said. "I think you're thinking of Britney Spears."

"Well."

When I met them, I could see how they raised someone like Eric. His parents were best friends, but they were also in love. My parents were just best friends. Meeting them showed me you could be both.

One night in June, Eric was reading something that quoted a Pablo Neruda line he repeated to me: "My soul is an empty carousel at sunset." A poem in just one sentence. It stayed with me. I'd felt like that for a long while. Waiting for somebody to come along so I could be of use. But now I was a girl who ran to the carousel, gliding through the lights and the music, holding my breath as the horse went up and down. I felt exactly what I should: happiness. I wanted to go on this ride again and again, and I was always first in line to get back on, laughing as I whipped around one more time.

IN THE MIDST OF THIS, I'D PLANNED A GIRLS' TRIP TO ITALY'S ISLE OF CAPRI for my thirtieth birthday in July. As we got closer, I realized how much I was going to miss Eric. My housekeeper Evelyn is the one who told me that I had to take him with me. "You'll regret it if you don't."

I flew us out to Capri along with Ashlee, my parents, and about a dozen girlfriends, and we had a gorgeous hotel high on a cliff. We girls all partied so hard the first night, Eric could barely keep up. With Ashlee and my crowd fully melded into one, we had become a happy-go-lucky band of ladies, just enjoying life.

I rented a yacht to take us from Capri to Pompeii. I'll be honest, I wanted to see the stone phalluses that are peppered throughout the city's walls and streets. So the day was basically one long penis joke. Someone had warned me that I had to wear sneakers because of the cobblestones. Now, I don't even have flats, so I definitely didn't have sneakers. So I got Asics and wore them with jean shorts and a muscle tee. I looked absolutely ridiculous. Meanwhile, Ashlee and all my friends were dressed for the cover of Italian *Vogue*. It was the least sexy I have felt in my entire life at a time when I was embracing the beauty of sex. But I had to laugh because I *was* having great sex.

On my birthday, we all had dinner at a restaurant, sitting outside by the sea. It was all my favorite people at one table, their beautiful faces lit by candlelight. Adrienne had a tradition where we each went around talking about what the birthday girl meant to them. I had never made a big deal about my birthday before, so this was the first time I was the focus of the ritual. What people said was so amazing. I think we move through the world assuming people know what they mean to us. But so often those assumptions fall short. I am one of those people who has a lot of best friends—I just love them all differently. But for some reason, a lot of those people just consider me their one best friend.

I was so moved, but I kept it together until we got to CaCee. CaCee is so quick-witted, I expected a funny story.

"I am proud of you, Jessica," she said. She talked about watching me bloom recently, moving away from fear and becoming a strong woman.

I began to weep, because I thought I had failed her in my divorce. She had come in and out of my life around John, and I thought I had broken *her* heart when I left Nick. With her speech, I felt released from that guilt—it was the best gift she could have given me. If someone I looked up to so much said she was proud of me, I had to be doing something right.

My friends and family surprised me with a cake, a gorgeous circle of icing flowers and one pink candle in the very center. I know I told you I believe in birthday wishes. As my friends finished singing "Happy Birthday," I looked into the glow of the flame, made my wish, and blew it out.

Later, in our room, I sat on the bed and watched Eric doing half-naked QiGong in a corner. I loved him.

"Babe," I said.

He looked over.

"I know we're not supposed to tell our wishes, but I can't keep my mouth shut about this one."

He said nothing, just stood at the edge of the bed.

"This could scare you off," I continued, "but I wished for a baby girl. And I would like to make that happen with you."

He leaned over and kissed me. Our sex was always powerful, because we were both very present in our bodies, but that night it was spiritually explosive. The kind of love that makes miracles happen.

From then on, we were inseparable. I told him to just move

in with me so we could start a family. We'd take it one day at a time, but our days went until four a.m. staying up talking. He brought his vintage record player and LPs, filling my home—our home—with his music, Bob Marley and reggae. And I made sure he knew every Willie, Waylon, and Hank I'd ever loved. The area where we always sat had a little fountain, and we lived in peace and gratitude that we'd found each other after not knowing we'd ever love again. When a dream falls through, you think maybe it's lost forever. And there we were, ready to scoop it up and get that second chance.

There was only one catch: Wharton. Eric had been accepted to business school at UPenn. On paper, it would be crazy not to take that opportunity, and I wasn't going to stop him. I even bought him a computer as a going-away gift, and I talked myself out of being disappointed when he went to visit Philadelphia to pick out an apartment. The weekend before he was set to leave, I had to go to Dallas to do some work for the Collection. Eric started packing while I was away, probably knowing it would be hard for me to watch him do that and keep my poker face. But as he packed, he later told me, he started getting upset. The whole point of going to Wharton was to anchor himself and meet people so he could build a community. He'd done that here with me and our friends.

When I came home, he said he was having second thoughts about business school. It was only then that I said my piece.

"I have a GED, and my business just cleared $750 million," I said. "We're closing in on a billion and trending up. A *GED*. You don't need to go to Wharton. You can hire someone who went to Wharton."

He thought long and hard and spoke to several mentors and

coaches from his past. Eric confided in them that he knew he would marry me, and we would raise kids together. If Wharton could jeopardize that future, it wasn't worth it.

"All right," he told me. "I'm going to Jessica Simpson Business School."

I was so relieved. The irony is that soon after, I told him that I was returning to the Persian Gulf. I said it so casually that he was confused. "Just a couple of days," I said.

Kidding aside, in October, I went back to the USS *Truman* to pay a visit to the troops. Back then, it seemed crazy that the war in Afghanistan had been going for nine years, and the war in Iraq was then at six years. I didn't want service members to feel forgotten. I was working on a second Christmas album, recording it quickly for a November release. I really wanted to do a duet of "I'll Be Home for Christmas" with a service member. I chose that song because I believed they should all be able to come home. My dad arranged for it, as only he could. The crew of the *Truman* had an *American Idol*–style competition, and when I flew in, I would judge the final eight with the winner becoming my duet partner.

It was beautiful. I watched eight sailors and marines perform, and the clear winner was Petty Officer John Britt. I remember he was on his fifth or sixth tour. We recorded his part of the record in the announcement room of the *Truman*, and I invited him to also perform with me at the Rockefeller Center Tree Lighting appearance I had scheduled for later that month. He wasn't sure he could, and my dad said he'd make it happen for him. He did, and John's wife and child were able to come to New York to see him perform with me. I was so proud of that and of my father for making it happen.

The media didn't give my trip the coverage I wanted it to bring the service members, but I was resigned to that. But then I accidentally handed them a headline: "Jess's Run-in with Nick!"

So a girl walks into a Mexican restaurant with her boyfriend and her crew from the Collection. My mom and all the girls had been working so hard, so we thought we'd all leave the showroom one night and have fun in the form of margaritas at Red O. They brought us to a table, and as soon as we sat down, the energy at the table got really awkward. Someone whispered to my mom, and she scanned the room quick.

"Jess, Nick is here," she said. "He's with Vanessa."

I looked up, but I didn't see them at all. "He's spotted you," my mom said. I couldn't for the life of me see him. The restaurant was dark with gold and red lighting, but it wasn't *that* dark. My heart started going into overdrive, and I began drinking heavily, thinking it would help everybody loosen up. When even the waitstaff started to seem anxious, I realized this was ridiculous.

I stood up. "I'm just gonna go say hi and make it not awkward," I told the table. "Where is he?" People made subtle head nods in the direction of what seemed to be the entire restaurant, which, while subtle, was not helpful. "Well, I'll find them," I said, smoothing my shirt. I'd been working, so this was hardly how I imagined looking when I spoke with my ex for the first time in years, but hey. Growth.

I walked further into the restaurant, squinting and craning my neck to see him. Finally, I stopped and did a 360 scan of the place. I couldn't see him. I turned back to my table, and everybody's eyes were wide open, staring at me.

"I don't see him," I said, just loud enough that my voice would carry to my table. "I don't!" So I marched back.

"Jessica, you were right there next to them," my mom said.

"You guys, I swear I did not see them," I said. "And I am not wasted. *Now* I'm gonna drink because I feel like a freaking idiot."

I started crying, so Eric and I left. My mom went to them to try to smooth things over.

"I don't know why Jessica didn't see you," she told Nick.

"It was probably for the better," he said. He might have been annoyed, but he was graceful to my mom, and I appreciated that.

I still don't know why I didn't see him. Maybe God put blinders on me so I wouldn't be tempted to look back and just keep moving forward.

23

SINCE I'VE BEEN LOVING YOU

NOVEMBER 2010

I love TV. I didn't get to watch much as a kid, so I made up for it as an adult. Before bingeing shows was a thing, I could lose myself in TV, watching episode after episode. *Friday Night Lights, Weeds, Californication*... At this time, our show was *Parenthood.* I called it our show, but Eric isn't someone who can just sit and watch a show like me. He needs to be moving around. On the morning of November 11, I was mainlining the second season on DVD, crying with the Bravermans in Eric's big Yale sweatshirt and the underwear I called my ruffle-butt panties. I heard Led Zeppelin blaring from the direction of my bedroom upstairs.

He came into the living room and saw me literally crying from the television show I was watching.

"You gotta see what Bentley did upstairs," he said. Bentley was his dog, an Airedale terrier I had grown to think of as mine, too.

"Babe, I'm totally lost in the middle of this," I said.

He went upstairs and called down. "There's something wrong with Bentley!"

I jumped up and *ran* up those stairs now, worried about Bentley. But when I got to our bedroom, Bentley was fine, and Eric was out on the balcony, and there were rose petals all over. I realized my favorite song was playing, Led Zeppelin's "Since I've Been Loving You," from the *How the West Was Won* live album.

I walked to him, slowly realizing what was happening. When I got to him, he got down on one knee, presenting a beautiful diamond-and-ruby ring.

I was so overcome I sat down on his knee. "Whoa," I said.

"I know it's only been six months," he said, "but I know that the rest of my life is yours. If you'll have me."

It was an immediate yes. I enjoyed him, my best friend, in the hard stuff and the fun stuff. I didn't ever want to sleep without him next to me. We understood each other when nobody else ever seemed to.

Eric timed the proposal for exactly 11:11:11 on November 11. He knew 11:11 has always been a special time for me for some reason. I happen to look at the clock at that exact moment and freak my girlfriends out by telling them to make a wish.

"I know you would not want to be anywhere but your home when I asked you," he said. Anybody who knew my heart knew that was true. I would not have wanted to say yes to forever in front of anybody else or anywhere else.

"But how did you know that I wanted a ruby?" I almost yelled.

"Because I know you," he said. "It's your birthstone, and I know what's sentimental to you." He told me my mom helped him pick out the ring, and she told me he paid for it himself. It's so funny, because he lived so simply that I always assumed he had no money. But all those years playing in the NFL, he'd saved. We kissed, and by then the record had gone through "Stairway to Heaven" and started Eric's favorite, "Going to California."

"Your bags are packed," he said. "I'm taking you up to San Ysidro Ranch." It's a hotel that's one of the most romantic places in the world. He'd confided his proposal plan to Lolo, because she'd brought us together in the first place, and she suggested it as the perfect getaway.

"How did you do all this?" I asked. How long had I been watching *Parenthood*?

"I just did," he said. It was about a three-hour drive to San Ysidro, and we called all our loved ones on the way. He told me he'd asked my parents' permission, and they'd given their blessing. None of my friends were shocked, or at least nobody said they were. Everybody knew we were meant to be together. We already had a plan: we would get married the following year, so our wedding date could be 11/11/11.

I remember looking out on the coastline, thinking that now more than ever I wanted that wished-for baby girl. *Trust God's timing*, I told myself. She'll appear.

THE FOLLOWING SUMMER, A YEAR INTO TRYING TO HAVE A BABY, I KEPT A stash of pregnancy tests in the downstairs bathroom. I didn't want them in my bathroom, because I would constantly see them. I just needed to know they were there when I was ready.

When I had the surgery to remove my right fallopian tube as a teenager, the doctor had said I would likely only be able to get pregnant every other month. Then, it didn't seem like a big deal. Now it seemed like it cut my chances in half. It was summer, a month where I would be ovulating on my left side, where I still had a fallopian tube. Those months were always full of hope. I had been trying ever since Capri. I know that there are people who've waited longer or been told more definitively that they will not be able to conceive or bring a baby to term. I am in no way comparing heartaches. For me, passing the year mark was hard. I wasn't ready to start monitoring when I was ovulating, because I was afraid of realizing I had a real issue. But I took a pregnancy test every month, just in case, and this time the Not Pregnant sign on the test hurt my heart.

I needed Eric. He was outside at the glass table with Master Wang, who was visiting. They were sipping tea, and Eric was listening intently to his old mentor. Master Wang was a powerful man, somehow young and old at the same time, and able to command any room he is in with silence. Eric always said he gave it to him straight and had no time for the trappings of ego or excuses.

I went outside to Eric, crying uncontrollably, a year's worth of tears coming out. "I'm not pregnant," I said, "and I'm never gonna *be* pregnant. And I just want to be a mom."

Master Wang paused a long time, seeing the hurt in my eyes. He softened.

"Let me try a treatment on you," he said. "An adjustment."

I'm not a doctor, chiropractor, or nuclear scientist, so this is not advice. But we went inside, and he somehow knew that my issue was on my right side, where my fallopian tube had been removed. He did an adjustment that I can only describe as popping my pelvis. I asked God to make this work.

The summer continued, and I saved photos of wedding dresses on my phone for a November wedding. In August, Eric and I headed to Watch Hill, Rhode Island, for a getaway with his parents. He was intent on getting me on a bike to tour the area. I resisted and was irritable about it. I just felt a little off. But Eric won out, taking me out on ten- to twenty-mile bike rides. It's beautiful there, with old Victorian-style "cottages" that are really these sprawling mansions by the ocean. We watched the sun set, and I was proud that we'd gotten through our bickering and gone riding. Go team.

When we got home, we still had the cycling bug, and we made plans to see Eric's friends in Venice. It was morning, and Eric was upstairs in the shower. I was standing in the kitchen when I had this strange feeling. It was so striking, so clear, that I said the words aloud:

"I don't feel alone."

Some instinct put my hand toward my lower stomach, and my heart started beating fast. I slowly walked to the bathroom, pulling open the drawer where I kept my pregnancy tests. I'd had my period, and this wasn't even a month where I would be using the fallopian tube I had. I heard my girlfriends' voices in my head telling me I was crazy. Asking me why, if I had my period, did I insist on taking pregnancy tests and putting my-self through the pain of the bad news. But the voices faded. I peed on the stick and read the instructions in the same ritual I always followed, even though I knew the drill by heart. "Place on a flat surface . . . windows facing up . . ."

I did. And I waited, thinking, *Should I have waited for Eric? Was it wrong to do this alone?*

No, I decided, if this is a baby, it's just me and this kid right now. We have these minutes to find each other, or not. Finally, I looked.

Pregnant.

I ran upstairs screaming. We'd found each other. Eric thought something was wrong because I was crying. I couldn't talk, just handed him the pregnancy test. What I'd known for that minute, he now knew, and I watched the excitement and relief wash over him.

We called *everybody*. My sweet mother almost tried to turn around on the highway to get to me sooner. Everybody wanted to come over, and we welcomed them. I'm sorry I didn't call you, but I would have if I'd had your number.

One of my girlfriends who knew my cycles asked if I wanted to take a second test. I didn't want to pee on another stick, because I didn't want it to say anything different. If this was some foolish dream, I wanted to live in it longer.

I called my dad. I love my father, but he responded as a manager of a talent who had a lot of deals in the works.

"Well, what are you gonna do?" he asked.

"What do you mean what am I gonna do?" I said. "Um, I'm having the baby?"

"No, what are we gonna do? I have all these things."

"I'm sorry," I said. "Maybe do some things for *you*. I'm not gonna work for a bit, how 'bout that? We're just gonna grow the business of the Collection, and I'll do design meetings. And I'm not gonna go on the road."

Creatively, I had been my parents' outlet for so long. My having a baby felt like an opportunity for my mother to take even more ownership of the business and for my father to put his energy and ideas into other things.

I called my doctor right away, and they were scared at first because they said I was at high risk for a tubal pregnancy. They wanted me to see a specialist immediately at Cedars-Sinai Medical Center. When we left the gate, we had ten cars of paparazzi following us. There was no way we could get to the hospital without putting an even bigger target on my back. Anytime a female celebrity goes to a hospital, it's like sending up a flare that paparazzi should be on high alert for a pregnancy. We were already being more cautious about protecting what we prayed would be a healthy, happy baby, so Daisy Duke's evasive driving maneuvers were no longer going to fly. We turned around, and my heart sank.

We made another appointment for exactly twenty-four hours later. We'd have time to do planning with rental cars and hiding in backseats. Another trick was to leave a rental car waiting in a paid parking garage, then drive out in a different car. We would do whatever we had to do.

But, more important, we prayed over my belly for that twenty-four hours. The prayers amounted to one word: *Stay*.

"IN ALL MY YEARS OF PRACTICE, I'VE ONLY SEEN THIS ONCE," THE SPECIAList said as she walked in the office. The egg traveled from the ovary on the right side of my body to use my one fallopian tube on the left. "It's a miracle," she added.

Since that word came from a doctor, I decided "miracle" was a technical term, and I carry it with me still. And that pregnancy felt like a miracle. I loved every minute of it. I would get headaches, but never felt morning sickness. Within two weeks, Eric and I already had names picked out for a boy or a girl. I am sentimental, so the names needed to come from family. If we had that baby girl, we wanted a combination of our mothers' maiden names to honor them, Maxwell Drew. For a boy, Ace Knute—our grandfathers' names—would be perfect. We found out early that we were having a girl, and I was thrilled. My wish had come true. When I was pregnant with Maxwell, every sad thing in my life was forgotten or put into a healthy perspective. I know that was so much to put on her, but I couldn't help it. She saved me from all the worries, all the overthinking, all the dwelling on the past.

That's why I had absolutely no problem stopping drinking during my pregnancy. I was able to turn inward instead of doing my usual escaping. I didn't want to look outward, because I was just so astonished by what my body was capable of. Creating life allowed me to awaken my spirit.

We decided to put off the wedding to focus on the pregnancy. We wanted to keep it our secret for a while, but there was no hiding her from the media. Pretty early on, she wanted to be seen, and I had a bump I couldn't hide. For weeks people guessed, and Eric and I decided to end the speculation by announcing the pregnancy on Halloween. I posed for a photo dressed as a mummy, old-school with the white bandages tight over everything but my face and hair. I posted the shot of me cradling my stomach with the caption, "It's true—I'm going to be a mummy."

When I was four months, I felt Maxwell kick for the first time. I was like, Whoa! Something is really in there. It was the weirdest and most amazing feeling. My little girl was already clear about what she wanted: a combination of salty and sweet. I craved cantaloupe, but with salt all over it. Then I went through a stage of peanut butter and jelly sandwiches, toasted. I would put salt on my hand like I was taking a tequila shot, take a bite of my sandwich, then a lick. I ate what my body told me and would gain about sixty pounds. But I wasn't worried, because I had been approached by Weight Watchers to be an ambassador when the time came to lose the pregnancy weight. I liked their message of self-empowerment, and I knew how good I was at following directions. If you tell me how to do something, I'll do it.

Whenever I did an interview during my pregnancy, I was asked how I was adjusting to putting on weight. The interviewer would "helpfully" tell me people were commenting about my weight, even though, duh, I was pregnant. "Are you held to a higher standard because you were a sex symbol?" a male reporter asked me on a morning show.

"I think I still *am* a sex symbol," I answered. "I know to my husband I still am." I was just so confused by the "were." Excuse me? And what I said was absolutely true. During my first pregnancy, I was finally fully in my body, and I felt sexy to a point that I wanted to have sex four times a day.

Maternity clothes were not fun for me, so I put them off as long as possible. I lived in Eric's sweatshirts, and if I had to do an event, I'd throw a jacket on a stretched-out designer dress. I joked that I was going to give birth in my YSL heels. I noticed that I could find maternity clothes that were either comfortable or cute, but never both.

"Mom, we're just gonna have to do this ourselves," I said. And so, the idea for the Jessica Simpson maternity line was conceived. I was so proud of how my mother had grown the business, and how the business had become such a family affair. My sister, Ashlee, even pitched in to do a campaign shoot while I was pregnant. The Collection has always reflected the stages of my life, and for this I have my mother to thank. I was able to publicly do so at my baby shower, telling her how I hoped to be half as good a mother as she was to me. Everything I had was because of her faith and love.

I didn't know our lives were about to completely change, and not because of Maxwell. In late April, three weeks before my mid-May due date, I was in the hospital to monitor the baby. Because of her size, my doctors wanted to schedule a caesarean section two weeks before my due date. I was scared.

And that's when my dad chose to tell me he was planning to leave my mother. He thanked me for showing him the way— leaving a life in which I felt trapped and finding the one I was meant to have. They were fighting all the time, her nitpicking everything he said.

I was completely blindsided, as I knew my mother would be. I take on the problems of my friends and family, and now I was burdened with this secret that I felt responsible for. Of course, my mother knew there were problems in her marriage, but this was all she had ever known. For my survival, and my daughter's protection, I buried this news. I refused to deal with it and instead focused on welcoming Maxwell. I have perspective now. Or at least the hope of perspective. I know people shouldn't be miserable, but my father's timing added a layer of terrible sadness to what had been a joyous time. For a long time, I harbored a lot of resentment about the way he told me the family I knew was over.

The night before the scheduled May 1 C-section, Eric packed a record player and a selection of his old Bob Marley records to play at the hospital. I, of course, had to have my Roberto Cavalli caftan, which I had taken to wearing all the time, flowing about like some Stevie Nicks earth mother. They were right about her size: Maxwell entered the world on May 1 at nine pounds, thirteen ounces. My miracle baby. When I held her for the first time, I couldn't believe my luck. Eric and I stared at her, knowing we had been given the truest, most precious purpose of life.

When we got home, our lives revolved around Maxwell. We'd place Maxwell in a bassinet, and we'd sit outside in a shady spot by the fountain. We barely went out, preferring the world come to us. Eric took to fatherhood as his calling. He could feel that Maxwell didn't like to be bounced, just held in stillness. He's so strong, so just one of those hands that were so famous at Yale could hold Maxwell while doing QiGong or gently walking around the yard.

We hired a night nurse, Ann Marie, to come from 7 p.m. to 9 a.m.—this perfect English nanny who we peppered with questions all night. It was so odd, this feeling that someone who has been part of you for nine months is now next to you in a bassinet. We got up with the night nurse, and we'd all watch old movies together, so even with the benefit of a nurse, I was sleep-deprived. I would google the weirdest stuff in the middle of the night. Suddenly the lightest rash was "Should we call the doctor?" To avoid creating even more anxiety, I started night-shopping. The things I would order. Maxwell had like ten different bathtubs because I would either forget I bought one or, *ooh, this one has a scale!*

We stuck to a schedule like gospel, but breastfeeding didn't come easily to me. Not enough people talk about how tough it is, so hear it from me: it's okay if it doesn't come naturally to you either. There's enough pressure keeping this perfect little creature alive. Just do the best you can, whatever your best is. For me, breastfeeding was a time to pray over her and connect with her. You can do that while you're giving your baby a bottle, too.

Carol Vanderslice, my old Sunday school teacher, came to help me. I sometimes measured my mothering skills by how much she smiled while looking at me. I loved having her there. Eric and I were fortunate to have help and be there for every first. Those first months, there was so much magic happening in our home that I had a beautiful distraction from my parents and their drama. In August, my mother discovered that my father had betrayed their marriage, just as she and I thought things were turning around for them. She had just told me what a nice time they had together on their anniversary, and she thought maybe they had turned a corner. I thought so, too. When she confronted him, my dad began calling me, and I would not pick up. One time he called while I was in my closet, looking to see what I could fit into. Maxwell was in the bassinet next to me. I watched the phone ring until it mercifully stopped. I sighed. A minute later, Eric was there.

"Jessica, your dad's here," he said. *No, he's not,* I thought. He just called. He is far, far away.

"What do you mean 'Your dad's here?'" I said. "What's he gonna say to me?" He had called from out front. I still thought

I could hide. I looked at my baby. "Okay, Maxwell, it's you and me, kid."

But suddenly my dad was there, spouting in full denial mode. After all those times he'd flirted with the idea of rescuing himself, he couldn't do it. "I'm not with anybody else," he said. "I love your mother."

My anxiety made me freeze. I turned words over and over in my mind, trying to find just the right ones to express my pain.

He said he didn't want to hurt me, and that's when Eric stepped in. He said something like, "Each time you deny your own truth, something intense happens. You have to listen to the signs and take care of it yourself. Jess has no extra energy to give to you right now." I could tell that got through to my dad. It was the type of thing he might have counseled someone back in Richardson.

My parents filed for divorce that August. Dad moved on quickly, and maybe he'd planned it so long that he had a running start ahead of my mother. He tends to have conversations with himself for so long, and then he suddenly talks about something as if we're all supposed to be up to speed. He starts in the middle, and it can make people—well, my mom—feel lost. So, I admit, I took care of my mother. In many ways, she had lost her best friend. She was twenty when she got married. She was the youngest child, and he gave her the world. She's said that he didn't just give her identity, Joe Simpson *was* her identity. He took her out of her comfort zone. He helped her be adventurous, to see the world. Her everything had become nothing.

My mom had a hard time with Ashlee and me even seeing

our father, and I was incapable of not telling my mother when I'd spent time with Dad. So, for a long time, this daddy's girl stopped seeing him. I told him I loved him, but it was easier this way. Strong Ashlee was the one who stepped up, refusing to limit herself. She and our father formed a new relationship. I am proud of her.

Sadly, this is when I had to fire my father, one of the hardest things I've ever done. The worst part was that I had do it five times because he would not accept it. Too often I was circling back to people, only to find that Dad had made some move without telling me. People agreed to bad terms, thinking that was what I had demanded when, really, I had no idea. It left a lot of hurt feelings I didn't know existed, and I knew I had to make the move to go forward with ownership of my own career.

I did one thing to make sure my dad knew I loved him. His father had always sat in a big leather recliner. My grandfather loved that chair, and I loved to sit by it and tickle his toes to make him laugh. Dad always wanted one, but my mom's interior-designer instincts wouldn't allow it. "I am not putting a leather recliner in our house," she'd say. I bought him one. Now he could do what he wanted.

While I chose to see my mother over my father, I also felt the lightest barrier forming between her and me. It was self-protection. She was hurting, and someone who's read as many self-help books as I have knows, hurt people hurt people. She would say something cutting to me, and I would later turn it over in my head like a puzzle. It took me a long time to realize that when she did that, it was because she didn't like herself in that moment. She didn't want to make me cry, she only wanted to take me to the same dark place where she was.

But that took a while for me to figure out. In the meantime, I focused on my little family of three. Creating my own family within that loss was a beautiful thing. And I was about to be blessed again.

24

LET'S GO DANCING
IN THE LIGHT

Of course, I turned my Weight Watchers meetings into parties. They sent me this great mentor, Liz Josefsberg, to make the plan for me, and I shared it with all my girlfriends. There was something celebratory about our weekly weigh-ins, not punishing. I was on fire, losing three and half pounds a week, and on a serious health kick.

And yet, I felt off. We had our normal gathering for Halloween, and I felt so nauseous. I had given up breastfeeding, thinking it would make me feel better, but now I felt awful. I flashed on a recent time when Eric and I had made love, and how we looked at each other and I said, "I think we just made a baby." But no, Maxwell was only four months old . . .

I went to the downstairs bathroom, where I still had my stash of pregnancy tests.

Pregnant.

Eric was upstairs in our bedroom and Maxwell was napping. Again, I raced up the steps, but this time I wasn't screaming because the only thing bigger than a mom's need to yell is her baby's need to sleep. I was shaking when I showed Eric the test. Of course, we were thrilled, but it was *such* a shock. Again, I got pregnant on a month where the egg had to cross over to my left fallopian tube.

Immediately, I went into mom-of-two mode. "Well, this house is too small," I said. "Where are we gonna put this baby?" It was heartbreaking to realize we had to leave our house, because it was so special. The place where I'd found my forever. But my real forever was Eric, Maxwell, and now this little person, who I was suddenly very worried about. I knew I had to see the specialist right away again to rule out a tubal pregnancy. She was shocked that my eggs had pulled off this trick a second time.

"I think it was some really powerful sex," I said. "Eric must have meditated right before."

We delayed our wedding a second time, this time tabling the whole plan. Our only concern, once we knew our next child was healthy, was focusing on Maxwell. We wanted to spend as much alone time with Maxwell before she had to share our attention with another baby in the house. When we told friends, some people—okay, a lot of people—were like, "Oh my gosh, are you gonna do this? Back to back?"

"Well, we don't have a choice, you know," I'd answer. "We're gonna do this and they're gonna be best friends." When we found out we were having a boy, we were thrilled. We already had that perfect name, Ace Knute.

Now I needed to stop throwing up. I had morning sickness, but for me, it was also afternoon and night sickness. The day would slowly edge into misery. I wondered if it was karma for all the interviews I'd done talking about how blissful pregnancy was. Maybe because it was a boy, my hormones responded completely differently this time around. Isn't that the old wives' tale?

In a move that will go down in history as not one of our better ones, we booked a three-week trip to Hawaii for the end of December and beginning of January. We announced the pregnancy on my social media, this time with a Christmas photo of Maxwell on the beach with "Big Sis" written in a heart in the sand in front of her. I also had to announce that I was stopping the Weight Watchers diet but would return to it as soon as I could.

We had three waves of family and friends coming to visit the house in Hawaii. It was rainy, and I spent most of the trip in the theater room of the house we rented, Eric joking that as people came to visit, I became more and more like Howard Hughes. The hermit tycoon hiding in the dark room, only rubbing her belly.

Right before we left for the trip, we fell in love with Ozzy Osbourne's house, which was for sale in Hidden Hills, so we spent much of the trip sealing up the details with our realtor. I had always liked Hidden Hills when I'd lived nearby in Calabasas. Ozzy also had his own studio in the house, and I thought it was just perfect for our family—once I redecorated, of course.

That spring was about transitioning to the new house, with Willie Nelson and Neil Young albums as the soundtrack to our lives. I even had a tapestry embroidered to hang over Ace's crib with a verse from "Harvest Moon," one of my favorite Neil Young songs.

When June 30, the day of his C-section arrived, they asked me in the OR what kind of music I'd like to have playing. *Oh, I should play Neil Young,* I thought. Ace would recognize that music from hearing it so much at home. But I wasn't thinking clearly.

"Neil Diamond," I said.

The nurse paused. "Like 'Sweet Caroline?'"

"Oh gosh, no no no no," I said. "Neil *Young.* 'Harvest Moon.'"

He was seven pounds, four ounces, a little guy in comparison to his big sister. We took him home to our new house, and again Eric rose to the occasion. Maxwell, who was about fourteen months, started pretending to diaper her dolls to be like mommy and daddy.

When you have a second child, you wonder if your heart will divide to accommodate another child, but it just expands and gets bigger. Each time I put them to bed, there was a feeling of gratitude. I couldn't believe they were all mine, and I had made these perfect beings with my best friend.

I held on to that gratitude, sometimes gripped it tightly to withstand a sudden, unexpected wave of anxiety. I'd been pregnant back-to-back for two years, and now I was no longer able to turn inward in a positive way. I felt overwhelmed by the return of my old demons. I am wired to stay awake until everything is complete, and when you have two kids under two, there is always something to worry over. I have more sympathy for myself now than I did then, which I know is the story of a lot of women's lives. We are kind in hindsight.

I had these two babies, and I was trying to catch all these firsts and savor every second. I wanted to still be intimate with my husband as my system tried to reset itself—and once the hormones stopped fluctuating, I had no idea what that would even look like. Even with the children outside my body, we were still so strongly connected that their emotions and needs crowded out mine. Was I anxious because of something I was feeling, or was I picking up on Maxwell's distress about not having a need met in that one second because I was trying to breastfeed her brother? Where did I end and begin? Did it even matter?

I was able to talk about these feelings with Eric on our walks, getting in my steps as I rejoined the Weight Watchers program, working my way back to a healthy weight. The investors in the Collection gave me a grace period before I got back to the business of being famous and out there. My mother had poured all her heartbreak and creative energy into building the brand. She was phenomenal, but the brand needed its face back.

"We need you to be relevant," someone told me. Oh, that word. *Relevant.* I turned that one over in my mind. How was I irrelevant? Being relevant to them was about my going places and being photographed, whether it was appearances for the collection or being some aspirational version of Jessica Simpson. I also put pressure on myself because I was fully aware that I needed to be fully connected to my brand. It was my face that sold it. But *this*—being a mom—was the person I aspired to be. But "relevant" dug into an insecurity I had: Other than planning a wedding, I really didn't know what was next.

Eric and I didn't need a big wedding to prove our love. We

had each had our dream weddings already. And then my publicist and best friend Lauren told me a magazine wanted to buy the exclusive and said what they were willing to pay. The offer would cover a huge celebration, not so much for us, but for all our loved ones.

"Hunh," I said. "I guess I'm having a big wedding then."

We were already in the habit of hosting huge parties at our house. Two- to three-day extravaganzas where all our friends gathered to share one another's company. Any excuse would do, and we always had a blast. We had it to share, and this wedding would be like one of those parties on steroids.

There was one last thing I wanted to do. When I next visited my beloved Nana and Papaw, it was for the Thanksgiving after Ace, Papaw's namesake, was born. At that point, Papaw was suffering from dementia and was unable to retain information. I watched my strong grandmother, my prayer warrior, being so protective of her husband of sixty years. We sat in the living room, and she held my hand. I shared my memories of Papaw, and him taking the snakes from the grass for us. I looked up at her wall, which still had pictures of me and Nick.

"Nana, I love you so much," I said. "But you have to let me help you take those pictures down. I have babies with another man. Eric is going to be my husband. He already is in my heart."

She nodded. She would do that for me.

My grandfather, Acy "Ace" Drew, passed away on December 4. The *Waco Tribune-Herald* ran a big obituary. One of the lines read, "Coach Drew's grandchildren were the apple of his eye." It was so meaningful to me that he was alive when my dream of a family came true and that he and his namesake shared the same earth, if only for a short time.

25

EVER AFTER

Just be in the moment, I told myself the morning of the ceremony. *Be here. Be present.*

I woke in our cottage at San Ysidro Ranch and looked out at a garden of roses. I had chosen this place to start our marriage because it felt like our first home: everywhere you looked there were flowers or ivy climbing a wall. As if a good witch had spun around, raising a collection of enchanted cottages from the earth. For a while I had been blocked on what I wanted my wedding to be. I didn't want it to be opposite of my first wedding, but it had to reflect who I was. I found myself going back to the book I loved, *Great Expectations*, and its 1998 film adaptation. The movie captured what I loved about the book, a delicate beauty that's been worn and softened with the passing of time.

Eric, always moving if he was not perfectly still in meditation, was already outside welcoming the day. Carol was looking after our kids in her cottage. They adored her and called her Cici. This was the slight calm before the storm of the day, probably the last minutes I would have alone. I had spent six months planning every detail for this wedding weekend for 275 guests. I let myself get too stressed about it. It was the wrapping-paper thing I do—where I overthink how I package a gift for someone when they're only going to tear through it to get to what matters. I overworked myself on every detail, but Eric and I did really want this wedding to be for our friends. It was a thank-you and a love letter in one, a hug back for the support they'd given us in love and in parenting. This was as much about them as it was about us.

In many ways, this was an opportunity to have the family I grew up with back together. I asked my father to officiate the wedding, and my mother and Ashlee were both my maids of honor. My parents had trouble being in the same room, and now I was going to make them stand next to each other up there with Ashlee just so I could look at them.

My father called me three days before we left for the wedding to tell me he was bringing his friend Jonathan, a young model he often shot for his new photography business.

"He wasn't on the list," I said. There was a pause. I reminded myself that I needed to accept my father for who he was as he worked it out in real-time.

"Okay," I said. I wasn't sure how to handle my father now, so I worked with the information he was ready to give me. Maybe I wasn't ready to listen, I don't know. My mother was bringing someone, too, her own Jon, the landscaper who'd made my Hansel and Gretel cottage so beautiful. He was kind and treated her well. People move on, even if I couldn't.

"Dad, whatever you do, don't forget your Bible," I said. "I want your Bible there, the one you preached with."

We set the wedding for July 5, with everyone arriving July 3 to have time to spend with close family. We booked all of San Ysidro Ranch for our guests, wanting it to be private and special for everybody. On Independence Day, we hosted a Texas-style barbecue for the guests. Eric's grandparents were able to come, and we were able to let them stay in the Kennedy Cottage, where then Senator John F. Kennedy and Jacqueline Kennedy stayed on their honeymoon. Eric idolized his grandfather and modeled his own strong, masculine presence on him and his dad, Stephen.

I wasn't alone long that morning. My mother led a team of fairylike bridesmaids to fetch me and start the preparation process. Carolina Herrera had made me a champagne-colored gown with gold embroidery, and I gasped when I saw it hung in a window, backlit next to the little one she made for Maxwell. She was my flower girl, and Ace would be a ring bearer along with Ashlee's son, Bronx. I didn't want to wear straight white, but I couldn't help but want a princess dress that flared. A bit of Texas in San Ysidro fairyland. My stylist Nicole Chavez and I spent months picking out gowns—gauzy shades of the lightest blue, lavender, and green—for my twelve bridesmaids. We'd look on all the runways and ask nicely if we could maybe borrow a dress. It was like high school, when I would help girls get ready for a party. I worked with all of them to choose how they wanted their hair for the day. I wanted every one of my girlfriends to feel their most beautiful.

I saw my dad right before the ceremony, holding an iPad outside the chapel we'd built for the day. He'd forgotten his Bible. His iPad was about to die, and he would just have to wing it. *Jessica, it's okay,* I told myself. Maybe that's what we all needed to learn how to do better. To wing it. I'd put a lot of pressure on my father to be the man I knew in Dallas. I wanted him to move people through his words. And yes, I wanted people to think that he was okay. That our family was okay. But there was a time when I was figuring out who I was, and now it was his turn. *Wing it, Jessica.*

To begin the ceremony, I had an eighteen-piece orchestra playing selections from the score of *Great Expectations*. Yes, I know that is a lot, but you should know by now I don't do things halfway. Once the procession started, the kids received standing ovations. Ace was unsure at first, but then Eric crouched down low to stretch out his arms. He went right to Eric. When it was my moment to walk down the aisle, the orchestra began the song "The Day All My Dreams Came True." It plays in the movie when the hero, after going through so much, is finally happy. The song couldn't have been a more perfect choice.

Be here in this moment, I told myself. Through the lace of my veil, I saw my family all together and my loved ones, all waiting for me, framed by gorgeous hanging greens and flowers. But Eric. There was a look of uncertainty on his face that he couldn't hide. It was the pull of his smile. He could fool everyone else but not me. *Oh gosh, does he not like my dress?*

I left it. *Be here, Jess.* My father did a wonderful job. People were crying, and as he talked, I glanced at Ashlee and my mom.

Here we were, all grown up together. Each forming our own path. When my dad pronounced us husband and wife, a big cheer went up. I could hear Maxi and Ace's voices among them.

"Babe," Eric whispered. "I split my pants completely when I grabbed Ace."

"I knew something was wrong!" I yelled, then whispered. "Lemme see."

Sure enough, his tuxedo pants were split from his crotch to the top of his butt. The whole time, he wasn't sure if people were seeing his underwear. Once everybody was gone, we went behind a curtain, and he took his pants off. We had a seamstress come and sew them while he stood in his boxers. People were waiting for us, and I know there was a lot of "Where are they?" Someone piped up with, "Well, Jessica's definitely had sex, so it's not for that."

Once we were introduced as Mr. and Mrs. Johnson, it was like the lid was lifted off the wedding. Eric did a speech greeting everyone and spoke about his grandfather and his pledge to take care of me and the kids forever, just as his grandfather had done for his wife and family. It was so sweet and emotional. Then I could just relax. Eric and I didn't want to do a lot of the party-stopping traditional things like a first dance or cutting of the cake. We wanted everybody to have a blast. We had a huge band with seven different singers, and there was a moment when the four of us were holding hands on the dance floor. I don't remember the song, but I remember the weight of Ace in my arms, the twirl of Maxwell's dress, and the sureness of Eric.

"Hi, husband," I said.

"Hi, wife," he said.

That never got old. Four years and two babies in, we were husband and wife. I had a running joke, "I want to get married, but I keep getting pregnant." But the truth is that it made perfect sense that we were all together to share our wedding day. I wouldn't have had it any other way.

26

I ONCE WAS LOST

There's a Before and an After, but I have had a hard time pinpointing when exactly things changed. As I write this book, I've been having heart-to-hearts with all my friends, and each has a different moment in which they began to worry about me.

I know when *I* started to worry, though I kept it to myself. I was convinced I could make it work. It was after the holidays, which had been hard. Maxwell and Ace were only three and two years old, and when I hosted family gatherings, I realized that they would never know a time when their grandparents were together. Eric's parents were wonderful and had even moved out west to be closer to us. But I wanted my mom and dad to be together for my kids, like I'd had with my grandparents. My parents were so enmeshed in my life and career, and when I needed them most, it felt like they'd abandoned me to start their lives over.

The anxiety that had so long colored the edges of my life began to take hold of me. There had been so much happening to crowd out those feelings: trying to get pregnant, then having two babies under two, a new house, and a wedding. The Jessica Simpson Collection expanded to over thirty categories, and we were at the point where we cleared a billion dollars in sales. Even if I wanted to think about my parents' marriage crashing and what it meant about all I'd held as the foundation of my life, there was no time.

As life calmed down, there was time. At first, the feelings would come like a chill, the kind where you quickly rub your arms up and down and shake it off. I'd get up quickly or run my hands through my hair to pull it back tight, physically moving to push the thought away. "Somebody has just walked over my grave," we used to say about those unexplained shivers of foreboding.

But I knew what was buried. This feeling of being alone and scared in the dark was one I'd had since I was abused as a child. As this new loss brought me closer to the original one, when I lost my trust, I was a girl again, frozen, unable to use her voice to tell someone to stop. Thinking this darkness had sought her out because there was something wrong with her.

First, I numbed the pain with a drink. As soon as I felt it creeping in, I filled one of my closed gold-glitter tumblers with a straw. This wasn't to hide it—I never did—but maybe to mask from myself how much I was actually drinking. I'd forget, go to pick it up, and the emptiness would surprise me.

Like it had just evaporated. But I knew. *You're drinking way too much,* I would think as I took the next sip of a new one.

Then I started drinking in advance of those feelings, like taking a seasickness pill before bumpy waters. And do you know what? For a while, it worked. I kept it up, no matter what time it was. I could be absent while in the room with my parents at gatherings, but the second my kids needed something, I would be right there, laser-focused on them. I would be hungover, braiding hair, making lunches, fighting to be present.

We hosted more and more parties, which were still fun. I don't regret any of them. I just wish Eric and I didn't drink so much at them. We began to get disconnected. He would pick up on the energy of others, acting like he was Jim Morrison living out this rock-and-roll life, and I would stay in one spot while people around me passed out. I'd put blankets on them to tuck them in. I was jealous that sleep came so easily to them, but also grateful they were there.

I was able to drink so much when others couldn't because I had a secret. I'd found a doctor, what in L.A. you call a rock doc. "What will help me lose the most weight?" was my very first question.

It's awful to remember me saying those words, but my vanity had returned, despite all the work I had done to accept myself. Frankly, I liked how people treated me when I was skinny. Any extra pound would add to my vulnerability, and I was feeling fragile enough as it was because the family I'd grown up with as my rock had disintegrated. I thought if I was skinny, I was powerful.

He prescribed a stimulant at a high dosage. The stimulant

kept me alert, no matter how much I drank. Alcohol is a depressant, but the two substances didn't balance each other out in my body. No, they competed in some terrible chemistry experiment on my liver. I should have passed out from all the alcohol, but my body kept going because of the stimulant. Then I would shut the whole system down when I went upstairs. An Ambien brought the runaway train to a screeching halt.

I had no idea what I was doing to my body. And then I found out.

I WAS TURNING THIRTY-FIVE IN JULY, SO I PLANNED TWO GIFTS TO MYSELF: A trip to Saint Bart's for all my friends and a partial tummy tuck. The surgery wasn't for weight loss—I weighed 107 pounds when I planned the surgery. I wanted to get rid of the stretch marks and loose skin left sagging from my back-to-back pregnancies. I was so ashamed of my body at this point that I wouldn't let Eric see me without a white T-shirt on. I had sex with it on and even showered with it on. I couldn't bear to look at myself. I need to say this: if you have stretch marks from pregnancy, I hope you can be proud that your body created life. I was not strong enough. It touched all my insecurities, and I couldn't handle it.

I planned the procedure for two weeks after I got back from Saint Bart's, a trip I wanted to be an adults-only blowout. I hired a private jet to take thirty of us down for a weeklong stay at Le Sereno, which is right alongside a beautiful turquoise lagoon. I invited my mom, who had just gotten engaged to her boyfriend, Jon, so I decided not to invite my dad. Ashlee stayed home because she was pregnant and due at the end of the month. Because the trip was for my friends, I spared no expense, renting his and hers yachts, Jet Skis, the whole nine yards, and then thrown in nine more. I got my girlfriends the same glittercups I drank from, each emblazoned with her name and the number 35. I was not sober for a minute of the trip.

On my birthday, my assistant Stephanie got a call. It was my doctor.

"I have to talk to Jessica right now," he said.

Stephanie said it would have to wait. "It's her birthday."

"I am her doctor," he said. "Put her on."

"Okay." She came and got me.

He was direct. My plastic surgeon may have approved me for the surgery in two weeks, but he would not. "I am looking at your liver levels," he said. "You could die."

I had a drink in my hand. I sipped. "What?"

"Jessica, you need to stop everything for three months before you can have this surgery. *Everything.*"

That seemed somehow more definitive than "you could die." I was killing myself with all the drinking and pills. "Okay," I said.

I hung up and told the girlfriends around me what the doctor had said. I sipped again. *Stop,* a voice said. I ignored it. I would stop when I got home in a couple of days. It was my birthday after all.

I told Eric. We were in a sort of shared spiral, both of us in denial about how much we were drinking. I'm sure we were wasted when we talked about it. I would deal with it later, I decided. Why ruin a trip? I had lived in this state of emergency for so long that it felt comfortable.

We went out that night, all of us boarding a bus to take us to a burlesque bar. It was a fun night, and I was able to further distract myself from what the doctor said. Eric drank too much tequila and got argumentative with one of his friends. He resolved it, but on the bus back to the hotel, he started laying into me about the doctor's call. It was like he realized what it meant and wanted to shock me into taking it seriously. He accused me of neglect, not so much as being a bad parent, but because a mom shouldn't be so selfish that she would risk her life. "Don't leave us," he said, right there in front of my mother and my friends.

He still says it was not his finest moment.

When I got home, I cut down on everything, like someone cramming for a test. I disregarded what my doctor said and kept the surgery date. The morning of the operation, my mom tried to get me not to go. I had never shown her my stretch marks and skin.

"Mom," I said, taking off my dress in front of her. I stood there, nekkid before the woman who birthed me.

"Let's go," she said.

The surgery went fine, but I wasn't happy with the results. I still had loose skin that hung over my pants. I had a recurring thought: people had been so cruel to me when I was onstage at 120 pounds. What were they going to say when I raised my arms, caught in some moment where I forgot myself in the music, and they could see my skin sagging over my pants? I could bank all the self-esteem in the world, but I wasn't ready to face that laugh-and-point cruelty again. So I scheduled a full tummy tuck for two months later.

This surgery was more involved. There was a sense that something was going to go wrong from the get-go, even though I stopped drinking to prepare. The day of the surgery, Eric was puking his guts out because he was so nervous. He had to leave the hospital, and my mother stayed. She did not want me to do the surgery—nobody did. CaCee was of course googling every complication she could find to prep for the worst.

The surgery took two hours longer than planned. Post-op, I was sent to recover at a luxury hotel near the doctor's office. I know, people call it Hollyweird, but it's a thing here that folks recover from plastic surgery with aftercare services at hotels. I couldn't believe they just did the surgery and practically sent you home. I still had two drains with pouches to collect blood.

It did not go well. I got an infection—colitis—and was vomiting so much I thought I was going to bust my sutures. My mom and Eric were so worried. They had to rush me to Cedars, and I secretly stayed there for nine days. Doctors talked seriously about me needing a blood transfusion. It was so hard on Eric, who was convinced he should have talked me out of going through with the surgery. Eric loved me at any size or shape, even if I couldn't.

I recovered, and yes, my stomach looked great. I felt like myself again. But I can tell you that plastic surgery does not cure what's inside. Really, it's about how you feel emotionally, and I was still just as hard on myself once those stitches were out. I still had work to do.

I DECIDED THAT 2016 WAS GOING TO BE THE YEAR THAT I COMMITTED TO my music and to songwriting. I needed to save myself, get to know myself again. I wanted to start journaling again, pick up a pen and confront who I had become and challenge myself to be better. I had mostly stopped when I was so tormented by John. The longer I waited, the more of a reckoning it would be.

I was in a position where I had my own studio in my house, and I could pay producers and songwriters to come and work with me. This way my kids could see what their mom actually did for a living.

But opening that new Mead notebook to write with other people in the room was like summoning all my ghosts. "Places everyone." I was taking my memories, trying to put them to music in a room with people I had never met in my life. I know that there are songwriters who treat it like a job. For me, it's ministry. I sat on the floor of the recording studio, trying to write the story of my life so that I could help others. About the heartache of a failed marriage, of giving yourself over to someone who tortured you. Songwriting takes me to an honest place, and honestly, I was in a dark place. I just didn't know it until the words came out of me. Before I even knew how heartbroken I was about my parents, the words spilled out of me. *Wait, I'm heartbroken?* I thought.

To prepare, I drank before the songwriting sessions, and during, and then after to recover. The alcohol helped me go to the painful place, but then it started to hold me back. When I sang, it wasn't the same as when I was younger. I was scared, and fear kept me from being wholly there.

I kept putting the music off, then coasted into the next year as I focused on the kids and the Collection. It was easy to invest my time in kids and the business. As much I was my own worst enemy, I did everything I could to be present for my children.

In September 2016, my father called to tell me that he had been diagnosed with prostate cancer. He'd been told that if he didn't have surgery, he had six months to live.

"So, you're having the surgery," I said, gulping from a glittercup.

"I'm not sure," he said.

I couldn't believe my father would consider not fighting. He was spiraling, and I didn't know how to help him, I wasn't a doctor, so all I could do was remind him what he taught me to do. To have faith and know that it's all going to be okay. But you have to fight. You can't give up. I was still recovering from losing him as a manager, but losing my father altogether was something I just couldn't fathom.

He set the date for the surgery. My poor mother still loved him, and I know she felt powerless. For thirty-five years, she'd helped him, nursing him through every cold and flu. And now, when he needed her most, he didn't want her there. I felt the pressure to take her place. To be that mother figure, a wife to my own dad.

The morning of the surgery, I brought alcohol with me to the hospital. Seven a.m. and I was drinking to calm my anxiety. Ashlee was there, along with Jonathan and Dad's best friend Randy. The doctor told us that during the surgery, they discovered the cancer had spread to his lymph nodes. He had stage IV cancer.

Through the anxiety, I tried to be present and take in the information. I was supposed to be filling in for my mom. As he got treatment, I would relay the information to her, feeling like I was failing them both somehow by not doing enough. I realize now that when I thought I was escaping my feelings of responsibility by drinking, I was actually making things so much worse. It was a dark time, but not being sober for it exaggerated every problem when I just could have dealt with it head-on. Still, his recovery forced a needed reconnection for me with my dad.

Soon after, my doctor informed me that he could no longer prescribe me both the stimulant and the Ambien. I think he was afraid that I'd die. I had to choose, and for me it was to sleep or not to sleep. It was a come to Jesus moment, where I had to ask myself, *Which controls me more? My vanity or my fear?*

I chose to keep the Ambien. I was terrified of not being able to hit the Off switch at night.

As soon as my prescription for the stimulant ran out, my drinking caught up with me. I would pass out, so I made a concerted effort to stay "with it" until the kids' bedtime. I was less focused and increasingly unable to hide the effects. So *I* hid, staying out of the public eye as much as possible.

I did take one trip, visiting Nana in Texas for her eighty-fifth birthday. It was harder now for her to get around. She'd gone into a nursing home, but she didn't like it and left. Her whippersnapper heart rebelling even with her slowing body. Back home, she used a walker and would amble with it to the driveway, park it next to her car, and slide into the driver's seat. "I drive around for an hour," she said, "then come back, and the walker is right there waiting for me."

"I don't know how safe that is, Nana," I said. But I knew the feeling. When your world shrinks, you make adjustments. My anxiety had shrunk my world to my house.

When I did go out, I didn't have a sense of how clear it was that I was having issues. In late May, I went on *The Ellen DeGeneres Show* to promote the Collection, making an appearance I have never watched. I admit I drank beforehand and was also on steroids for a chest infection that made me hoarse. I was nervous, but I'd always been able to turn it on for talk shows. Instead, I couldn't find Ellen's rhythm, mumbling and second-guessing everything I was saying.

At first, Ellen tried to help, and then she gave up. Her blank stare at my conversational freefall was tough love. Ellen didn't say anything to me after. I awkwardly walked off the stage and took in the look on the face of my publicist and friend Lauren.

"Uhh," she said.

"Did I not do good?" I asked, knowing the answer.

"You could have done better," she said, which is probably the most critical thing this kind woman has ever said to me. I want to say it here to Ellen and the viewers: I'm truly sorry. I disrespected them by trying to make an appearance when I had no business doing so.

My friends began their plans for interventions. I picture them two by two, first dancing around the subject with each other, then gripping each other's arms in solidarity. They felt powerless, afraid that if they confronted me, I would shut them out. Lauren put together a plan of action for when I was ready, discreetly collecting the numbers of people who specialize in rehab and counseling.

On my thirty-seventh birthday in July 2017, two years after a doctor told me my life was in danger, I had my friends over for a daylong party at my house. At the end, while my friends were all downstairs, I sat on my bed and cried. Another friend had just gone to rehab. She was a mother, and she found the strength to face her pain and anxiety instead of dousing it in alcohol to numb it. She did what I knew I needed to do. I was humbled, because she chose what was best for her family. I knew I needed to stop drinking, and I couldn't. I had alcoholism in my bloodline, and I was carrying it around. Our kids were five and four. How could I protect them? How could I lead them away from this, and break the cycle?

I prayed, which I realized I hadn't done in a long time. I had stopped taking those moments of stillness for myself. A remembered Psalm floated up from within me. *The Lord is close to the brokenhearted,* I told myself. *He saves those who are crushed in spirit.* But if I was so broken, why did He feel so far away? He'd protected me my whole life, given me a light and a calling to use my voice to help others. Now I couldn't face this fear in me, and I was dimming my light, and hiding from the world He had long ago told me to change.

There was a tiny light still in me, though, a little flame for me to make my birthday wish on. I whispered my request, asking God for the help and mercy I wouldn't give myself.

It would take three and a half months. But God would save me so I could come home to myself.

27

BUT NOW I SEE

Twice a week, my therapist and I sat across from each other in our study, exorcising demons. My kids were at school, and Eric would busy himself to give me space. I told her the stories that I've shared with you, and in the beginning, I could rattle off the facts of things that happened, standing outside of the girl next door as she went through the experiences. Eventually, I could examine that girl's feelings closely enough to better understand them and how they informed her choices. With work, that girl and I were one again, and I allowed myself to feel the traumas I'd been through. The sessions left me scooped out, and my kids got used to me being extra huggy on certain days. Not just needing the sureness of them but valuing it.

Any homework she gave me, I wanted an A-plus-plus-plus, so when my therapist prescribed an antidepressant, I took it right away. But I didn't like how it made me feel and went off it under her supervision. I sensed that, for me, I needed to work to figure out the roots of my problems, and they weren't chemical.

"I think it's situational depression," I told Eric on one of our post-therapy walks around the neighborhood. "It was just a long situation."

Without alcohol, the clarity I had feared turned out to be a continual gift. When I was drinking, I had been confused by how I was going to juggle work and parenting. Because it was exhausting, the way I would drink. It took time away from real life. Now I had room for so many wonderful moments that I would have missed, either because of the carelessness with which I treated my body, or because I was too numb to appreciate them. I took mental snapshots to keep in my heart: sober for the first time ever in my studio and seeing Maxwell grab a guitar. Ace in pajamas he put on himself, proudly putting a sticker on his bedtime chart. My husband and I rediscovering each other, feeling that same gratitude over finding each other that we had when we first met. That my husband stopped drinking with me was powerfully romantic, even if Hallmark doesn't have a card for it. Or maybe they do. It saved our marriage, or at least saved us from the stupid fights that didn't need to happen. Things said that didn't deserve to be said because it was the alcohol talking, not the heart. I was sober and I was *feeling*. This was what it felt like to be living. This is what I was running away from?

I began to open up to people and came out of hiding mode. One of the first tests was a girls' night out at a restaurant. I think we were all nervous about how we were going to handle me not drinking when we were all together. The first minutes were strange. Everyone could read how anxious I was. Then the waiter came over with the wine list. They all started to say it at once: "I'll have water." I cried happy tears, and just like my birthday, they each told me how grateful they were that I had saved myself.

Still, I dreaded hosting Thanksgiving and Christmas, unsure that I could handle the holidays sober. I was so happy my father had beaten that bout of cancer. Still, seeing my parents together but apart would be like surgery with no anesthesia once again. There was no alcohol in the house, so I didn't know what I would do.

Instead, at each gathering I watched them be careful of each other, still doing the dance of trying to avoid prolonged contact but doing so in a respectful way. *It was you, Jess,* I thought. They were more over each other than I was over them being apart. It was me who needed to catch up.

I collected days sober along with all these new memories. When I hit ninety days, I went right into the studio after to write. A new song, "Heartbeat," came out so easy, and I finally felt unblocked. I could put words to feelings again and make them mean something for other people. That was what would matter now, and my prayer was constant: "Lord, use me." I'd been selfish with my time and careless with my life. Now I wanted to give back and have a life of purpose again. In my life, I want to be a role model for people—especially my children. They have to know that they can always count on me. I am so grateful that I stopped in time and resisted the forces that were carrying me away from them.

I made plans with my friend Koko, whose husband is in

the service, to do something to help military families. In April, to honor the Month of the Military Child, we went to a Dillard's in Nashville to host a day of pampering for army wives and daughters from Fort Campbell, right on the Kentucky-Tennessee border. We gave them all hair and makeup services, and I got to style each one in our spring 2018 line and our Girls line. I brought Eric along, and even though he was right there with me, I kept retelling him all the stories women shared about what their families had gone through. He was looking at me differently. He'd seen me, the real me he remembered, back in action.

But sometimes I still threw him. The following month, I announced that I wanted to take the kids to Disneyland.

"Are you kidding?" asked Eric. He is not an amusement park kind of guy. He also knew that I'd been thinking a lot about my failed Mickey Mouse Club audition and all the times I'd worked Grad Nites, watching kids my age go off to live normal lives. "Why would you want to go back there?"

"It will be part of my healing," I said with a completely straight expression. "I need to face my demons."

He gave me a look of *Seriously, is she okay?* and then I let myself laugh. "I think the kiddos will love it."

We got in late in the afternoon and planned to do the park the next day. We were at the pool in the hotel, and this middle-aged woman came up to me. She was frantic.

"*Oh my God, Britney Spears,*" she yelled in a midwestern accent. "I love you so much."

My kids were in the pool, staring at the scene. I was like, of course this would happen to me. Britney steals even this Disney moment, right there in front of my kids.

"Ma'am," I said calmly. "I am sorry, but I am not Britney Spears."

"Yes, you are," she said. "We are taking a picture."

"But I swear I'm not—" She already had her face next to mine, her arm outstretched to get a good selfie with Britney. I was not about to say, "I'm Jessica Simpson." So I smiled and laughed about it for the rest of the night.

The next day I wore the vintage Mickey Mouse shirt they gave us at the first day's tryouts in Dallas. I brought Ashlee along, just like I'd done back then, and she brought her two kids. I wore Minnie Mouse ears and kept them on the whole time. My excitement had a lot of people looking at me, and instead of shrinking, I smiled and said hi to everybody, hugging characters along the way. Eric had never seen this side of me, and I was the most overenthusiastic Disney mom there ever was.

"I think you're having more fun than the kids," Eric said. I had only gone in and out for work whenever I'd visited, so I hadn't realized how much walking was involved. I'd worn heels, of course—sky-high platform heels—but by the end of the day, I had to give in and buy some twenty-dollar Star Wars flip-flops from a little kiosk. As I was inside trying to decide between Princess Leia or Yoda Havaianas, I heard a voice behind me.

"Oh, my God, I am so embarrassed."

I turned. It was the woman from the pool. She was with a man I guessed was her husband because they matched. "I literally thought about this all night," she said, coming closer. "You're Jessica Simpson."

I smiled, and she kept going. "I prayed to God—me and my husband—"

"We had to pray a lot," he said.

"That we would see you so I could apologize," she said.

"It's really not a big deal."

"*Jessica Simpson*," she said, solemnly. "Can I have a picture with you?"

"Only if you smile," I said.

She handed her husband the phone, and we took a picture. I hugged her goodbye and held up the Yoda flip-flops. "May the force be with you," I said.

That night, I was in such a good mood that at ten o'clock I wasn't having any of the nerves that nighttime usually brought me. Our children were all in bed asleep, worn out by the day. Ashlee and I were kids again, snuggled on a couch.

"Jessica, I don't want to make fun of you or anything," she said slowly. "But you still have your ears on."

I reached up to feel the Minnie ears and smiled as I took them off. "I love you, Ash," I said, snuggling closer to her. "I'm so glad you're here with me."

"Me, too," she said.

I thought back on how all those years ago, we were each other's protectors in the night. Me saving her from abuse, and after, her keeping the demons of the dark away for me. I am so grateful for the bond we have.

I STOOD BACKSTAGE AT THE PACIFIC AMPHITHEATRE, SMOOTHING MY dress and shuffling in my cowboy boots. It was August 9, and Willie Nelson had invited me to perform with him at his OC Fest show. I'd talked to him about what I'd been through, and I was so glad that my first time onstage in so many years would be with him.

Maxwell and Ace, six and five, had never even seen me perform, and they were with Eric in the audience. I was so excited for them to see me. "Oh, *that's* what Mommy does," I imagined them realizing. They played my Christmas albums all summer, but this would be different. Willie and I were going to sing "Your Fool," a song I wrote with producer John Shanks after pouring my heart out to him about what my friendship with Willie has meant to me. It has a line I came up with in Maxwell's room, putting her to bed. She had stars on her ceiling, and I always told her I'd lasso them down for her.

Backstage, I listened as Willie sang his songs for the sold-out crowd. I cried a little through "Always on My Mind" and dried my tears during the fun instrumental "Twelfth Street Rag."

"We got a real special treat coming up for y'all," he said. "Our good buddy Jessica Simpson and I are gonna sing a song together, and we'd like to get her out here today."

I walked onstage, shy at first, but all the cheers and Willie's smiling face made me realize I was home. As I started to sing our duet, "Your Fool," the cheers and whoops got louder, and I spotted Eric and the kids in the front. "I'll be that one true friend," Willie sang to me. "You know you're stuck with me."

I was so grateful to be in that moment. As the song ended, I said, "Thank you, Willie."

"I love you, Jess."

I floated offstage. He closed the concert with a fast medley of "Will the Circle Be Unbroken" and "I'll Fly Away," two songs that remain near and dear to my heart. They used to make me sad in uncertain times in my life, but now they made me happy, because I'd found my forever in my husband and children.

After the concert, Ace looked at me like he had no idea I was a superhero, and I picked him up to hug him. "I love you so much," I said, and his eyes shined. Maxwell peppered me with questions. "That's the man I listened to when I was a baby?" she asked.

"Yeah, honey."

"And you said you'd lasso the stars, just like you told me."

"Always," I said, hugging her. "Always."

Eric hugged me, placing his hand on my stomach. I put my hand over his and smiled at him. We had a secret, one that had come as a happy surprise to us. When we found out, what we'd been through made sense. We needed to clear the way for a new life.

We were about to be a family of five.

28

BIRDIE MAE

MARCH 2019

I was so ready to have this baby girl.

I had spent the last several therapy sessions talking about how I needed her out of me. I honestly couldn't think of anything else. She was laying on her side in me, and she was so big that they scheduled a C-section for March 19 when my actual due date was April 15. But first there had been the shock that at age thirty-eight they considered this a "geriatric pregnancy," which is the oldest you will ever feel.

I was like, "*What?*"

"Really it's just a box to check," said a nurse. "It just means you're high-risk."

I chuckled. "You are full of good news," I said. "What else you got? Thoughts on my hair?" We laughed, and she told me not to worry. But this was kind of the pregnancy from hell. When I wasn't being hospitalized for bronchitis—I had it four times—I was breaking a toilet seat leaning back. At least I was really open about it. In January the Ten-Year Challenge was a big thing on Instagram, where you posted a 2009 photo next to a current one.

I posted my old skinny legs next to my incredibly swollen ankle. It was so sweet, because I heard from many, many women who've been through the same thing.

The pregnancy was a crazy painful journey. And you were with me the whole way. I spent a lot of nights in our study working on this book, with just you and my little girl there to keep me company. So, you are cordially invited to her arrival.

The nurses and doctors at Cedars-Sinai told me they'd never seen a bigger group of people in the birthing suite. In about thirty minutes, they'd wheel me in for the C-section, and there were about twenty people packed into the room, friends and honorary family carrying on like it was a party. My friends were leaning back on my bed to take selfies with me, and my kids were peppering me with last-minute questions.

"Mom, how long's it gonna take?" Ace asked.

"About an hour? Maybe?"

"Is it through your belly button?" Maxwell asked.

I pointed lower. "No, right about here, honey."

"So, it's not down where you pee?"

"No, but some mommies do that. It's all good."

Someone suggested people write down their guesses on the weight of the baby, like it was a jar of jellybeans.

"I'm thinking eight pounds," said CaCee.

Everyone took one look at my belly and laughed.

"No way," said my mom.

"Yeah, much bigger," said my dad.

I smiled at them, smoothing my hand over my belly. I looked around the room. Eric's parents, Ashlee, my second mom Carol, all my girlfriends. My parents were each here with their significant others, and it was okay. All the stuff that would normally bother me, just didn't. This was my new normal. And maybe that was okay after all.

It was only awkward for the nurses. One of the veteran ones said she needed to take me to the bathroom, and as we moved, she whispered, "Can I get these people out of here?"

It hadn't even occurred to me. "Oh yeah," I said. "Sure."

"Okay," she yelled. "Can we clear the room? Give Jessica a second before she gets sliced open and has her baby."

"You'd be a good bouncer," I said.

They took me into the operating room. Eric had to wait about twenty minutes before coming in because they do the spinal tap and epidural when you're by yourself. It was just me and my baby—and the doctors that came in scrubbed up in blue with their hands in the air. It looked like they'd raised their hands in prayer.

"Do you have a birth plan?" one asked.

"Uh, I'm here," I said. "Have you guys done this before?"

"Are you going to eat your placenta?"

I laughed. "Nope," I said. "No. You can throw it out."

There was so much going on, and I was numb from the chest down. I could kind of lift my arms, but I was thinking, *Don't fall off.*

"What kind of music do you want?"

My mind went blank. "Whatever y'all want to listen to that makes this go by, that's great," I said. "Just get her out." So, they put on the *Grey's Anatomy* soundtrack and cued up "How to Save a Life." *Oof.*

"Okay, we're ready," a doctor said.

"But Eric is not," I said. "Don't forget my husband!"

"Oh, he's just getting scrubbed up," a nurse said.

Just then, he came in. "Babe, I'm here."

"They asked me about music, and I forgot to say Zeppelin!"

He held my hand, and I started crying. I just wanted her to be okay after everything we'd been through. After the incision, I felt a hard tug, and she was out.

Why isn't she crying?

It was not even a full second. But that second was the longest moment of my life. She started to yell, and I don't think I've ever cried more cleansing tears.

Birdie Mae Johnson was named for my father's grandmother Bertie, and in tribute to songs that have carried me through my life: "His Eye Is on the Sparrow" and Dolly Parton's "Little Sparrow." I don't know what it means for her life, but I know she gave me the strength to go back out onstage and write this book. Birdie entered this lucky world weighing ten pounds, thirteen ounces. No one guessed her weight high enough, but Eric's dad came the closest, so he won. Maxwell was not happy that Birdie was bigger by a pound than when she was born. But she was so excited to see that they had the same stork bite birthmark in the same place, right between their eyes. Immediately, it was like, "This is my sister, and this is our thing." Ace has smaller ones, and not in the same place as theirs, but he can brag that he has five of them. You only see them when the kids get upset. I always called them "angel kisses" because a stork bite sounds pretty aggressive in my opinion.

We took Birdie home, our family of five all together at last. Birdie was welcomed by so many people, but one of the best presents was a package of photos I received from Casa Hogar Elim, Mama Lupita's orphanage. They sent us a letter welcoming Birdie, along with tons of pictures of the kids having fun and learning at school. They have the same spark of joy that my children have and seeing that was one of the best gifts Birdie and I received.

I'M WRITING TO YOU IN THE THICK OF SUMMER NOW. WE SPENT THE DAY OUT back with the kids, and it was Birdie's first time in the pool. She loved the water, and the kids were excited to be able to take turns carrying their little sister. I watched her in the water wondering if she would take to it like her brother and sister. She did, her dimpled smile growing as she splashed her hands in what must have seemed like a giant bathtub.

I have fallen more in love with my family watching them love our Birdie. She came at just the right time for us. Sweet Ace is so quiet with her, always wanting to hold her. He is so intuitive, knows so much about people without even spending a lot of time with them. He will know his sisters so well, and always look after their hearts.

Maxwell is not the junior diaper changer I thought she would be, but she loves her little sister so much. The other day I caught her singing to Birdie about Peter Rabbit. The baby had just woken from a nap. I stood in the doorway, listening with my heart about ready to burst.

I laugh because they all need me, and poor Eric, we all need him. I'm so happy not to be pregnant anymore that I still just lay on his chest and breathe these big sighs of relief. When I am with him, wherever we are I feel at home. When I hold his hand, I feel like I can just step forward into the future with grace and strength. Music is part of that journey again. Teresa, who helped protect me as an artist all those years ago, is back in my life. I am so proud of the work we are doing together.

Finding peace with total quiet is possible, but I do still struggle with insomnia. All my fears and doubts do come once everyone is asleep and there is nobody to distract me. When thoughts come, I've learned that they're okay. I can't say I've made friends with them, but lying in bed I can at least shake hands with them now. Like, "Okay, I see you. I'm aware of you, and now you be aware of me. Good night."

I have been letting those closest to me read passages from this book. I was most scared to show my father. Just as I was scared to play him music on that Halloween that changed my life. He wrote me yesterday. "I wish I could have held you more in so many of those dark hours," he said. "Please forgive me for being a better manager than a father."

I told him he was the best father I could ever have had. "I wouldn't change any moment." It's true. I wouldn't change a single thing about my story, because I finally love who I am, and I can forgive who I was.

I knew that I would be ending this book tonight, and for a long time I feared this very moment. There's a permanence to getting your thoughts down that can feel like a last testament. The reason I started journaling at fifteen years old was because we lost my cousin Sarah and she left behind her diaries. I worried that writing a book represented the end of something. Now, I see my life is just beginning. I have a better footing now for retracing the steps that got me here.

I have thought of you so much as I wrote this book, wanting to give you things to carry on your own journey. Every night I go to bed next to that angel figurine given to me in Iraq. It comforts me, but also calls me to be more. I wanted this book to be something like that for you, and now that it's ending, these parting words seem so important.

So, I got out all my journals tonight and piled them on the

table next to me for inspiration. I pulled one out at random to see what message I was supposed to leave you with. I opened the page to this: "Sometimes we are all so afraid to be honest with ourselves because we know that honesty will lead to somewhere." I wrote this ten years ago. "Can fear walk us to something better?"

I can say now that the answer is yes. I knew that then, too, but I still had to phrase it as a question because I wasn't ready. I had to walk through my fear to be here writing to you about the painful moments of my life. "Pain is where all the tools are," I said to my therapist the other day. If you're someone who has a lot of tools, I'm sorry, but I am also hopeful for you. You have so much to work with. I think it's important, whatever your situation, to turn inward. So often we turn away from ourselves, and just numb our feelings to get through the day. You can do that with anything, not just with alcohol. It's so easy to overwhelm yourself with too much to do in a day, where you never have enough time for yourself. We need to own our weakness, our hurt, our pain, and say it out loud so that we can name what is coming up and why. You deserve it. You deserve to feel the heartbreak and the pain so that once and for all you stop holding yourself back from feeling whatever it is you've tried to mask.

No, it's not easy but you are worth the work. And if you do not have a stable presence in your life, take the time you need to become that stable presence for yourself. To find that stillness within you, no matter what storm you are in.

Leaving you now, I feel the way I do seeing my children off to school. I start to sputter all these things to them at the door. Do you have your water bottle? Here, let me straighten your collar. Remember to be kind. Listen to your teachers. Sit with someone lonely. Make good choices.

And, most important, I love you.

acknowledgments

Like my life, this book—one of pain, loss, forgiveness, persever-
ance, hope, light, fear, laughter, beauty, and abundant joy—has
been inspired and led by my cousin Sarah. At seventeen, her wise
soul took flight to change the world as she sat next to her true
companion, our Lord and Savior Jesus Christ. I was fifteen when
she introduced me to myself, inspiring me to find my purpose, my
calling, by picking up a pen to communicate to God and to her.
They held me accountable, so that I could be who I am today:
Me. All of me. When I was upset or ashamed, I didn't walk away
from God, I walked toward him. Faith was never a choice, it was
the essence of my life because of her. Sarah led my way, and now I
hope to lead with her, providing hope to those that need to find a
friend in themselves.

I am grateful to HarperCollins Publishers and Dey Street Books for valuing my sense of purpose in creating this book. Thank you to Liate Stehlik, Ben Steinberg, Kendra Newton, Anwesha Basu, Kelly Rudolph, Andrea Molitor, Renata De Oliveira, Caitlin Garing, Suzanne Mitchell, Mumtaz Mustafa, Andy LeCount, and Tatiana Dubin. To my editor, Carrie Thornton, thank you for understanding how important this book is to me, and allowing me to make sure every word, detail—and bird—was just right.

Lauren Auslander, you are my champion and the gatekeeper to my heart. I could never have done this book without you believing in my intuition. In times when most people would think I was out of my mind, you always know how to listen to my heart. Your passion and loyalty have given me the confidence to take on the world with strength and gratitude. Thank you for pulling me out of the dark and helping me rediscover the power of the light. I love you. You are the creator of LUNA, and I would also like to share my thanks with your amazing staff. Kylee Kilgore, Kevin Smith, and Erin Cullen, the endless ways that y'all as a team make talent shine is a treasure.

To Lacy Lynch, my literary agent. You poured your heart into this book from the moment it was just an idea, and your faith in me as an author has meant the world to me. You believed in a fellow Texas girl, and I am indebted to you for being such a good advocate for me. Thanks also to the entire Dupree Miller team, especially Jan Miller and Dabney Rice.

Kevin Carr O'Leary, you are the Shakespeare to my thoughts. Thank you for teaching me that the hidden places of my heart are the most powerful to find and share. God sent you my way, and together we have become part of a real and true purpose.

To the tribe of ladies that make the Jessica Simpson Collection a true labor of love, thank you. Not just from me, but all the confident women around the world that y'all have helped to feel beautiful. We are a family business, one who lives and breathes the value of a woman's worth. Tina (Mom), Beth, Norma, Juliann, Lolo, Dre, Peggy, and Koko . . . Going on fifteen years and we've only just begun!

CaCee, everyone needs someone like you in their life so they can exist to their full potential. You bring truth, courage, confidence, laughter, and whole lotta love. You are my constant, forever more. I love you.

Koko, I couldn't get through a day without your friendship. Thanks for always being the joy in the room. Nobody can get things done quite like you. Your passion for the collection and my life makes me excited to keep doing as much as I possibly can.

Steph, thank you for always helping me find the beauty in broken moments and reminding me to look to God for answers. We have been friends since the beginning and will be to the very end. I love you.

Adrienne, the depth of you is beyond human. Your extraordinary perspective has always given me clarity. I truly respect and adore your wise ass.

Lolo, my fairy. You are the connector of all beautiful things.

Turkey, there is so much magic in your heart. Thank you for breaking the mold. You always are fearlessly yourself. I love you, weirdo.

Erin, thank you for always teaching me that I deserve whatever my heart desires. You have given me insight to a very authentic part of myself, one that pushes boundaries to find a greater artistic depth. I love you and Dylan!

Jessie: BFF, wildflower, loving soul. Your love is family.

Kathy, thank you for always checking in and being the best listener.

Nicole C., you always see me as I am. You embody style and you're a lover of life.

Jen—the Queen of Venice; there is nobody on this planet who doesn't want to soak in your radiant glow.

Morgan, thank you for your willingness to help at any moment and for always being your true self.

Jon and Jonathan—my extended family. Every day I am grateful for our purposeful connection. Love y'all.

Trish, Bonnie, Renee, Kev, Laura, Ann Marie, and Stella: Thank you for giving me the space to focus on this book, all while being present for my children. Without y'all I could never be the mom I am today.

Anna, I am so blessed to have you by my side every day. Thank you for always being so selfless and full of integrity. You get this family through all of the craziness with structure and love. This has been one of the most challenging years of my life, physically and mentally, yet you are with me holding my hand, making it all seem possible to manage. Love you, lady.

Evelyn, Sonia, and Marlene: All day, every day I appreciate how you take care of me and my home, my sacred place. This family loves y'all so deeply.

To Kristin, the queen of collages. Thank you for documenting all of my moments. When I look back on this life, I will be able to see the entire metamorphosis as an artistic memory you've captured.

Driver Dan: Copy that, 10-4. Love you.

David, thank you for loving me like your own and believing in the power of a woman. I love you.

Cate, your support is endless. I adore you. Thanks for making sure my bills are paid on time! I promise I will make returns. Ha ha.

Teresa, thank you for not just listening to my voice, but actually hearing how it could impact the lives of others. You have a way about you that can move anyone into the heart of a song. There is not one person in the music business that compares to you.

Bart, you are the best vocal producer I have ever worked with. Thank you for allowing me to break down to break through, every single writing and vocal session. I love you.

Carol, you bless my family enormously every day with your devotion, unconditional love, and prayer. That heart you possess is bigger than Texas, and I hope to be half the woman of God you are in this lifetime. God listens to all of us, but somehow, I know that your tap on the shoulder is the most familiar to Him. I love you as much as you love me and my children, which I know is as much love that exists.

Randy and Beth, you have been my valiant protectors since childhood. You are family to me, and have proven time and again that you'll do anything it takes to ensure that I am safeguarded. I trust you both with everything I have.

Aunt Debbie and Uncle Boyd, I am so grateful that you gave me your blessing to share Sarah's story and example. You have been models of strength and mercy for me on my journey through life. I love you.

To all my aunts, uncles, and cousins in our beautiful family: I was blessed to grow up with you in Texas, and to continue to have you in my life now. I thank you for every shared moment. I love you.

Mary Jo and Steve, thank you for raising the greatest love of my life. Each and every day, I see how Eric embodies the nurturing values you taught him. You led by example in your marriage and family, and we all benefit from the love you showed him. I am also grateful that you moved out here from Boston so you could be present for the kids and so involved in their lives. They adore Mojo and Pop Pop Ringo.

Nana: You are my prayer warrior. Thank you for holding me so closely in your heart. You have taught me the beauty of surrendering my spirit so that God may do his work in my life.

Papaw: Oh, how I miss you. Our God reigns.

Nanny: His eye is on the sparrow, and I know he watches me, right along with you, my butterfly. Sweet caretaker, you are with me, so I will sing because I'm happy, I will sing because I'm free.

Papa: I never got to hear you preach. My father learned from you, and he was the very best. Thank you for teaching me through him up there on that pulpit.

Nana Maxwell: You are the true essence of beauty and poise. You will last longer than me in high heels celebrating your ninetieth birthday.

Pop Pop Maxwell: You are deeply missed, but seen in every eagle that takes flight.

To my sister, Ashlee, a force of nature. Without hesitation you are the brightest star in the galaxy. Your arrival was the greatest gift of my childhood, and I only adore and respect you more as we go through life together. You overflow with an abundance of twirls and leaps through life, leaving everyone feeling as if they have danced along with you. It is an honor to be an aunt to your deeply loving children. Bronx, you are a superhero with the depth of Socrates. I love you and your philosophical mind. Jagger, you are beauty and love with an extra flavor that is only your own, nobody else's.

Evan, thank you for giving your heart to my sister and sharing your loving family with ours. Love you.

Dad, you are the maker of my dreams. Your guidance through my life has taught me that there is absolutely nothing I am not worthy or capable of. You are the first I have ever loved, the first I have ever admired. You taught me that "pride comes before a fall" so that I remain humble and steadfast in my journey. You have always given me a safe atmosphere in which to connect to my purpose, You will never have to let me go, nor I you. We remain as we were from the beginning, always and forever. I truly wish there were more words for love, because you deserve them all.

Mom, you are the leader to my destiny. I look to you as the strongest force of soulful ambition. You have made every sacrifice possible in order for me to find center stage with ownership of my voice. I belt out the high notes with ease because you have taught me that the hardest parts can be the easiest to master. I try to look at life through your eyes because of all the beauty you are able to see. You held my purpose inside of you thirty-nine years ago and live every day to help me see it through. The greatest of love is yours. Now that I am a mother, I understand the way you love me. My role model, mentor, best friend, and boss lady . . . we are not just the little engine that could anymore. We are proof that we can—no matter what gets in our way. Thank you for making all things possible. I love you.

Eric, you are the answer to every question, the completion to all equations. My love, you have helped me arrive to the pure abundance of soulful, connected ideas. You have grounded me with an extreme grace of patience while moving with the mosey of my steps as I get myself to this exact purposeful destination. You always trust my direction as God's because you can discern my heart's deepest desires. My sexual shaman, I give myself to you, fully. I will forever exist in your stratosphere. Your meditation with movement leads our family safely home, and loving you is like wearing a crown of light. I see life through you each moment, until the next, when we begin again. Thank you for giving me the miracle I have prayed for since I was a little girl, our children . . .

Maxwell, my first born, an arc of God's light surrounds you so bright, my fierce natural born leader. Thank you for elevating my intention and faith every night with your sweet prayers for the lonely who need God's hugs, the animals to find homes, the doctors to save lives, the country to live in peace, the firefighters to be brave, and for the mean people who hurt others to feel loved. Your innocence is depth, and your spirit is power. Mommy promises to lasso the stars and pull them straight into your heart every time God turns down the lights. I love you.

Ace, my only son, Mom's Cancerian soulmate, I get you. I understand you as much as I do myself. And then throw in the best characteristics of your daddy . . . You are a mastermind of observation, patience, mystical powers, intuition, gratitude, resilience, and explosive love that will indeed last a lifetime. Thank you for always saying you love me more, but I can promise you: No way, no how, bud. I wish I could give you everything you want in your childhood, but Mommy isn't getting you a Komodo dragon. Your imagination will take you wherever your beautiful heart desires, my Home Run King. There is nothing you can't do. I love you × infinity. Top that! I'm sure you will try.

Birdie: You, my baby girl, were chosen by God to reunite your mommy to the melody of life. In return, I will sing with open wings, giving all that I have inside me. Your life was an unexpected treasure I now can't imagine living without. The moment I felt you flutter around, I knew that your presence would claim the sky, with your head in the stars and your feet on the ground. You gave me strength as I carried you throughout the creation of this book. First in my heart, then within me, and at last in my arms. When I held you, you looked at me with a smile, your hand held mine and I knew, somehow, we had met before . . . I dreamed you into life.